JUSTICE DELAYED IS JUSTICE BURIED

(Bankers Fraud Story based on Real Life Incidents)

Author pen name

THE OPTIMIST

A Double Post Graduate with CAIIB, having twenty six years of banking experience

Four years of experience as regular Faculty,

Three years of Research Experience and

Twelve years of experience as Guest Faculty

INDIA • SINGAPORE • MALAYSIA

ISBN 979-8-88935-932-6

Contents

Preface

This book makes one realize how costly your official signature is, if you sign in good faith by believing the words of your boss, it may even completely stop your career growth. The entire story moves around an illegitimate penalty order imposed upon an efficient Bank officer Mr.LSR. Despite being the accused, Mr.LSR without getting depressed or demotivate, how energetically he studied the fraud loan case in its entirety and how he has brought to light all the wrong deeds committed by some internal officers of the Bank by colluding with the external fraudster in a NPA Bad loan are explained in a very logical as well as elaborate way by the author.

The Author of this book having done research while pursuing his PhD and having qualified for UGC's JRF and SRF, while reading this book, it looks like a research paper which is investigative in nature. Especially this book is an alert as well as an advisory to financial organizations as it talks about systems and procedures to be adopted while fixing staff accountability upon an officer by examining the incident in its entirety.

Having more than twenty five years of experience in Banking and having worked in various departments like credit processing, post sanction credit monitoring, vigilance, audit, recovery and as Faculty, all this experience helped the author to bring this book with all the technical points that a financial organization, especially a Bank shall not overlook and must ensure compliance.

It also talks about how to identify the internal fraudsters if any who caused loss to the organization by colluding with the external fraudsters, the procedure to be adopted while fixing the staff accountability fixation matters, how the enquiry process to be conducted upon an accused / charge sheeted officer, how objective the report of the inquiring authority should be and the need for arriving at the logical conclusions based on the documentary and other evidence duly ensuring transparency is discussed at length in this book.

The struggle faced by the charge sheeted officer who is a scapegoat, how he has brought all the facts to light so as to convince the Bank's management is presented in an interesting way. Despite the non-response from the Bank to accept its mistakes, the efforts that the charge sheeted officer continued by appealing several times to both external statutory authorities as well as to Bank's management are very interesting to read. Though it is not liked by the charge sheeted officer to file a case with High Court, the circumstances forced him finally to approach High Court, but the case has never come for hearing at all despite the time is lapsing and his service in the organization is coming to an end. Hence the author predicted the proposed judgment and presented in a systematic way. Justice delayed is justice denied was the old saying, where as in the present context of this charge sheeted officer's case, truly, justice delayed is justice buried, but the author is still optimistic.

K.U.M.Reddy

Deputy General Manager

Chapter-1

The Staff Accountability

Justice delayed is justice denied is an old saying, but justice delayed is justice buried is the right statement. It is generally observed in this specific case that the disciplinary proceedings initiated by the Bank are based on certain documentary evidences. Prima facie for any common man with basic understanding skills, it looks as if the procedures' adopted and actions initiated by the bank are in order until the affected person brings the facts to light in a correct angle. For example as per the data fed in Bank's HRD records, Mr. LSR joined the Bank on 29-12-2007 at its Hyderabad branch, but in reality Mr. LSR joined at its Kakinada branch on 29-12-2007 and subsequently posted to its Hyderabad branch and accordingly after getting relieved from Kakinada, he has joined at its Hyderabad branch on 25-02-2008 and after attending office for few working days, he had gone on transfer benefit leave (Joining time leave) for two weeks during mid of march 2008 for shifting household goods from Kakinada to Hyderabad. Bank considered his posting to Hyderabad as transfer order and as per his claim, paid all the transfer benefits to Mr. LSR including sanction of Transfer leave/joining time leave for two weeks. This fact of his transfer from Kakinada to Hyderabad is nowhere captured in his personal HRD records of the Bank and everywhere it is erroneously recorded as if Mr. LSR joined Bank directly at its Hyderabad branch on 29-12-2007 itself upon selection as AGM by the Bank.

It is generally observed that if a loan account becomes NPA (Non-performing Asset) i.e., if the over dues are not paid for more than 90 days, immediately the staff accountability part and staff involvement are examined by Banks. Certain important aspects need to be paid special and careful attention while examining staff accountability i.e., the reason/s for the account becoming NPA. Generally there are only two types of reasons for any loan account to become NPA i.e., 1) General reasons and 2) Fraud element.

With regard to general reasons, there may be genuine business failure of the borrower, job loss of the borrower, health issues, family issues, external aspects like certain government decisions etc. These general reasons which cause loan account to become NPA are not a failure on the part of the individual loan case dealing officer and he or she should never be fixed with staff accountability.

Within the general reasons, there are another type of reasons viz failure in doing proper market inquiries about the proposed borrower, not conducting visits to the borrowers business place and to the collateral securities, not observing certain important aspects like presence of grave yard, big drainage, hill area, slum area, boundaries of the property etc during visit to the immovable securities like buildings, open plots, flats by the Bank officer which may ultimately result in non-realization of security value in case of loan account turning NPA, failure in ensuring end use of bank loan portion as per the prescribed loan sanction conditions, failure in doing constant monitoring as per banks internal guidelines, failure in obtaining certain documents viz proof of business, licenses, permits, defective appraisal of loan proposal etc, can be attributed to the Bank officer as the reasons of failure in discharging his/her duties. However the volume of the business the concerned officer is handling and the supporting hands provided to him or her (i.e. manpower sufficiency) should also to be factored while fixing staff accountability on the part of the officer.

Before fixing staff accountability, it is also very important to investigate and identify whether there is any gross negligence of duty or mala fide intentions on the part of the officer because of which the loan account has turned in to NPA. The nature and integrity of the officer, his/her past professional history, mala fide intentions or gross negligence of duty reflected in the earlier instances if any, his length of experience in the present organization shall be given due weightage while fixing accountability. Length of experience of the officer is to understand how best he or she is acquainted with the systems, procedures' and internal guideline of the present organization.

It is pertinent to mention here that the charges framed upon an officer shall be strictly in accordance with the points based on which the accountability is fixed. In this instant case while perusing the minutes of the staff accountability committee meeting dt.16th August 2012, it is observed that the accountability is fixed upon LSR based on two points as noted below:

a. For not confirming margin money brought in and

b. For not ensuring end use of funds at the time of disbursement

Both the above points are definitely important to be complied with by any bank officer dealing with post sanction credit matters. In this instant loan case of SBEMPL (NPA account), the staff accountability committee of the bank has observed that the above two points were not paid attention by the officer LSR, hence the loan account of SBEMPL was turned in to NPA.

Upon perusal of the charge sheet issued to LSR, it is observed that the charges framed against him are majorly different from what is observed by staff accountability committee of the Bank in its minutes. Further it is observed that the basic documents (internal office notes) put up to staff accountability committee by the concerned HRD/department dealing officers was sought for by the charge sheeted officer LSR from Bank's HRD and Bank has refused to provide the same to LSR.

While submitted the internal office notes to fix staff accountability upon LSR, it can be presumed that those internal office notes must have projected LSR as the officer dealing with post sanction credit matters of SBEMPL loan case and to this extent they must have provided/enclosed some supporting document/s confirming that Sri.LSR was the dealing officer for this SBEMPL loan post sanction credit matters during the relevant period. This supporting documents either in the form of any works distribution order or other documents/office notes confirming LSR's role in this loan is a pre requisite for fixing accountability. Staff accountability fixation is such a serious and important matter as it helps

Bank in protecting its interest as well as affects the concerned officer's career. Hence this exercise shall be undertaken with due care and with all supporting valid documents with pragmatically drawn conclusions.

Staff accountability fixation is generally considered as one time activity except in exceptional cases. For example, post fixing of accountability upon any officer, if new facts come to light, the HRD officers of the organization shall go back to the next Staff Accountability Committee (SAC) meeting duly submitting modifications to their earlier internal office notes to revise the staff accountability based on the facts came to light. To err is human and it may happen with HRD officials also, hence HRD officials of the organization need not hesitate to go back to SAC, they must have courage to accept their mistakes and suitably guide the SAC in re-fixing the accountability if it is to be revised due to genuine reasons.

Failure to re-submit the new facts that requires revision in staff accountability amounts to crime and misconduct on the part of HRD officials. In fact such failure amounts to suppression of facts and it shall attract separate disciplinary action against the responsible HRD officials who resorted to such acts of misconduct.

Preferably the internal investigation needs to be conducted prior to submitting the office notes to staff accountability committee. The SAC shall take a holistic view rather than merely guided by what is mentioned in the office notes submitted to it. The SAC members should broadly discuss about the accountability matter among themselves, pose cross questions to the HRD and Dealing Group (DG) officials who have prepared internal office notes about the discernibility of accountability against any officer and should call for the additional information if required based on the internal discussions happened. In fact the office notes/internal memorandums prepared regarding staff accountability shall be supplied in advance to the respective SAC members for their perusal and broad understanding.

In this instant case of LSR, with regard to fixing staff accountability, it is observed as follows:

Documents considered as the basis to confirm LSR as the loan case dealing officer during the relevant period are either not examined properly or must have intentionally overlooked/neglected by officers who have prepared and put up internal office notes/memorandums to the staff accountability committee. ***For example his joining Bank at Kakinada on 29-12-2007 and stay there at Kakinada up to the end of February 2008 is either over looked or suppressed in the internal office notes/ memorandums submitted to the staff accountability committee.***

Mr.LSR is projected as the loan case dealing officer of SBEMPL in its post sanction credit matters whereas all the available documentary evidences are confirming that Smt.VKN was the dealing officer of SBEMPL loan case in its post sanction credit matters. ***It appears that all those documents evidencing presence of VKN and absence of LSR are either not submitted to SAC or intentionally misrepresented to SAC duly suppressing the factual information about the incidents took place from the date of sanction and the officers involved there in at every stage.***

As per his letter dt.04th May 2013, being the charge sheeted officer, Sri LSR sought for certain documents from the bank and out of which majority of the documents were not provided to LSR. This act of the Bank amounts to depriving him of the opportunity to recall and confirm what exactly happened during the period of incidence happened in the year 2008. ***This act of the Bank is against to the principles of natural justice.*** It is found that all that documents sought for by LSR are very much relevant and would help him in arriving at actual context during the year of incidence.

Accountability against LSR was fixed in the year 2012 and the matter in which the accountability was fixed is pertaining to the incidents of the year 2008. Bank cannot unilaterally decide any document whether it is irrelevant or not when it is sought for by the charge sheeted officer. There is no room for secrecy in such accountability fixing matters, because it is matter of professional career of an individual officer.

Bank should also examine the prescribed internal and RBI guidelines, circulars and other policies and should comparatively cross check whether compliance part is paid deaf ear by the officer concerned in adhering to those guidelines. Bank should prescribe certain points in chronological order so as to avoid misrepresentation of basic points to the SAC. For example:

1. Who has sourced the loan proposal and the due diligence aspect paid with regard to the market inquiries about the borrower, activity etc.
2. Who has conducted the pre-sanction visit to the securities, their visit reports and visit observations
3. Who has/have appraised the loan proposal and compliance to prescribed Bank's norms including the eligibility norms prescribed for the loan proposals to be entertained
4. Who has sanctioned the Loan and the observations and conditions stipulated by the sanctioning authority
5. Who has issued sanction letter and whether all the sanction conditions are incorporated there in the sanction letter or not
6. Legal title verification reports and valuation reports of collateral securities and the observations made there in by the respective advocate/engineer and compliance thereof and the details of the officer/s dealt with these matters
7. Who has conducted documentation and security creation and compliance to the prescribed procedures in this regard?
8. Who has conducted pre-disbursement visit to the securities both primary and collateral, their visit reports and visit observations vis a vis bank's internal guidelines stipulated in this regard
9. First disbursement note, its date and procedure adopted, draft office notes moved in this regard if any
10. Approved first disbursement note, sanction conditions complied and pending for compliance if any, officers involved there in
11. Approvals on hand from the competent authority to go ahead with disbursement pending compliance to sanction conditions if any as applicable.
12. Confirmations about the end use of Bank funds before initiating second and subsequent disbursements.

13. Progress reports and visit reports pertaining to the activity/purpose for which the loan is sanctioned, between each disbursement before going ahead with next disbursement

14. Confirmation about loan end utilization

15. Loan account operations monitoring

16. Fixation of drawing power in case of working capital loan and compliance to drawing power fixation norms as per Bank's internal guidelines

17. Who has conducted regular post disbursement monitoring activities and compliance ensured thereof and

18. Renewal/Review and enhancement matters and compliance to the procedures and guidelines prescribed by the Bank in this regard.

If the officers putting up internal office notes to the SAC or the SAC members themselves pay attention on the prescribed points noted above, it will really help in identifying the accountability aspect whether really discernable against any employee/officer or not.

In this instant NPA case, while examining the staff accountability, it is found that none of the above points were paid attention by the bank and its officers concerned including the SAC members before fixing accountability upon LSR. In addition to paying deaf year to the above mentioned points, it is observed that the Bank's dealing HRD officers were more enthusiastic in providing false information to SAC without any of the above mentioned points related supporting documentary evidences. Further Bank's officers who ever have put up office notes to SAC in this matter have committed big blunders by not even looking at the entirety of any document considered as basis for fixing accountability. For example the factual/actual date in the works allocation order adopted as important evidence in this accountability matter was misrepresented to the SAC and thus the HRD department officials reflected gross negligence of their duty which amounts to misconduct and attracts disciplinary action against them as its cost is professional career loss of an innocent officer.

Coming to second type of loan accounts which turned in to NPA due to the FRAUD element persisting in them, the staff accountability shall be examined with more focus on how the fraud happened, what kind of fraud it is, whether it happened with the cooperation of the internal officers, what is the modus operandi etc need to be paid special attention by the concerned Bank officers and a comprehensive note with all factual information supported with documentary evidences shall be submitted to SAC. This internal office notes shall also very specifically contain information about how the fraud took place, what are the internal guidelines bypassed that resulted into fraud happening successfully. Such bypass of guidelines if happened, whether it is due to oversight or intentional also shall be mentioned in the office notes submitted to SAC with proper justifications.

For example if there is a fraud element observed in the immovable property mortgaged as security, the following aspects attract special attention:

1. What are the internal guidelines prescribed by the bank with regard to accepting an immovable property as security and systems and procedures prescribed for mortgage of immovable properties as security
2. Pre-sanction visit reports of immovable properties, its content and compliance thereof by the dealing officers
3. Advocate's title investigation report, conditions stipulated by advocate like property tax receipt to be obtained, continuity encumbrance certificate to be obtained, mutation to be done in government/revenue records, name change in electricity bill, water bill in the name of the mortgagor etc and compliance thereof exercised by the dealing officers shall be examined.
4. Empanelled valuer's reports on the immovable properties, nature of land whether agri or non-agri type, proposed master plans if any and the probability of loss of full or part of immovable property in road widening, buildings/shed structures if any existing in the immovable property and its details etc and compliance thereof exercised by the dealing officers shall be examined.

5. Other conditions if any stipulated by both the advocate and valuer in their respective reports and compliance thereof exercised by the dealing officers in this regard shall be examined.

6. Due diligence exercised and confirmations obtained by the dealing team on the following aspects also need to be paid attention viz Genunity of the Title deeds confirmation, search report on the title deeds at respective sub-registrar's office, Encumbrance certificate etc.

7. In addition to the above, it is also to be observed whether the pre-disbursement visit to the property location was conducted and the observations made in this regard also to be verified while recommending to SAC.

8. Guidelines already issued by Bank vis a vis point to point compliances to be submitted to SAC preferably in a table format.

9. Other fraud elements like fake identity cards, fake salary slips, fake PAN cards, fake IT returns and defective field investigation reports by the external agencies engaged etc needs to be separately mentioned in office notes submitted to SAC for examining the Staff Accountability.

In addition to the above, SAC shall also broadly take in to account and should pay special attention on the following:

1. The experience of the dealing officer in the activity/job role and the works allocation orders available if any, his or her access to files and his or her access to core banking software

2. ***Whether he or she has newly joined the Bank, if so, during the first one or two years of the service, these newly joined officers would be on probation and all that acts and deeds committed and duties discharged by these officers on probation are subject to verification and authorization by the respective senior officers or supervisors in the organization. Hence the discernibility of accountability does not arise against those newly joined officers who are on probation unless there is clearly proved mala fide intention on the part of the newly joined officer who is on probation.***

3. Inquiry reports and investigation reports available if any, observations mentioned therein about the NPA loan and acceptability of the investigation report after examining them in their entirety and

4. The errors or mistakes committed if any by the dealing officers shall also to be examined with respect to mala fide intentions and gross negligence of duty.

Bank's should also take care that the staff accountability notes are prepared by the individual officers who have sufficient knowledge about the job role/ working knowledge of the area/function upon which the need aroused to prepare staff accountability. For example an officer from HRD without having credit knowledge or who have not worked in credit department shall not be asked to prepare staff accountability note to be submitted to SAC.

With regard to the officers on probation or newly joined the organization, if their supervisors or senior colleagues commit any irregularities/frauds by misusing their power over the newly joined officer, banks shall respond in the following manner:

a. If the respective documents is jointly signed by both the newly joined officer along with his supervisor, accountability shall not be fixed upon the newly joined officer

b. Similarly the computer entries where ever maker and checker concept is there, the checker shall be held responsible if the maker is a newly joined officer

To sum up in a nut shell, the SAC shall be provided with the information in chronological order from the date of sourcing the loan proposal along with the details of all that internal officers / persons involved there in, noncompliance to internal guidelines happened if any at each stage until it became NPA, the officers responsible for the same and the true reason/s for NPA duly focusing on the fraud element if any shall be addressed along with the internal/external investigation reports if available and as applicable.

Chapter-2

The Charge Sheet

The following charge sheet dt.28-02-2013 along with its enclosures produced before the author is examined and observed the following:

At the beginning of the articles of charges, Bank addressing LSR mentioned that "During the course of your duties and tenure as AGM and Officer SME Credit administration at Bank's City SME Center (CSC) Hyderabad ***from December 29, 2007 till December 9, 2010***, various acts of misconduct, as hereinafter mentioned, are reported to have been committed by you;

That on October 25, 2007 M/S SBEMPL was sanctioned financial assistance of Rs.354 lakh (Term loan and Cash Credit). In gross neglect of your duties and responsibilities, you had without observing proper due diligence, recommended for disbursement of both Cash credit limits and Term loan to the company despite deficiencies, you also failed to ensure end use of funds lent by the Bank both by way of Cash credit limits and Term loan and to monitor the cash credit account of the company in as much as,

i. Charge-1: "You failed to seek clarification from the company on the observations recorded by our officials in the pre-disbursement visit conducted on 23-2-2008 before approving the disbursement of cash credit limit."

ii. Charge-2: "You failed to ensure that payments were made to the suppliers/vendors directly from the Term Loan amount disbursed and instead disbursing the amount by crediting the funds disbursed to the current account of the company."

iii. Charge-3: "You have failed to ensure that from the term loan amount disbursed, payments are made to the supplier/vendors, which were named by the company in its project report and also failed to seek documents/proof of creation/acquisition of fixed assets from the funds lent by the Bank."

iv. Charge-4: You failed to ensure that the account was closely monitored and clarifications from the company were obtained regarding transfer of funds to the individual accounts of promoters and also failed to ensure that the funds lent by the Bank are utilized for business purpose only.

v. Charge-5: "You failed to ensure that post disbursement visits, as envisaged in the terms of sanction, were carried out to confirm acquisition/creation of fixed assets as per the project report" and

vi. Charge-6: "You as Post Sanction Credit monitoring officer failed to obtain stock and debtors statement from the company at monthly intervals and set the drawing power on the basis of such statements"

Based on the above, as instructed by the Bank, LSR has submitted his written statement of defense dt.13-03-2013 denying all the charges. The details of the same are as follows:

1. The disbursement note of Cash Credit limits dt.08-03-2008 was not routed through me and I have not recommended the same, my signature is also not appearing on the same. Hence I am denying this charge.

2. On 31st March 2008 evening, after returned to home and when I was on the way, I was called over phone by the then DGM Mr.VSV who was the head of SME department up to January 2008 and was heading another department in the same Bank as on 31st March 2008. He asked me to come back to office and meet my present boss/ DGM Mr.NRC. I have returned to Bank as instructed by VSV and upon reaching office I was asked to meet VKN and after some discussions VKN made with me, I approached NRC, he told me that they have to disburse SBEMPL Term Loan (TL) urgently and instructed me to sign the TL

disbursement note urgently. Further he told that the WC limits of the same borrower were already disbursed many days back and Mrs.VKN is having more than 20 years of experience in the Bank and as she has been dealing with loan cases, she knows all procedures/guidelines and assured that both of them (NRC & VKN) will take care about adherence to procedures and instructed me to sign the TL disbursement note.

Upon receiving such instruction and assurances from my immediate supervisor NRC, ***I have reluctantly signed the TL disbursement note as nothing adverse was observed upon perusal of the same***. After signing the TL disbursement note, I have told to Mrs.VKN in the presence of NRC, not to bypass any procedural guidelines even due to oversight. Further they have assured me that they will issue pay orders/demand drafts etc to the respective vendors/suppliers as per the project report/loan appraisal memorandum.

During the same time NRC told me that the TL disbursement proceeds would be temporarily parked in the current account of the borrower to maintain 31st March financial year-end target balances and he had given me a debit voucher which is already signed by him for crediting the TL disbursement amount in to the current account of SBEMPL and instructed me to sign that debit voucher also. As I am generally aware about Bankers financial year end targets and commitments and ***as NRC had already signed the voucher, I too signed the same as instructed by him.***

In view of the above, it is evident that the officers who are supposed to ensure the payments to suppliers/vendors are VKN and NRC. Hence I request you to with draw this charge framed against me.

3. Mrs VKN was the direct dealing officer for this SBEMPL loan case in the post sanction credit matters. While disbursing the TL, VKN and NRC have given me oral assurance that they will ensure adherence to all procedural guidelines including payment as per project to the supplier/vendors. As she was directly dealing with is

loan case and directly reporting to DGM NRC, both of them have to ensure end use of funds and should obtain documents/proofs of creation of assets out of the TL disbursement proceeds. Hence I am denying this charge and it should not be framed against me.

4. All sorts of monitoring work in this loan case including monitoring of account transactions in finacle core banking software is pertaining to VKN as she was the loan case dealing officer in post sanction credit monitoring aspects of this SBEMPL loan case up to the end of January 2009 (for a period of almost 15 months). Bank is requested to verify the records with regard to my reporting structure, VKN reporting structure and about the date of providing finacle user ID to me by the Bank during May 2008. In view of the above, I deny this charges and Bank has mistakenly framed this charge against me. In view of the above I request you to withdraw this charge.

5. As per the email dt.23-1-2009 I was made Head Credit Monitoring of CSC, Hyderabad, the subject loan case was allocated to Mrs KRB to deal with its post sanction credit matters. Until then it had been handled by VKN for a period of fifteen months from the date of its sanction and she had been directly reporting to DGM NRC.

   After becoming Head Credit Monitoring of CSC, Hyderabad, we have contacted Mr.SPR the promoter of SBEMPL (Borrower Company) several times over phone and vigorously followed up for recovery. During our recovery follow up over phone, several times we have asked Mr SPR to arrange/accompany for a visit to the Unit, but every time Mr SPR avoided/postponed visit to the unit stating that the forest department had seized the vehicles, and he was making efforts to get them released and presently there was nothing to show even if he take us for field visit. Further many times Mr SPR had given some other unsatisfactory excused to us over phone to avoid field visit.

   I have also advised Mrs KRB to conduct field visit and submit report. In addition to the above, several times we have called Mr SPR and had discussions with him seeking his action plan for clearing over dues. Documentary evidences pertaining to the same are available in the concerned loan files along with the email correspondence done with him. In response to the same Mr.SPR had also given promises in the form of repayment action plans but every time he did not fulfil his promises.

Please refer letter dt.7-7-2009 signed by me evidencing that I have made vigorous efforts for recovery of dues in the capacity of Head, Credit Administration. Since my email data was crashed during Nov 2010, I have lost many of data/correspondence happened in this regard both with the borrower as well as with the then dealing officers regarding visits, recovery etc, I request you sir to retrieve my email data so that it would help me in providing much more information and supporting documentary evidence about the due diligence I had ben exercising in this instant NPA loan case.

The content of my letter dt.7-7-2009 noted above is evidencing that I have made several telephonic discussions and correspondence with the borrower prior to July 2009 also. Due to the non-cooperation extended by the borrower, we have conducted several visits to the collateral securities also so as to initiate action as per SARFAESI act and during those visits the discrepancy in the collateral security was observed by me and accordingly we have moved one internal office note for initiating appropriate civil and criminal actions against the borrower and mortgagors in view of the over dues as well as suspicious fraud angle in the collateral security. In view of the above, I submit that i have discharged my duties very diligently by conducting visits as well as making vigorous efforts for recovery from the date of becoming as Head Credit Administration. Hence I deny this charge.

6. I was not the Post Sanction Credit monitoring officer for this NPA loan case. From the date of its loan sanction till 23-1-2009, Mrs VKN was the Post Sanction Credit monitoring officer to this loan case and subsequently it was Mrs.KRB doing Post Sanction Credit monitoring w.e.f. 23-1-2009.I was never the direct Post Sanction Credit monitoring officer for this loan case.

After I was made as the Head of Post Sanction Credit monitoring team, myself and my team have made best efforts to impress upon all the borrowers including SBEMPL to submit the stock and debtor statement. Despite our best efforts, SBEMPL did not submit the same.

By the time, this loan case came under our purview as on 29-1-2009, the CC a/c was already overdue/ over drawn for a period of four months and the promoters were not ready to submit the stock statements and to clear the over dues. However due to our vigorous follow up with the borrower, with in a span of two months, i.e. by march 2009 we could able to bring down the CC outstanding amount below the sanctioned amount by recovering the over dues. Thus up to June 2010, we have recovered an amount of Rs.14.10 lakh from this NPA borrower. Other recovery and monitoring efforts including the efforts made by me for obtaining stock statements are evident in various emails I have sent to my Post Sanction Credit Monitoring team members as well as to this NPA Borrower. In view of the above, I deny this charge and request you to withdraw the same.

Based on the above charges framed by the Bank and charge specific replies submitted by LSR, it is observed as follows:

While submitting internal office notes to the Staff accountability committee, it appears that the dealing officers who have prepared those notes must have projected Mr. LSR as the loan specific Post Sanction Credit monitoring officer since 29-12-2007 i.e. since the date of his appointment.

The documents considered by the Bank as the basis to confirm Mr.LSR as the loan specific Post Sanction Credit monitoring officer are not listed in the charge sheet dt.27/28-02-2013.

The denial of the first charge by Mr.LSR saying that he has not signed the Cash Credit disbursement note dt.08-03-2008 and his claim that it is not routed through him is giving scope to suspect whether the officers who have drafted this charge have genuinely verified the supporting documents like cash credit disbursement note, drawing power fixation note etc. Further it is very specifically alleged in the first charge that Mr.LSR has disbursed cash credit limits without seeking clarification from the company on the observations recorded by the Bank officials in the pre-disbursement visit conducted on 23-2-2008.

While framing the first charge, it is presumed that Bank officers who have prepared this charge sheet must have seen/verified 1. Cash Credit Disbursement note Dt.08-03-2008, 2) Visit report of Bank Officers Dt.23-02-2008. Whereas upon perusal of these two documents it is observed that the signature of Mr.LSR is nowhere appearing in those documents.

In view of the above it is observed as failure on the part of the Bank officers who have prepared this charge alleging Mr.LSR that he has failed to seek clarification from the company on the observations recorded by bank officials in the pre-disbursement visit conducted on 23-2-2008 before approving the disbursement of cash credit limit. *Such false allegations without supporting documentary evidence attracts penal action against those officers who have prepared/drafted such baseless charge alleging an officer.* It is useless and time waste on the part of the Bank seeking clarification from the CSO about such baseless charge. As explained in detail at the 1st chapter of this book on the guidelines to be adopted while fixing staff accountability, appears to have been paid deaf year by the Bank and its responsible authorities.

With regard to charge number 2 to 6, as it is evident that all these charges are pertaining to the duties of Post-sanction Credit Monitoring Officer, it is observed as follows:

As on the date of incident happened, bank should justify its charges by providing supporting internal guidelines in the form of circulars or policy copies etc confirming the procedure prescribed for disbursement of Term Loan amount, periodicity of visit to be conducted and the important aspects that should be captured in the visit reports and the procedures and guidelines of loan account monitoring. It should also provide the supporting document confirming that the CSO LSR was the person supposed to adhere to those internal the guidelines and ensure compliance as per the works allocation order issued to him if any.

Upon perusal of the charges framed by the Bank and the replies submitted by CSO LSR, it is observed that the Bank has not enclosed/ not provided the following interesting supporting documents to CSO LSR along with the charge sheet issued to him:

1. Bank did not provide any specific internal guideline prevailing as on March 2008 prohibiting parking of TL disbursement funds in to the current account of the Borrower
2. Bank has neither provided the list of suppliers/vendors to whom the TL disbursement amounts were supposed to be transferred nor has provided any project report in this regard to the CSO confirming where he has failed in discharging his duties.
3. Bank failed to provide any office order or works distribution/ allocation order issued to the CSO LSR as on the incident happened date or prior to it fixing the responsibility of account monitoring, conducting of visits, obtaining stock statements etc upon the CSO LSR.

However by looking at the nature of activity involved pertaining to all the six charges framed against CSO LSR, it is broadly understood the he was considered as Post sanction credit monitoring officer by the Bank for the subject NPA Loan case. Whereas in all the replies submitted by LSR to the charge sheet vide his reply letter dt.13-03-2013, he has been repeatedly saying that he was not the Post sanction credit monitoring officer to this loan case.

Upon examination of letter dt.13-03-2013 (replies submitted by LSR denying the charges framed against him), the following important points attract attention:

He joined Bank at its Kakinada branch on 29-12-2007, but in the charge sheet it is mentioned that he has been working at its SME department, Hyderabad branch since 29-12-2007. He is quoting the office order no: 1862 dt.15-2-2008, based on which he was relieved from Kakinada branch on 23-02-2008 and reported for duty at Hyderabad branch on 25-02-2008. Further he is confirming that this office order dt.15-2-2008 was considered as Transfer order by Bank's HRD and accordingly he was paid all the general transfer benefits amounting to Rs.76494/- on 06th May 2008 and availed transfer joining time leave also after reporting at Bank's Hyderabad Office. Upon perusal of his SB account statement, the same is proved correct as he was paid his transfer bill claim amount. If he has been continued at its Hyderabad branch from day one of his joining the Bank on 29-12-2007 till the year 2010, payment of transfer claim bill to him does not arise at all.

Hence upon receipt of his replies, ideally Bank should have perused the factual information by verifying his account statement, transfer bill etc to confirm whether what he had written in his replies to charge sheet is correct. If this aspect would have been paid attention, the need would have aroused for the Bank to recheck and modify certain contents in the charge sheet mentioning that he has been continuing at its Hyderabad office since 25-02-2008.

Whereas bank neglected to cross check the factual position and it rather believed what is mentioned by it in the charge sheet regarding the tenure of LSR at its Hyderabad office is correct. If the same would have been cross checked by the Bank, the actual position would have come to light about his dealing with the subject loan case in its post sanction credit matters.

He has while submitting his replies enclosed the copy of works distribution order dt.23-01-2009 issued by the then DGM SVS and confirmed that until then he was doing works on piecemeal basis as and when entrusted by the DGM/s as he was on probationary period of his service in the Bank.. It is general practice and fact that if any officer has newly joined any organization, he or she would not be specifically assigned with particular works and they are generally given opportunity to acquaint themselves with the systems and procedures of the organization up to six months or one year from the date of their reporting. ***Further during the first one or two years of the service, these newly joined officers would be on probation and all that acts and deeds committed and duties discharged by these officers on probation are subject to verification and authorization by the respective senior officers or supervisors in the organization.***

The CSO LSR has attached the following documents with his replies dt.13-03-2013 with certain clarifications and explanations, the gist of the same is noted below:

An attendance sheet was signed by all the individuals present while conducting loan and security documents execution. This sheet is signed by the representatives of the Bank as well as by the borrower/mortgagor/guarantor and the Bank's empanelled advocate. Upon verification of the same, it is observed that the same is signed by (1) VKN (2) NRC (3) Borrowers and (4) Bank's advocate. As alleged in the charge sheet, if CSO LSR was the officer entrusted with the duties pertaining to post sanction credit matters in this subject loan case, he too must have been the part of this attendance sheet, but his signature is not appearing on the same.

After the competent authority sanctions any loan, the first exercise to be done is preparation of loan sanction letter and issue of the same to the borrower and the next exercise is obtaining and verifying the supporting documents like valuation reports and Title investigation reports of the securities stipulated, obtaining the approvals if any required if there is any deviation from the sanction terms. After satisfying that everything is in order as per sanction terms/approvals, the dealing team should conduct documentation in their presence to be executed by the borrower/s, mortgagors/guarantors etc. As a general practice in those days to make it an evidence in future if required, this attendance sheet signed by all the concerned while conducting documentation will be produced in the court of law so that the parties who have executed the documents/created security cannot say that they have not signed/not executed those documents.

The CSO LSR's presence is neither found in the Loan sanction letter nor in the documentation attendance sheet. This is the first and very important point supporting his version saying that he was not entrusted with the responsibility of Post Sanction Credit matters in this subject NPA loan case.

With regard to other documentary evidences available pertaining to post sanction credit matters, the working capital disbursement note dt.08-03-2008, the drawing power fixation sheet pertaining to the same, pre-disbursement visit report pertaining to the same subject NPA borrower, the pre-disbursement verification office note, the Term Loan

(TL) disbursement note and the TL repayment re-fixation office note are examined by this court with reference to the denial of charges submitted by CSO LSR. Upon perusal of all the above documents, it is observed that all these documents are dealt exclusively by both VKN and NRC except the TL disbursement note which is signed by all the three officers i.e., VKN, LSR and NRC. Coming to the chronology of documents based on their dates of presentation and approval, it is evident that the TL repayment re-fixation office note is the last one dated 22-04-2008.

To cross check the claim of the CSO LSR who said that he was not the Post Sanction Credit Monitoring officer for this subject loan, the available exhibits as produced by him are presented in the following table:

Sl no	Name of the exhibit	Date of Exhibit	Officers signed the same
1	Sanction Letter	02-11-2007	VKN & NRC
2	Pre-disbursement visit report	23-02-2008	VKN & NRC
3	Documentation Attendance sheet	05-03-2008	VKN & NRC
4	Working capital CC disbursement note	08-03-2008	VKN & NRC
5	WC Drawing power fixing sheet	08-03-2008	VKN & NRC
6	Pre-disbursement vetting office note	17-03-2008	VKN & NRC
7	Term Loan disbursement draft Note	31-03-2008	VKN & NRC
8	Term Loan disbursement Note and its voucher	31-03-2008	VKN & LSR & NRC
9	Finacle screen shot parking TL funds in CA account (voucher prepared by VKN)	31-03-2008	VKN & NRC
10	Term Loan repayment re-fixation note	22-04-2008	VKN & NRC
11	Account Monitoring and its control	During the relevant period of diversion and siphoning of funds up to 30-04-2008	VKN & NRC

Upon perusal of the above documentary exhibits in Post sanction credit matters of the subject NPA loan, Mrs.VKN and Mr.NRC have been commonly present in all the document and they have presented/approved all of them. Parking of TL funds in Current Account (Sl No: 9) was done by NRC and its voucher was prepared by VKN as per the hand writing appearing there in. Whereas the presence of CSO LSR appeared only in TL disbursement note. The TL disbursement note (Sl No: 8) is neither beginning nor ending of the chronology of post sanction credit matters in this NPA case. Further the presence of CSO LSR in SL no: 8 document above is not duly excluding VKN but it is including VKN. There are no other documentary exhibits other than mentioned in the above table pertaining to post sanction credit matters in the subject NPA loan during the entire year 2008.

Based on the above, it can be understood that it was VKN & NRC who have dealt with all post sanction credit matters in this NPA case during the entire year 2008. The above factual information is repeatedly mentioned by CSO LSR in his replies dt.13-03-2013 submitted to the Bank. Since he has enclosed all the above documentary evidences to his replies to charge sheet and thus he has made bank's job easy to cross check the documentary exhibits. If Bank was not satisfied with the above documentary exhibits, it was at liberty to find out other documents if any available in the loan files of the subject NPA case that establishes the responsibility of post sanction credit matters upon CSO LSR. However bank has accepted that all the above documentary evidences are the only documents pertaining to post sanction credit matters in this NPA case during the entire year 2008.

In view of the above, both logically as well as legally it can be concluded that post sanction credit matters in this NPA case during the entire year 2008 were dealt by VKN & NRC. In this context it is equally important to find out how the signature of CSO LSR appeared only in the Term Loan disbursement Note and its voucher (Sl.No: 8 above) and how bank has arrived at the conclusion that the CSO LSR was solely dealing with all post sanction credit matters in this NPA loan case.

Mr.LSR has mentioned many more points in his reply dt.13-3-2013 which cannot be neglected from consideration; he has expressed that he was getting doubt about the following:

When VKN herself along with KRB undertaken pre-disbursement visit to the borrower's unit in Karnataka on 23-02-2008 and found no activity at the field location and submitted a report to this extent,

- What made her to conduct documentation of the same borrower on 05-03-2008 despite her adverse observations during the visit?
- What made her to recommend the WC disbursement note on 08-03-2008 to NRC despite there has been no activity at the borrowers works location for the past one year.

VKN submitted her visit report to NRC and NRC had noted all the observations of visit report including the comment about nil/no activity. Despite being aware of this,

- What made both VKN and NRC to prepare and disburse WC limits to CC account of the borrower without capturing the adverse observations of the unit visit in the WC disbursement note? And
- How they have arrived at drawing power in CC account despite no stocks at the work site and no eligible book debts at all as the activity was already stopped one year back itself.

Further it is mentioned by LSR that after signing the TL disbursement note on 31-03-2008 around 6 pm, he had observed that his colleague Mr.EKL was still there in the office in his seat, hence LSR approached him to say bye to him for the day once again. In that context Mr. EKL asked LSR why he has again came back to office and LSR told him about the TL disbursement. On hearing the same Mr.EKL informed LSR that after 5 pm on the same day after LSR's first departure to home, VKN approached EKL and requested him to sign the same borrower's TL disbursement note. He has agreed and asked VKN to bring the loan files and other supporting back papers for his perusal. However VKN did not turn back to him but suddenly LSR surprisingly returned back to office. LSR expressed that when EKL was telling him that, he did not take it seriously, but while correlating the incidents happened, now after receipt of the charge sheet, he is getting many doubts with regard to this TL disbursement and understood that VKN & NRC want at least one AGM's signature in TL disbursement note, irrespective of whether that AGM has any assigned role or not.

He has also expressed there in that he was unable to understand why VKN had not obtained EKL's signature despite having requested him for the same and what made VKN, NRC and* VSV *to call LSR back to office and obtain his signature without giving time/scope to him for perusal of connected back papers in this regard though he was not involved in this loan case in any manner.

Further at the concluding part of his replies dt.13-03-2013, LSR mentioned that though the receipt of this charge sheet has caused lot of pain and mental agony to him, in the best interest of the Bank he had conducted some discreet inquires in this regard and collected some audio recording evidences which would definitely help bank in identifying the real reasons and persons for the financial loss incurred by the bank in this NPA loan case.

He has also mentioned the gist of confirmations available in all the audio record evidences as noted below:

1. During the pre-sanction and pre-disbursement stages of this loan itself, NRC and VKN are aware that this is a problematic loan proposal.
2. NRC has clearly stated and admitted that LSR has no assigned role in this loan case and he is ready to admit and confess the same before any authority/committee.
3. Sourcing and bringing of this bad loan proposal to the Bank and its irregular disbursement were completely ensured by VSV and he had conducted visit to the borrower's work site also as mentioned by the borrower himself in his loan application.
4. NRC says that while recommending this loan case for sanction in the year 2007, VSV was the then Regional Head, SME, Hyderabad and he knows that it is a fraud loan case, that is why

he cleverly avoided signing this loan appraisal memorandum while recommending to sanctioning committee despite he signed other loan proposal sent to the same sanctioning committee during same time, but cleverly got this loan sanctioned without he signing the appraisal memorandum.

5. VSV had put lot of pressure upon NRC and VKN to complete disbursement of this loan
6. KVD another officer in loan processing team said that VSV was sourcing unworthy loan proposals through ABPS a Chartered Accountant and had been pressurized upon her to process such unworthy loan proposals.
7. VKN said that both NRC and KVD knows that this is a problematic loan before its sanction and disbursement itself
8. ***VKN said that NRC asked her to change her pre-disbursement visit report positively***
9. NRC says that both he and VKN discussed several times that though this is a problematic loan case, VSV was putting pressure upon them for its disbursement.
10. VSV and ABPS have been close associates since the period of their working together at COAPIT
11. ABPS sourced many bad loan cases and got them sanctioned by the Bank through VSV and many of them have now turned in to NPA.
12. Mr RNR (borrower of another NPA case), VSV and ABPS have been close friends for the past twenty years and above.
13. VKN told that one Mr.GG (another AGM) warned her that this is a problematic case and be cautious while dealing with loan case. It happened when both VKN and GG were going together for a visit pertaining to SAL (another loan case).
14. NRC told that he has some other information about another problematic case where in discrepancies took place due to the involvement of VSV in his the then department in the Bank.

Despite such an elaborate reply dt.13-3-2013 along with documentary and audio evidences offered by LSR, bank did not satisfy, it did not withdraw the staff accountability fixed up on LSR and did not withdraw any of the charges framed against him.

What made the bank to be so rigid and not to revise its decisions will be discussed and explained at length in the forthcoming chapters of this book. However based on the replies submitted by CSO LSR, bank has ordered for internal departmental inquiry by appointing its GM PKK as the Internal Inquiry officer, Mr.BMM as the presenting officer from Bank's HRD side and few experienced senior officers as Management Witnesses for the inquiry proceedings including VKN as one of the Management Witnesses.

Chapter-3

The Internal Departmental Inquiry

In view of the replies submitted by CSO LSR to the charge sheet, Bank has ordered for an internal departmental inquiry to find out whether the charges framed against LSR are proved or not. Accordingly it was informed to LSR in writing by the Bank and he was assured of equal opportunity to defend himself with all supporting evidences and also by seeking additional documents if any required so as to ensure a transparent inquiry proceedings.

The Inquiry officer Mr.PKK vide his letter dt.25-04-2013 communicated in writing to LSR that the inquiry will be held by conducting Regular Hearings (RHs), accordingly he has conducted the first RH on 3rd May 2013. During the first RH, the IA PKK asked whether the CSO admits the charges framed against him and the CSO LSR replied stating that he has already denied all the charges vide his reply dt.13-03-2013 and informed that he would like to submit certain additional facts/information regarding the case and offered a letter with a pen drive attached to it reportedly containing certain important evidence in audio form. IA expressed his inability to accept evidence in audio form pending clarification from the Bank.

Important observation: The IA PKK has to take decisions independently with regard to accepting evidences in whatever form they are available and he should check the content there in as per the procedures available so as to finally arrive at whether the content in the evidence has to be given due weightage while submitting his inquiry report. Hence in the first RH itself the IA PKK could not act independently to the full extent and indirectly conveyed that his decision/s and acts would be as guided by the Bank.

The IA asked CSO to furnish the additional list of documents required if any and CSO informed that he will submit the list shortly. Accordingly the preliminary round of RH was concluded on 03rd May 2013 and the proceedings of the same in writing were signed by IA, PO, CSO and the Defense Representative (DR).

The RH-2 was conducted on 16th August 2013 in the presence of IA PKK, PO BMM, CSO LSR, DR VJ and MW-1 RSM. The brief content of the same is as follows:

PO submitted to IA the following Management Exhibits (ME):

1. ME-1 Sanction appraisal memorandum DT. 25th October 2007
2. ME-2 Loan sanction letter DT. 2nd Nov 2007 issued to SBEMPL
3. ME-3 Pre-disbursement visit report by VKN & KRB conducted on 23rd February 2008/report dt.26-02-2008
4. ME-4 CA certified stocks and book debts statement dt.29th February 2008
5. ME-5 Cash credit disbursement note Dt 8th March 2008
6. ME-6 CA certificate DT. 24th March 2008 regarding capital expenditure advances
7. ME-7 TL disbursement note dt.31st March 2008
8. ME-8 Statement of SBEMPL Cash credit account up to the year 2013
9. ME-9 Statement of SBEMPL Current account up to the year 2010 March

The important gist of the inquiry proceeding of RH dt.16-8-2013 for the questions asked by PO BMM and the replies given by the MW-1 RSM are as noted below:

MW-1 Mr.RSM deposed that while preparing loan sanction memorandum, the project report containing the details of the machinery to be purchased, specific brand names, make etc are generally to be mentioned therein, but in this instant loan case of

SBEMPL, these details are not mentioned in the loan appraisal sanction memorandum and the loan sanctioning authority has also not commented on this matter.

He has also deposed that as per the prevailing practice, the pre-disbursement visit report major observations have to be captured in the disbursement notes, but the same are not captured in both the disbursement notes of CC and TL dt.08-3-2008 and 31-03-2008 respectively and the approving authority has not commented upon the same.

He further deposed that the Cash credit account was not monitored in the way it should have been monitored which resulted in failure to ensure end utilization.

In the RH-3 held on 17th August, 2013, the important proceedings deposed and recorded are as follows:

Both the PO BMM and CSO LSR have asked several question to MW-2 VKN and she has replied to all those questions. The gist of the same is as noted below:

MW-2 VKN's Answers to various questions are as follows: Pre disbursement visit has to be conducted for verification of the works to be carried out, to assess the quantum of the loan amount to be disbursed in tune with the activity level being carried out and her visit report dt.23-02-2008 contains the sufficient information available as on that date.

While answering to question about the procedure and guidelines required to be followed while disbursing Working capital and TL loans, regarding various types of data and information to be captured in these disbursement notes, she confirmed that the dealing team has to ensure all the pre-disbursement conditions stipulated in sanction memorandum and Sanction letter are compiled and approval has to be sought for the deviations if any while disbursing WC and TL. ***Further she stated that the pre-disbursement visit observations have to be captured in the disbursement note.***

When asked to offer her comments on ME-3, ME-4 and ME-5 for operationalization of working capital limits and ME-6 and ME-7 for disbursement of full TL, MW-2 VKN replied stating that all terms and conditions of SL have been complied with and deviations were captured in the disbursement note for operationalization of working capital limits. Drawing power has been fixed based on the receivables statement submitted by the borrower as per ME-4.

All the terms and conditions of SL have been complied with and deviations were captured in the disbursement note (ME-7) and as per CA certificate (ME-6) 71% of promoters' contribution have been brought in by the borrower as stipulated in the sanction memorandum (ME-1). No specific directions are available in sanction memorandum and sanction letter with regard to the suppliers from whom the machinery has to be purchased. ***Hence the disbursement was released to the current account as per as per the prevalent practice, in the absence of any specific condition stipulated in the sanction memorandum (ME-1) and SL (ME-2).***

With regard to Pre-disbursement Verification (PDVC), MW-2 Mrs.VKN replied stating that PDVC should cover the compliance of terms and conditions of sanction, procedure followed for verifying the documents offered as security, loan and security documents executed by the borrower, security creation etc., and the officer who has carried out PDVC (Annexure to ME-7) certified that the same is generally in order.

With regard to the procedure to be followed while disbursing loan funds to the borrower, MW-2 Mrs.VKN replied stating that we have to ensure that all the pre-disbursement conditions as per the SL have to be complied with, and approval has to be sought for, for the deviations if any. Pre-disbursement visit observations have to be captured in the disbursement note. As no specific guidelines were available in the sanction memorandum and SL, with regard to the suppliers from whom the machinery has to be purchased, TL was released to the current account of the borrower as per the prevalent practice, in the absence of any specific condition stipulated in the SL.

While replying to question pertaining to the procedure to be followed to ensure end use of funds in case of WC and TL, MW-2 Mrs.VKN replied stating that the end use of funds for working capital is generally monitored through the buildup on current assets as reflected in the periodic stock statement (DP Fixation), regular submission of stock statements etc. the end use of funds in TL is monitored through creation of fixed assets acquired/purchased with the loan funds, including by way of physical inspection, collection of documentary evidence such as bills, receipts, CA certificate etc.

With regard to importance of WC CC account monitoring, MW-2 Mrs.VKN replied stating that monitoring the transactions in Cash Credit account is to find out the nature of cash out flows and inflows, analysis of stock statements and regular inspection of the unit, visit reports, dues position i.e., early warning signals for the likely NPAs etc play an important role in monitoring the borrower accounts. Exhibit ME-8 indicates cash out go to personal accounts of different persons. It needs to be verified whether they are suppliers of material to the company or not.

While replying to the question pertaining to conducting periodic visits to borrowers' place of business operations, MW-2 Mrs.VKN replied stating that periodical visits to the borrower's place of business operations and submitting the visit reports help in better monitoring of the account and to ensure that the project is implemented as per the schedule. In case of existing projects, the level of activity, inventory and other records like invoices etc can be verified to detect the early warning signals.

To a question pertaining to the importance of obtaining periodical stock statements, MW-2 Mrs.VKN replied stating that end use of funds for working capital is general monitored through buildup of current assets by verifying stock statements and fixation of drawing power. The stock statements are also used to assess the level of activity.

When CSO LSR asked "as mentioned in the Sanction memorandum (ME-1) whether MW-2 VKN along with KVD have conducted unit visit on 16-10-2007 (pre-sanction visit of SBEMPL? MW-2 Mrs.VKN replied stating that MW-2 ***Mrs.VKN was not part of the site visiting team.*** As a continuity question she was asked, if she was not part of that visit, whether she has seen any visit report conducted on 16-10-2007, her reply answer was NO. Further she was asked whether VSV had conducted any visit to SBEMPL as mentioned in loan application of ME-1 and she replied that she has no knowledge about the same. When she was asked whether she had visited SBEMPL work site pertaining to Singan Projects, she has confirmed that she has not visited any other work site except the site of M/S Noble Mining Company, Hospet.

While replying to the question whether the DP fixed for releasing WC for SBEMPL is in order as per the Bank norms, she replied yes. For another question about receivables considered for arriving DP includes the receivables subsequent to the date of ME-4 (Stock Statement) position date and do you agree whether it was correct, she replied Yes, however the DP was released on 08-03-2008 and the stock statement dt.29-02-2008 was including the book debts dt.04-03-2008 amounting to 35.00 lakh, hence the same was not excluded.

For another important question "do you think that the SBEMPL WC disbursing officers have neglected the observations of ME-3 signing officers, she replied ME-3 was conducted on 23-02-2008 and WC was released on 08-03-2008 based on the receivables position as on that date (ME-4). To one more important question, " whether the WC disbursing officers who have signed this disbursement note have brought the adverse observations of ME-3 (visit report) into ME-5 (WC disbursement Note)?, she replied saying that the observations of ME-3were not reflected in ME-5 as the disbursement format does not contain the relevant columns. As a continuity question, she was asked, if the above WC disbursement was done in the prescribed format of the Bank, please provide the format reference/circular, she replied saying that was the format generally followed at the time of disbursement in all the loan cases during that time.

When CSO LSR asked whether loan documentation and collateral security mortgage documentation of this SBEMPL loan case happened at a time in one sitting, MW-2 Mrs.VKN replied stating that she cannot comment based on the available exhibits.

With regard to PDVC (Pre Disbursement Verification Certificate), CSO LSR asked the following question to MW-2 Mrs.VKN and she replied as noted below:

Q: PDVC was supposed to be obtained prior to disbursement of WC in SBEMPL Loan case, whether WC disbursement officers have neglected this aspect?

VKN Answer: PDVC was obtained on 17-03-2008 and WC was released on 08-03-2008

Q: Whether the officers who have initiated the note to obtain PDVC have provided all the correct and relevant documents to the PDVC certifying officer?

VKN Answer: The PDVC indicated the details of the documents submitted to the officer in the report dt.17-03-2008.

Q: The item No: XIII (the valuation report dt.30-10-2007) in PDVC dt.17-03-2008 provided by the WC disbursing officer to PDVC certifying officer. Whether it pertains to the collateral securities already mortgaged on 05-03-2008?

VKN Answer: Cannot comment as per available exhibits.

Q: Whether the Legal opinion on the title of the properties was obtained before recommending WC disbursement?

VKN Answer: Yes as per the Annexure-II page 5, item no: 18 of the Exhibit ME-5.

Q: Is it not important to provide these legal opinion reports for conducting PDVC?

VKN Answer: Yes

Q: Whether the WC disbursing officers have provided these Legal opinion reports on the title of collateral securities to the PDVC certifying officer?

VKN Answer: Cannot confirm based on the PDVC Certificate (Annexure to ME-7)

Q: Whether the PDVC certifying officer in her report commented on the legal opinion of the collateral securities?

VKN Answer: PDVC officer commented that the PDVC is generally in order.

Some other questions were also asked by CSO LSR and MW-2 VKN replied as follows:

Q: Whether the margin to be brought in by the borrower for TL is stipulated in Loan Sanction Letter (ME-2) (SL)

VKN Answer: No margin was stipulated in SL, however it was mentioned in the means of finance in the Sanction memorandum (ME-1) as 31% of the project cost.

Q: Whether the officer preparing the TL disbursement has obtained any draft approval for the same before finalizing the TL disbursement note?

VKN Answer: Cannot comment as per the available exhibits.

Q: Can you identify the hand writing appearing on the TL disbursement voucher (who has prepared) i.e., annexure to ME-7 (DC NO: 82339) dt.31-03-2008?

VKN Answer: It is not mentioned on the voucher that who has prepared the same.

Q: On verification of CC account statement (ME-8), whether any diversion/siphoning has taken place between 08-03-2008 to 31-03-2008 of WC disbursement amount?

VKN Answer: ME-8 indicated cash outgo to individual accounts of different persons.

Q: Your observation to the above question, while preparing ME-7 on 31-03-2008, whether the officer who has prepared TL disbursement note has brought it to light in the TL disbursement note about siphoning of WC funds between 08-03-2008 to 31-03-2008?

VKN Answer: Not reflected in TL disbursement note

Q: While disbursing the WC limits on 8-3-2008, whether the officers who have recommended WC disbursement have commented anything about visit to the collateral securities in ME-5?

VKN Answer: NO

Q: Whether WC disbursing officers, as per ME-5 have obtained collateral security visit report from any internal officer?

VKN Answer: Cannot comment as per available exhibits.

Since the RH proceedings for the day are not completed with the above, it was proposed to have one more RH at a future date to complete cross examining MW-2 VKN by CSO LSR.

With regard to the RH held on 30-08-2013, CSO LSR submitted the following Defense Exhibits (DEs)

1. DE-1 Bank circular dt.20-02-2007 (regarding Risk department approval) prior to sanction of loans
2. DE-2 Re-fixation of TL repayment schedule office note dt.22-4-2008
3. DE-3 Zintec confirmation DT. 13-06-2013 about Finacle user ID given to CSO on 05-05-2008 (marked as B-4 document by Bank)
4. DE-4 Investigation report of Sri.RSS
5. DE-5 VKN's cybercrime email dt.22-06-2008
6. DE-6 SAC Minutes dt.16-08-2012 of the Bank
7. DE-7 CSO LSR Bio-data as per Bank's HR record
8. DE-8 CSO LSR appointment order dt.27-11-2007 posting to Kakinada
9. DE-9 Bank's office order No:1862 dt.15-02-2008 posting CSO LSR to Hyderabad
10. DE-10 SBEMPL loan documentation transaction (attendance) sheet dt.05-03-2008
11. DE-11 TL disbursement draft note
12. DE-12 TL disbursement finacle snap shot dt.31-03-2008
13. DE-13 Recovery follow-up letter by CSO LSR to the Borrower company

14. DE-14 Internal office note dt.13-11-2010 by CSO LSR recommending for criminal case to be filed against the borrower
15. DE-15 CSO LSR email to VKN dt.13-3-2013 requesting VKN to give it in writing confirming that CSO LSR was not assigned with any role in this NPA loan case
16. DE-16 CSO LSR email to NRC dt.13-3-2013 requesting NRC to give it in writing confirming that CSO LSR was not assigned with any role in this NPA loan case and
17. DE-17 (Proposed) CSO LSR sought for from the Bank the project report of the company SBEMPL as referred by Bank in its charge no: 3 framed against the CSO LSR. The same is named as the Feasibility report submitted by company SBEMPL along with its application for loan.

CSO LSR cross examined MW-3 Sri.RSS on 30-08-2013 and gist of the same is noted below:

Q: Whether there is any mention about obtaining Risk Department approval for rating in new SME rating model in ME-1 as per circular dt.20-02-2007?

Answer MW-3 RSS: NO

Q: Whether any officer can monitor finacle transactions without having finacle user ID and pass word?

Answer MW-3 RSS: No, officer cannot monitor finacle transactions without having finacle user ID and pass word

Q: Other than Hospet, is there mention about other work sites of SBEMPL in ME-1?

Answer MW-3 RSS: Other than Hospet, no other worksite is specifically mentioned in ME-1

Q: Whether legal opinion obtained from empanelled advocate on the title of the properties should be provided to PDVC certifying officer for verification?

Answer MW-3 RSS: Yes

Q: Whether CA certificate position date dt.29-02-2008 (ME-4) can contain book debts dt.04-03-2008?

Answer MW-3 RSS: No

Q: Before recommending WC disbursement is it necessary for the officers who have recommended/approved WC disbursement to seek clarification from the company on the adverse observations recorded by the visiting officials during pre-disbursement visits?

Answer MW-3 RSS: Yes

Q: Whether any disbursement format of WC or TL is prohibiting to bring the visit findings in to the disbursement notes?

Answer MW-3 RSS: NO.

During the RH held on 04th October 2013, the gist of the inquiry proceedings is as follows:

CSO LSR questions to DW-1 EKL (the then AGM now GM) and his answers are as follows:

Q: On 31-03-2008 evening whether you were approached by anyone to sign TL disbursement note (ME-7) of SBEMPL, if so what happened afterwards?

Answer of EKL: Yes, Smt.VKN the then Manager has requested me to sign the TL disbursement note of SBEMPL for which I had requested to provide back papers for perusal. She said she would get the papers but did not come back. Thereafter after around half an hour CSO LSR returned to office. It was informed by him that he was called for making urgent TL disbursement for SBEMPL being financial year end.

Q: To your knowledge, in the year 2008, who was the post sanction credit monitoring officer for SBEMPL?

Answer of EKL: Smt.VKN was the post sanction credit monitoring officer for SBEMPL

Q: To your knowledge, to whom Smt.VKN was reporting in the year 2008?

Answer of EKL: Smt.VKN was reporting to DGM NRC

Q: Whether at any point of time, you have discussed with NRC and SVS (DGMs) in the year 2008 about the reporting of officers in SME department and what was their response?

Answer of EKL: During 2008 it was discussed with NRC, he assured to finalize the same but did not do, subsequently after joining of SVS as DGM, this issue was further discussed, after which he made reporting arrangement for credit appraisal team. However for post sanction credit monitoring it was informed that the officers (VKN & KRB) being seniors (length of service wise in Bank) were not willing to report to CSO LSR, accordingly he made them to report to SVS directly as how it was during NRC's tenure as DGM.

Q: During the year 2010 have you seen or heard VKN furnishing TL draft disbursement note of SBEMPL Photostat copy to the CSO LSR?

Answer of EKL: In the year 2010, after detection of Collateral security fraud, VKN informed in an open discussion that she had a photo copy of draft TL disbursement note of SBEMPL, which she later handed over to LSR on his request.

Q: As per your knowledge, how the loan files were maintained after sanction in SME, Hyderabad in the year 2008?

Answer of EKL: after sanction generally the running files were in the custody of VKN under lock and key.

PO BMM Questions to EKL:

Q: As on 31-03-2008 who were the officers posted to SME, Hyderabad and what were their responsibilities?

Answer of EKL: NRC DGM & Head SME dept. Hyderabad, EKL AGM, KVD MGR, VKN MGR, KRB AM, PST AM, RPR AM and CS AM. During the above period there was no specific work allotment however EKL was asked to carry out credit officer Checker work, LSR was asked to carry out other works on piece meal basis as and when entrusted by DGM, KVD credit officer Maker, VKN post sanction credit monitoring officer, PST Credit officer Maker, KRB, RPR and CS

AMs were carrying out MIS and other miscellaneous works as and when entrusted by DGM.

Q: Would you have considered signing the TL disbursement note had all the back papers been produced?

Answer of EKL: Considering the exigency due to financial year end, after going through all the back papers, I would have considered signing the TL disbursement note, if found in order. I would like to mention that the post sanction credit monitoring officer VKN did not turn up with the back papers.

Q: In relation to CSO LSR's question to you w.r.t. Whether at any point of time, you have discussed with NRC and SVS (DGMs) in the year 2008 about the reporting of officers in SME department and what was their response? What was the back ground of your discussions with your DGMs on reporting relationship of officers SME, Hyderabad?

Answer of EKL: As there were no specific officers reporting to AGMs and it was difficult to get the works completed, I along with CSO LSR had approached DGMs for specific allotment of work responsibilities to the officers of SME, Hyderabad.

Q: When was the work allotment finally put in place? And till then, how the same particularly the post sanction credit monitoring works were carried out?

Answer of EKL: formally post sanction credit monitoring works allotment had happened in the year 2009, till that time they were carried out by VKN.

Remaining proceedings of the RH adjourned on 17th August 2013 pertaining to the questions asked by CSO LSR and answers given by VKN was continued on 4th October 2013. The details of the same are noted below:

Q: Before disbursement of working capital on 08-03-2008, whether NRC has asked VKN to change the visit report ME-3 positively?

Answer by VKN (MW-2): I don't remember any such thing

Q: As per DE-10 (attendance sheet dt.05-03-2008 while conducting documentation) whether VKN was physically present during mortgage documentation?

Answer by VKN (MW-2): The loan and security documents were executed on 05-03-2008 and it is evident from DE-10 that VKN was present.

Q: The names of the mortgagors were handwritten in DE-10 instead of appearing in print, in view of this, whether mortgage documentation was conducted in the Bank building premises in Hyderabad?

Answer by VKN (MW-2): There were no specific guidelines with regard to preparation of transaction sheet, as a matter of practice we record the names of the persons who were present during execution of loan and security documents.

Q: Whether VKN can identify the mortgagors?

Answer by VKN (MW-2): Definitely not, after more than five years from the date of execution.

Q: Whether MW-2 VKN has prepared and put up draft TL disbursement note (DE-11) to NRC?

Answer by VKN (MW-2): Yes, it appears from DE-11 that the same has been modified initialed by NRC.

Q: Whether DE-11(draft TL disbursement note) was routed through CSO LSR?

Answer by VKN (MW-2): No as per DE-11.

Q: In DE-11 (draft TL disbursement note) whether the margin money brought in was already confirmed by NRC?

Answer by VKN (MW-2): Yes.

Q: Whether VKN (MW-2) had initiated note for re-fixation of repayment schedule of TL (DE-2)?

Answer by VKN (MW-2): Yes as per DE-2.

Q: Whether VKN (MW-2) can comment about why DE-2 was not routed through CSO LSR?

Answer by VKN (MW-2): Cannot comment based on the exhibits available, however though approval was obtained, the same was not given effect in finacle.

Q: In the opinion of ME-2 VKN, whether all the facts about utilization of WC and TL funds should be commented in in DE-2 (re-fixation of repayment schedule of TL)?

Answer by VKN (MW-2): Not captured as per DE-2 (re-fixation of repayment schedule of TL).

Q: In the charge sheet DT. Feb 27/28, 2013 issued to CSO LSR, it is mentioned that out of Rs.80.00 lakh WC funds, Rs.70 lakh was transferred to individual accounts of promoters etc during March 2008 itself. Whether this fact was captured in DE-2?

Answer by VKN (MW-2): Not captured as per DE-2.

Q: Whether officers signing DE-2 have intentionally suppressed these facts?

Answer by VKN (MW-2): DE-2 was prepared for re-fixation of repayment schedule of TL. However the same has not been given effect in finacle.

Q: Whether Sri.GG (the then SME AGM) had alerted MW-2 VKN about SBEMPL stating that it was a problematic case (while both of them were visiting another loan case Steadfast Apparels Pvt Ltd)?

Answer by VKN (MW-2): I don't remember any such thing.

Q: While preparing WC disbursement note (ME-5), whether MW-2 VKN and NRC discussed that though it was a problematic case, they were being unnecessarily pressurized to disburse it?

Answer by VKN (MW-2): I don't remember any such thing, however the note was prepared at the instructions of my superior official.

Q: The stock statement format and its covering letter format to be submitted by the borrowers were already prescribed by Bank and are available in Banks intranet with effect from March 2005. Based on the above fact, in the opinion of MW-2 VKN, whether debtors' statement alone submitted by CA should be accepted for fixing drawing power?

Answer by VKN (MW-2): MSME Credit policy has come in to effect from May 2008, earlier the stock statements submitted by borrowers were accepted for drawing power fixation in other cases also which were disbursed during the relevant period.

Q: Whether the debtors' statement without containing the particulars related to bills discounted, stocks, sundry creditors etc can alone be considered to fix drawing power without seeking clarification from the borrower?

Answer by VKN (MW-2): In terms of SL (ME-2), cash credit needs to be released based on receivables and in the instant case, considering the nature of activity, there might be no stock which were quantifiable.

In between, the CSO LSR vide his letter dt.04th May 2013, sought for certain important documents from the bank through the IA PKK, out of which many of the documents were not provided to LSR. The details of the same along with its status whether provided to CSO LSR or not is mentioned below:

As replied by Bank

Information requested by CSO LSR	Bank's comment on Relevance of the document sough for	Status
1. Please provide me the copies of all the replies submitted by VKN and NRC along with copies of explanations called for from them by our Bank in the year 2012 and 2013 in this subject NPA loan case. Those letters and replies will give me opportunity to bring to light the false allegations if any made by them against my role in the subject loan case.	Information requested by CSO LSR is not relevant to the charges	May not be made available to the officer
2. Please provide me the copies of sanction recommendations of all the loan cases sent by Bank's CSC, Hyderabad to respective sanctioning authorities during October, November 2007, specifically the pages containing the signatures of the officers who have recommended the credit proposals to respective committees/sanctioning authorities.	Information requested by CSO LSR is not relevant to the charges	
3. Please provide me the minutes of the Zonal committee Chennai while returning back this subject loan case to Hyderabad for want of rating in SME model instead of CART model, also provide me the copy of appraisal memorandum submitted first time for the sanction to the committee	---------	Marked as B-2/3 enclosed

Information requested by CSO LSR	Bank's comment on Relevance of the document sough for	Status
4. Please provide me the proof showing the date on which I was provided with Finacle user ID after my joining Bank. On 05-03-2013 I have already requested Bank through my email and reminded for the same again vide my email dt.07-03-2013 but I did not get any reply.	---------	Marked as B-4 enclosed
5. Please provide me the pre sanction unit visit report conducted by the officers of CSC, Hyderabad as mentioned n the sanction appraisal memorandum of this subject loan case	----------	Not available on record.
6. Please provide me the pre sanction unit visit report conducted by VSV, because in the loan application the borrower himself mentioned that Mr VSV has undertaken visit to the works site of this subject loan case	----------	Not available on record.
7. Prior to issuing charge sheet to me in this loan case, provide me the copy of investigation report available if any	--------	Marked as B-7 enclosed
8. Please provide me the minutes of the SAC imposed accountability upon me	--------	Marked as B-8 enclosed
9. Please provide me the documentary evidence if any allocating loan cases among the officers in the year 2008 for monitoring post sanction credit activities.	-----	Marked as B-9 enclosed

Information requested by CSO LSR	Bank's comment on Relevance of the document sough for	Status
10. Please provide me the reporting structure in CSC, Hyderabad of all the officers as per HR records in the year 2007 and 2008.	Information requested is not directly related to the charges	However we may give officers profile with HRD marked as B-10

Based on the perusal of Management Exhibits, Defense Exhibits, PO's brief, the IA PKK asked CSO LSR to submit his overall presentation and accordingly LSR vide his letter dt.30-11-2013 submitted his overall presentation and the gist of the same is mentioned below:

Chapter-4

CSO LSR's Overall Presentation

As per the SAC policy of the bank and as per the Officers Conduct Rules, normally any officer deserves punishment if they reflect any mala fide intentions or gross negligence of duty. In this subject loan case there are no allegations against me (CSO LSR) about any mala fide intentions and the charges framed are not pertaining to gross negligence of duty as I was not the post sanction credit monitoring Officer for this SBEMPL loan case in the year 2008. I have obeyed my supervisor's instructions based on the assurance and confirmation given by him on 31-3-2008 and I have all the supporting evidences for the same. Further, I was a newly joined Officer with hardly one month experience in Bank's SME department Hyderabad as on 31-3-2008 and I was on probation for one year i.e. up to 29-12-2008.

The staff accountability was mistakenly fixed upon me by wrongly believing that I was the post sanction credit monitoring Officer for this loan case in the year 2008, but I was not the post sanction credit monitoring Officer for this loan case in the year 2008. This fact was confirmed by Shri.EKL, AGM/DW-1 during the regular hearing conducted on 4-10-2013 vide his witness reproduced below:

CSO:Q no:2: To your knowledge, in the year 2008, who was the post sanction credit monitoring dealing officer for SBEMPL loan case?

EKL -DW 1 answer: Smt.V.K.N. was the post sanction credit monitoring dealing Officer for SBEMPL loan case.

The then officers present in SME, Hyderabad branch in the year 2008 Shri.N.R.C, Smt.V.K.N and Smt.KRB have also confirmed in March, 2013 that LSR was not the post sanction credit monitoring dealing officer for this loan case in the year 2008. The audio record evidences to this extent are readily available with me and I have already requested the Inquiring Authority to accept the same as evidences. There are many more documentary evidences too which are clearly confirming that Smt.V.K.N. was the post sanction credit monitoring Officer for this Loan case.

It was wrongly mentioned in the Charge sheet reference and in DE-7 [CSO's bio-data supplied by HO] that I have joined Bank's SME department at Hyderabad on 29-12-2007. Please peruse DE-18 {email of Shri.GJ the then BH of Kakinada branch during 2007-08 and the scanned images of attendance register of Bank's Kakinada branch for December,2007, January 2008 and February 2008, along with DE-8 [Bank's offer letter & DE-9 [office Order No:1862 of HR dt. 15-02-2008 posting me to Hyderabad]}, the same are confirming that I have joined Bank at Kakinada on 29-12-2007 and subsequently relieved from Kakinada on 23-2-2008 and reported at SME department, Hyderabad on 25-2- 2008. Hence the DE-7 [CSO's Bio-data] provided by Head Office is not correctly reflecting facts about my joining this Bank in Hyderabad. If the DE-7 was taken as the basis to frame charges against me, that is incorrect and the charges should not have been framed against me.

As per DE-5 [the fake cybercrime email of Smt.V.K.N. dt.22-6-2008], it is wrongly concluded and wrongly believed by Bank's Head Office that the loan cases allocation in SME, Hyderabad happened in the year 2008. This is also not correct. In fact the Loan cases allocation was done on 23-1-2009 by forming post sanction credit monitoring (Credmin Team), until then Smt.V.K.N. was the Credmin Officer for this SBEMPL loan case. This fact was further confirmed by DW-1 Shri.EKL, AGM during regular hearing held on 04-10-2013.

The DE-11 [draft note for TL disbursement] was neither initiated by me nor routed through me, because I was not the Credmin Officer for this loan case. Please find the following witness given by MW-2 Smt.V.K.N. on 4-10-2013 in support of the same:

CSO Q No 37: Whether DE-11 was routed through CSO [LSR]?

MW-2 answer: No, as per DE-11

In addition to the above, my role has not appeared anywhere in the following office notes/reports of SBEMPL pertaining to its post sanction period:

- In ME-2 [Loan Sanction Letter]
- In ME-3 [pre-disbursement visit report],
- In ME-5 [WC disbursement note],
- DP fixation [excel sheet] in Cash Credit
- Note for identifying officer to conduct PDVC
- In DE-2 [Re-fixation of repayment schedule in TL] and
- In DE-10 [Attendance / Transaction sheet for conducting Loan Documentation]

All the above evidences/exhibits are confirming that they were neither initiated by LSR nor routed through LSR. This is because LSR was not the Credmin Officer for this SBEMPL loan case and it is Smt.V.K.N who has initiated all the above office notes of SBEMPL as she was the Credmin Officer of this loan case during the year 2008.

I was made as Head, Credmin w.e.f 23-1-2009 for all the Loan cases of SME/Hyderabad. In this connection, I feel it is very important to explain the actions initiated by me in SBEMPL loan case and the efforts made by me to protect the interest of our bank to recover the dues by following up with the borrower, by following up with the Credmin team members and by initiating appropriate office notes to the higher authorities to protect the interest of our Bank w.e.f 23-1-2009. In addition to this, I am herewith submitting the clarifications and explanations once again in detail to all the charges framed against me with justification as to why I was compelled to sign ME-7 [TL disbursement note].

It is mentioned in the charge-sheet that our Bank is exposed to substantial financial loss as a result of my acts of negligence. It is true that our Bank has incurred financial loss in this loan a/c, but the reasons for the financial loss are not my acts of negligence but the collateral security fraud committed by the Borrower and the mortgagors. The fraudsters have already successfully committed the fraud and cheated our Bank as on 8-3-2008 itself, where in I was nowhere in the picture. If the collateral security is a real and marketable immovable property, our Bank would have easily recovered the entire dues without any loss, but the Bank had incurred financial loss as the collateral security is a non-existing fake property fraudulently mortgaged to our Bank.

On examination of the entire history of this subject loan case, now after examining all MEs and DEs, I could infer many irregularities taken place in this subject loan case against our Bank guidelines right from sourcing stage till disbursement which enabled the borrower and the mortgagors to commit the fraud successfully. Hence, it is very important to identify and catch hold the internal fraudsters also, if any, that have extended their cooperation to the borrower in successfully committing this fraud, thus caused substantial financial loss to our Bank. Surprisingly by ignoring this aspect, making me the scapegoat with false allegations is not justified. In fact I am the officer who has detected this fraud in the year 2010 and reported to the higher authorities to protect the interest of our Bank.

I wish to submit that I have reported for duty as AGM at SME Hyderabad branch on 25-2-2008. As on the date of disbursement of TL to this subject borrower, I was having hardly one month experience in SME department, Hyderabad without Finacle user ID and without Finacle knowledge and I was not the Credmin Officer for this loan case. Prior to my reporting in SME, Hyderabad itself, this subject Loan case was sourced, processed, sanctioned, Sanction Letter issued and pre-disbursement visit was also conducted and subsequent to my joining SME, Hyderabad, documentation and security creation was done, WC limits were disbursed, PDVC was completed, TL disbursement draft note was moved and approved and the note for re-fixation of TL repayment schedule was also sent to head office for approval. ***I was nowhere in the picture in all the above stages***. All these notes were moved/recommended by Smt.V.K.N the then Credmin officer for this loan case. ***Basically this subject loan borrower has approached Bank with an intention to cheat. He knows that the collateral security offered to***

our Bank is a non-existing fake property. Intention of the borrower to become a defaulter and to make the loan a/c as NPA is pre-decided in pre-sanction and pre-disbursement stages itself. In this connection, it is important to see and understand the chronology of events that made borrower's job easy in cheating our Bank, then only one can identify the real reasons for the financial loss to our Bank.

The chronology of events that have helped the fraudulent borrower to cheat our Bank and the subsequent efforts made by me to unravel the hidden facts to enable the Bank to punish the real culprits of this fraudulent loan case are as follows:

1. In the Loan application 'Basic Information Sheet', it is confirmed that Shri. VSV [the then Head, SME, Hyderabad] has undertaken visit to the work site of the applicant. The credit appraising officers have not examined this visit report nor made any comments about this visit in the credit appraisal memorandum [ME-1]. In fact the visit report of Shri VSV is not available on record in the Loan files. Whether Shri. VSV has not submitted the report or has not conducted the visit or anybody has tampered this report is not established. This is a very important aspect because as per ME-3 (VKN visit report), activity at the borrowers unit was stopped since April, 2007 itself but the loan proposal sourced during September/October-2007, hence entertaining the loan proposal itself is irregular when there was no activity at all since April, 2007.

2. The Project Report/feasibility report [DE-17] is not containing the details of the vendors/suppliers to whom the TL is to be disbursed. This is basically in contradiction to the principles of Term Loan appraisal.

3. Before sending this loan proposal for sanction, as per DE-1 [HO circular] Credit Rating has to be approved by the Risk department, Head Office, but ME-1 is clearly reflecting that the DE-1 guidelines are not adhered to by the Appraisal team of SME, Hyderabad. Hence the sanction of this loan case itself is against to the circular guidelines of our Bank. Whereas, for another loan proposal [i.e.], "SD Agencies" submitted by SME, Hyderabad to the same sanctioning Committee on the same

day, Risk department approval was obtained as per DE-1, but not for SBEMPL. Further, in ME-1, it is clearly mentioned that the rating is initiated by Shri. VSV in the subject loan proposal. Hence, it is important to know how the sanctioning committee was misguided and how the loan was sanctioned in contradiction to the circular guidelines of the Bank without Risk department approval. Whether there was any deliberate act to bye-pass Risk department, HO and misguide the loan sanctioning committee is to be established.

4. In ME-1, it is mentioned that the Pre-sanction visit was conducted jointly by Smt. KVD and Smt.V.K.N on 16-10-2007. Whereas during Regular Hearing held on 17-8-2013, the MW-2 Smt.V.K.N has witnessed/deposed that she was not part of the pre-sanction visit on 16-10-2007. Please find the same reproduced below:

   CSO Q 1: As mentioned in the Credit Appraisal, whether Smt.V.K.N along with Smt. KVD have conducted unit visit on 16-10-2007 [Pre-sanction visit of SBEMPL]

   MW-2 Answer: No, Smt.V.K.N. was not part of the pre-sanction site visiting team.

   The above answer draws our attention to the following points:

   - Whether, what is mentioned in ME-1 about the visit is false or whether the above answer of Smt.VKN [MW-2] is false?
   - If ME-1 is a false record, who has recorded this false information in ME-1 to misguide the sanctioning committee?
   - If MW-2's answer is false, why she has given this false answer and what is her motive and intention behind giving such answer?
   - If the answer given by MW-2 is a lie, then where is that visit report?
   - Whether MW-2 Smt.VKN has attempted for tampering of office records by removing that report from the loan file?

[Because she was the dealing Credmin officer for this loan case in the year 2008]

- If the tampering of record is true, whether she has removed this visit report alone or any other papers are also taken out by her from the file? [Because the subject file was in her lock and key custody in the year 2008 and Shri VSV's visit report is also not available in the file.] In fact the pre-sanction visit report dt.16-10-2007 itself is not available in the Loan file of SBEMPL.

Based on the above, two things are clearly evident here i.e., either Smt.V.K.N may be giving a false witness in the capacity of Management Witness or the appraisal team might have misguided the sanctioning committee about the pre-sanction visit. However ultimately all these irregularities have resulted in giving birth to this fraud loan a/c in our Bank.

5. Please find below the partly reproduced content of the collateral valuation report dt.16-2-2008:

"For calculation purpose, the land rate is Rs.47500/- per Sq. Yd. (average) i.e., Rs.4,25,31,500/- and government SRO rate vide card no: 620 dt.15-10-2008 is Ra.30000/- per Sq. Yd. and it is informed that in April 2008 the rate may be Rs.40,000/- per Sq. Yd."

As per the above it is evident that, the empanelled valuer has obtained the government value of the collateral security on 15-10-2008. The valuation report dt.16-2-2008 should not contain government rate dt.15-10-2008, because it is a future date. If the year 2008 is a typographical error, instead if it is 2007, how come the valuer had already obtained the government rate on 15-10-2007 itself on this fraudulent collateral property when this immovable property was not proposed at all as collateral security by that date? The collateral security reflected in ME-1 is different from that of what actually taken as collateral security. This is giving scope to suspect that the borrower, the mortgagors, the valuer along with the Bank internal Officers Smt.V.K.N & Shri.N.R.C are in advance aware about this collateral fraud.

6. ***The valuation and the Legal opinion reports submitted by the empanelled valuer and empanelled advocate respectively are reflecting that these two properties offered as securities are open Plots without any building structures, but Smt. V.K.N & Shri.N.R.C while conducting documentation, accepted the original property documents [gift deeds] where in it is clearly reflected that these two collaterals (open plots) are having building structures also there in. The color photograph of these houses are there in the respective gift deeds as part of documents. Without seeking any clarification on this point from the mortgagors/borrower and empanelled valuer and advocates, both Smt. V.K.N & Shri.N.R.C have completed the equitable mortgage formalities on 5-3-2008 [as evidenced in DE-10] by suppressing this big blunder and allowed mortgagors/borrower to defraud the Bank by irregularly disbursing WC limits on 8-3-2008.***

    Please examine the Legal opinion report on the collateral securities where in the empanelled advocate has clearly written that the names of the mortgagors are not mutated in the revenue records. Smt.V.K.N has suppressed this fact and did not move any office note to obtain approval for this deviation to go ahead with WC disbursement.

    Further, the empanelled advocate has clearly prescribed to obtain the 'Property Tax receipt' as one of the title deeds to be deposited while conducting equitable mortgage, but Smt.V.K.N has neglected this aspect and did not collect the property tax receipt. The intentions of Smt.V.K.N and Shri.N.R.C in extending their cooperation to the fraudulent borrower in suppressing the above facts, in taking deviations without any approval from the competent authorities for not obtaining property tax receipt are not suspected and not investigated by Bank to bring to light the true reasons for the financial loss to the Bank.

7. ***Further the reasons for not conducting the collateral security visit and for not obtaining the legal vetting by empanelled advocate as per circular guidelines is also not investigated to know the true reasons for the financial loss to our Bank.***

8. As per our Bank circular No. 37/PSD – 7 /2007-08 dt.24-5-2007 guidelines, legal vetting of the Loan and mortgage documents has not taken place in this loan a/c though it is done in other loan cases of SME, Hyderabad pertaining to the same period by our empanelled advocates.

9. In contradiction to the Circular No.97 / CBSD – 24 / 2006-07 dt.28-10-2006 guidelines existing as on those days, PDVC was not conducted before WC disbursement. However though the PDVC was conducted on 17-3-2008, the dealing team consisting of Smt. VKN and Shri.NRC have provided an irrelevant and unrelated valuation report of collateral security to PDVC certifying officer purposefully to misguide. The Legal opinion reports obtained from the empanelled advocate were not provided at all to the PDVC certifying officer by Smt.V.K.N and Shri.N.R.C. If these reports would have been provided to the PDVC officer, the irregularities in the collateral security might have come to light before disbursement of TL itself. Further if PDVC was conducted prior to WC disbursement itself as per circular instructions, this fraud cold not have happened at all in this Bank. In view of the above, it can be said that the PDVC is not in order and it is important to know why Smt.V.K.N and Shri.N.R.C have misguided the PDVC certifying officer.

10. Out of the total three debtors of SBEMPL, the Singan Projects and Laxmi Aruna Minerals are the two high value debtors as per ME-4 [CA certificate dt.29-2-2008 on debtors]. Entire drawing power of SBEMPL was derived from these two debtors only. In ME-1 [credit appraisal memorandum] and in DE-17 [project report/feasibility report], there is no mention at all about these two debtors. In spite of no activity at the borrowers unit since April 2007, these two new and high value fake debtors reflected in ME-4 and without calling for explanation about the same from the borrower, Smt.VKN and Shri.N.R.C have disbursed WC limits irregularly by fixing Drawing Power on 8-3-2008 vide ME-5. My role was nowhere in ME-5 as I was not the Credmin Officer for this Loan Case.

11. The following points mentioned in Circular no: Ref.No.HO. PSD/2006-07/198 Dt. December 22, 2006 were not complied with and many items of Basic Information Sheet of this circular are not obtained/not complied with by the Appraising Officers of SBEMPL. Please find few examples noted below:

    a. Site visit report duly signed by the visiting officers as per Annexure II of the circular not obtained

    b. Net worth certificates of the Promoters/borrower not obtained but net worth mentioned as Rs.225 laks and net worth details are not available as to how it is arrived and it is not obtained as per Annexure V of the circular

    c. Market Inquiries about the borrower not done prior to sanction. ME-1 is silent on the same.

    d. As per the Basic Information sheet [as per circular dt.22-12-2006] attached to the application which is supposed to be filled in by SME officers, important aspects like Proofs of approvals/permissions for undertaking mining activity were not obtained,

    e. Please find below the partly reproduced content of the Basic Information Sheet

    "2. BO's comments on Primary and collateral security – 1) Whether title investigation carried out 2) Whether valuation obtained wherever required and date of valuation report 3) comments on quality of Primary/collateral security on the basis of site visit (marketability, liquidity etc) in case of separate visits to for collateral securities, attach visit report/s".

    As per the above circular, as stipulated in the basic information sheet, the above visit aspects were also not complied with during pre-sanction stage by the SME dealing Officers of Hyderabad. The main reason for the financial loss to our Bank was non-compliance to the guidelines of the Circular Ref.No.HO. PSD/2006- 07/198 Dt. December 22, 2006 by the then dealing officers of SBEMPL.

12. Mortgage documentation execution was not conducted in the Bank premises, it was done in a hotel but Loan agreements documentation conducted in the Hyderabad Branch Premises. The necessity behind conducting the mortgage documentation in a Hotel is giving scope to suspect Smt.V.K.N and Shri.N.R.C. The same may be confirmed from Shri.G.V.S.R the then Manager, as witness, because one Mr.MR, a mediator between the borrower and the mortgagors has disclosed the same to Shri.G.V.S.R during the investigation/inquiry conducted after detecting this collateral fraud in the year 2010. Further, the DE-10 [documentation attendance/transaction sheet] is also clearly reflecting that the names of the directors of SBEMPL and our Bank Officers were printed in DE-10, but the names of the mortgagors are hand written in DE-10. Before conducting documentation, normally respective dealing officers will be knowing the names of the individuals that are coming for execution of documents and accordingly they keep ready DE-10 duly printed, but in this loan case, the names of the mortgagors were hand written because the mortgagors have not executed mortgage deeds in the Bank premises. This aspect was not investigated to bring the facts to light. In this connection, please find the RH Inquiry proceedings dt.04-10-2013 partly reproduced below:

    CSO Q 33: As per DE-10, Whether MW-2 VKN was physically present during mortgage documentation?

    MW-2: Answer: The loan and security documents were executed on 5-3-2008 and it is evident from DE-10 that MW-2 was present.

    CSO: Q 34: The names of the mortgagors were hand written in DE-10 instead of appearing in print. With regard to this whether mortgage documentation was conducted in Bank branch building at Hyderabad?

    MW-2 Answer: There were no specific guidelines with regard to preparation of attendance/transaction sheet. As a matter of practice, we record the names of the persons who are executing the loan and security documents.

Yes it is true that we record the names of the persons in DE-10 as a matter of practice, because it will stand as an evidence to show who the persons present during documentation were. The dealing credmin officer would be in advance aware of the names of the persons who are coming for execution of documents, accordingly as a matter of practice, DE-10 would have been prepared in advance in the computer system, taken print and kept ready for obtaining the signatures of the persons present during execution of documents. Hence, if MW-2 VKN was knowing that the mortgage documentation was also going to take place on the same day i.e., on 5-3-2008, she should have included the mortgagors' names too in DE-10, but she did not do so. It is because the mortgage documentation has not taken place in Bank's branch premises on 5-3-2008 and the MW-2 VKN was not physically present during mortgage documentation.

Please find the following for further confirmation of the same: RH Dt.4-10-2013:

CSO: Q 35: Whether MW-2 VKN can identify the mortgagors?

MW-2 Answer: Definitely not, after more than five years from the date of execution.

Please see the above answer, how confidently MW-2 Smt.V.K.N was saying that definitely she cannot identify the mortgagors. Due to the passing of time, sometimes we may identify the executants and some other times we may find it difficult to identify them. The question of whether we are able to identify or not able to identify arises only after seeing the executants. It is a matter of memory power. However, to the above question of CSO, even before seeing the mortgagors, the MW-2 Smt.V.K.N is definitely saying that definitely she cannot identify the mortgagors. The words 'definitely not' are said by her, because she has not conducted the mortgage documentation as per DE-10, but gave these mortgage documents to somebody else for getting them executed in a hotel. Hence I once again request the Inquiring Authority to get it confirmed from shri.G.V.S.R, the then Manager now AGM, as the reason for financial loss to our bank in this loan case is due to the collateral fraud by way of mortgaging a non-existing fake property.

13. I was not involved in Loan and Mortgage documentation on 5-3-2008. [Please examine DE-10]. I have already joined Bank's SME department, Hyderabad by that time i.e., as on 5-3-2008. If I was the Credmin Officer for this loan case, I too should have been part of conducting documentation, but DE-10 is not reflecting my name. Hence it is evident that I was not the Credmin Officer for this Loan Case and that is why, I was not involved in conducting documentation.

14. As per ME-1, there are no other work sites of the borrower other than Hospet, Karnataka. ME-3 [pre-disbursement visit report] is reflecting that there is no activity at the borrowers work site at Hospet for the past several months. ME-3 was primarily prepared by Smt.V.K.N and observations in ME-3 were approved by Shri.N.R.C [both of them have signed ME-3] but, still irregularly, WC was disbursed by Smt.V.K.N and Shri.N.R.C vide ME-5 in spite of knowing that there was no activity at the borrower's work site.

15. In this connection, either the visiting officers or the Head, SME, Hyderabad have not made any attempt to visit the other worksites of SBEMPL if any, because they know that there were no other work sites of SBEMPL other than Hospet, Karnataka where in the borrower has already stopped the activity since April,2007 itself. Further neither ME-1 nor DE-17 is reflecting any other work sites of SBEMPL other than Hospet, Karnataka.

16. On 17-8-2013, MW-2 Smt.V.K.N has replied as follows to one of the questions asked by the PO. Please find the same reproduced below:

    PO Q-3: Please offer your comments on procedure and guidelines required to be followed while disbursing working capital and TL assistance, various types of information, data that should be captured and presented in the disbursement note for these types of disbursements.

MW-2: Answer: We have to ensure all the pre-disbursement conditions stipulated in the sanction memorandum and SL are compiled and approval has to be sought for any deviations while disbursing the working capital and TL. Pre-disbursement visit observations have to be captured in the disbursement note.

In contradiction to her own answer noted above, the MW-2 Smt.V.K.N has not captured the pre-disbursement visit [ME-3] observations in WC [ME-5] and TL [DE-11 & ME-7] disbursement notes initiated and recommended by her.

17. ***During the pre-disbursement visit on 23-2-2008, as per ME-3, the visiting officers have stated that the borrower's activity stopped for the past several months. If the activity was not there for a longer time, then the debtors within 90 days does not arise at all. This is a simple commonsensical aspect that both Smt. V.K.N [MW-2] and Shri.N.R.C should have paid attention and should not have disbursed CC limits at all.***

18. Before fixing the Drawing Power in WC limits, it is the responsibility of the officers approving the WC disbursement to ensure that the activity of the borrower is running well so that the end utilization of funds for which loans are sanctioned shall be ensured. In contradiction to this basic approach Smt.V.K.N and Shri.N.R.C have disbursed WC facilities.

19. While operationalizing the CC limits, it is observed that the debtors' statement obtained in the form of CA certificate dt.29-2-2008 [ME-4] is containing the book debts dt.4-3-2008 which is also an irregularity. In this connection, please find one of the questions that I have asked MW-2 Smt.V.K.N and the answer given by her on 17- 8-2013 in RH:

    CSO Q no: 9: Receivables considered for arriving DP includes the receivables of subsequent to the date of ME-4 position date. Do you agree with this?

    Answer by MW-2 Smt.VKN: Yes, however the DP was released on 8-3-2008 while the statement included the book debts of

4-3-2008 amounting to Rs.34.92 lakhs. Hence the same might not have been excluded.

On examination of the above question no: 9 and its answer, one can easily understand that the ME-4 dated 29-2-2008 should never contain anything that is subsequent to 29-2-2008, but it is containing book debt dt.4-3-2008 which may be an irregularity or a typographical mistake. Whatever it may be, the ME-5 officers without seeking clarification from the CA or from the borrower, considering the book debt dt.4-3-2008 for fixing DP is the first mistake and without accepting this, the MW-2 Smt.VKN replied stating that the DP was released on 8-3-2008 hence they have not excluded that book debt dt.4-3-2008.

This reply is clearly reflecting that she was trying to cover up the irregularity taken place while releasing WC by giving unacceptable reply. Further her reply is confirming that she has knowingly done WC disbursement in spite of seeing book debt DT. 4-3-2008 in the debtors' statement dt.29-2-2008.

Smt.VKN has committed another big blunder by giving above answer, i.e. she herself recorded in her visit report (ME-3) that there was no activity since April 2007, then how come the debtors within 90 days are mentioned in the statement and how she has accepted the same and fixed drawing power despite knowing that there was no activity at all at the borrower's works site.

20. Stock Statement in the prescribed format along with the prescribed covering letter was not obtained while releasing WC. Hence the Drawing Power fixed was irregular as the details of Sundry Creditors, Bills discounted etc are not reflected in ME-4. The stock statement format along with the model covering letter to be obtained from the borrower are hosted in Bank's intranet, departments, SME w.e.f. March, 2005 itself. It is available in Intranet-Departments-SME and I have shown the same to the Inquiring Authority on 04-10-2013 during Regular Hearing [RH].

21. In Credit appraisal ME-1 and DE-17, no where it is mentioned about the two work orders i.e., Singan projects & Laxmi Aruna

Minerals, but suddenly these two names appeared as debtors in ME-4. Confirmation about the genuineness of these two debtors not done and clarification was not sought for about the same from the borrower by Smt.V.K.N and Shri.N.R.C.

22. In spite of my physical presence and availability in SME department, Hyderabad, I was not involved in ME-5 which is dated 08-3-2008, the reason being I was not the Credmin officer for this loan case? but, in the charge sheet, it is wrongly mentioned that I have approved ME-5 [working capital disbursement].

23. Smt.V.K.N knows that the WC funds in the CC a/c were already diverted /siphoned between 8-3-2008 to 31-3-2008, but she had not brought this diversion/siphoning aspect in to the TL disbursement note.

24. ***Smt. V.K.N and Shri.N.R.C know that I was neither having finacle ID nor finacle knowledge as on those days of TL disbursement and they took it as an advantage to obtain my signature in ME-7 hurriedly by misusing the power as Supervisor and by putting pressure on me. Please find DE-3 which is clearly reflecting that the finacle user ID was provided to me on 5-5-2008 whereas this TL disbursement has taken place on 31-3-2008 itself.***

25. In the year 2010, Smt.V.K.N told me that she had obtained TL disbursement draft approval on 31-3-2008 from Shri.N.R.C, but it is not available in the Loan file. She only gave me a Photostat copy of the same in the year 2010 which I have submitted as DE-11. Further during RH on 4-10- 2013, she has confirmed in writing that she had not routed this DE-11 through the CSO LSR. If I was the credmin officer for this loan case, this DE-11 must have been routed through me. It is because I was not the credmin officer for this loan case, this DE-11 was not routed through me.

26. The truth that the CSO LSR was not the Credmin Officer for this SBEMPL Loan case was further confirmed by Shri.EKL AGM & DW-1 in various recordings on 4-10-2013 during Regular Hearing [RH].

27. In DE-11, it is evident that the amount recommended by Smt.V.K.N for TL disbursement was Rs.195 lakh only, whereas Shri.N.R.C has modified the amount and recommended for full TL disbursement of Rs.274 lakh in one go at a time. Mr.N.R.C has put his initial also for the above modification/ recommendation. DE-11 may please be perused to establish the same. On 4-10-2013 during the regular hearing, the MW-2 has confirmed in writing that the hand writing and the initial appearing in DE-11 is of Shri.N.R.C. This is clearly evidencing that Shri.N.R.C has recommended for full and final disbursement of TL in one go on 31-3-2013 and he has confirmed the Margin too brought in by the Borrower in DE-11 itself [as witnessed by MW-2 on 4-10-2013]. D-11 was not routed through me because I was not the Credmin Officer for this Loan Case.

28. Smt.V.K.N had approached Shri.EKL, AGM on 31-3-2008 and requested him to sign the TL disbursement note of SBEMPL. [As confirmed by Shri.EKL in his witness on 4-10-2013 during regular hearing]. Please find the same reproduced below:

    CSO: Q 1: On 31-3-2008 evening, whether you were approached by anyone to sign TL disbursement note [ME-7] of SBEMPL? If so, what happened afterwards?

    DW-1: Answer: Yes, Smt.V.K.N, the then Manager has requested me to sign the disbursement note of TL of SBEMPL, for which I had requested to provide back papers for perusal. She said she would get the papers but did not come back. Thereafter, after around half an hour, Shri.LSR returned to Office. I was informed by him that he was called for making urgent TL disbursement of SBEMPL, being financial year end.

    This is clearly reflecting that somehow they want to take the signature of any one AGM in TL disbursement note, but not because that AGM was the Credmin Officer of SBEMPL and subsequently how I was trapped and how my signature appeared in TL Disbursement note [ME-7] are once again explained in detail against my charge specific presentation in this letter.

29. The Current a/c of SBEMPL was NOT lien marked on 31-3-2008 by Shri.N.R.C to the extent of TL funds to ensure end utilization of TL. Being the senior most officers having more than twenty years of experience in this Bank, both Smt.VKN and Shri.N.R.C should have lien marked the Current a/c of SBEMPL at least to the extent of TL funds, but by giving false assurance to me on 31-3-2008 both Smt.VKN and Shri.N.R.C have not ensured end use of TL funds. Please find the DE-12, the finacle snap shot of TL disbursement and Smt.VKN' s hand writing appearing on the Debit voucher of TL to confirm the same, because the TL disbursement debit voucher is prepared by Smt.VKN [her hand writing is evidencing the same] and finacle entry is verified by Shri.N.R.C as per DE-12.

30. DE-4[investigation Report] and its annexure are clearly reflecting the diversion/siphoning aspect taken place out of CC and TL funds. This diversion/siphoning aspect of CC & TL funds was not highlighted in DE-2 [note for re-fixation of TL repayment schedule] and by suppressing this diversion/siphoning aspect Smt.V.K.N and Shri.N.R.C have recommended DE-2 to the Vertical Head/ED, SME. DE-2 was not routed through me as I was not the Credmin Officer for this Loan Case.

31. In DE-6 it is mentioned that ME-3 is satisfactory. In fact in ME-3 it is mentioned that the activity at the borrowers unit was stopped many months back. Hence any mention in the note put up to SAC about ME-3 stating that ME-3 is satisfactory is nothing but misguiding the Staff Accountability Committee too.

32. ***The margin brought in by the borrower was already confirmed by Shri.N.R.C in DE-11, accordingly Smt.V.K.N has proposed and Shri.N.R.C has approved ME-7, but in DE-6 [SAC minutes], accountability is fixed on LSR for not ensuring borrower margin to be brought in. Hence it is not justified to fix accountability on LSR as the margin is already confirmed by Shri.N.R.C in DE-11 itself.***

33. DE-5, the cybercrime email of Smt.V.K.N dt.22-6-2008, the relevance under which this document is produced to Bank's Head Office need to be examined, because this cybercrime email of Smt. VKN has misguided our HO team to frame the charges against me by wrongly believing that I was the Credmin officer of this loan case in the year 2008, which has caused all this mental agony to me.

34. DE-7 in comparison with DE-18 is a clear example to show that my appointment and other details are wrongly entered in my HR Bio-data in oracle, because, DE18 containing the email dt.7-9-2013 of Shri.G.J, the then BH of Kakinada branch and the email dt.2-9-2013 of SOM, Kakinada and its attendance register scanned copy attachments are clearly reflecting the facts about my joining SME, Hyderabad on 25-2-2008 but not on 29-12-2007 as wrongly mentioned in the charge sheet about my tenure in SME, Hyderabad.

35. I have already explained in detail the circumstances under which my signature was obtained in ME-7 vide my reply dt.13-3-2013 while denying the charges which is further confirmed and proved during regular hearing on 04-10-2013 in the witnesses given by Shri.EKL, AGM DW-1 and Smt.V.K.N MW-2.

36. DE-12 [TL disbursement finacle snap shot] is clearly evidencing that Shri.N.R.C has credited the TL funds to the current account of the borrower but subsequently he has not taken care to ensure end use of funds.

37. ME-7 Attachment debit voucher hand writing is clearly evidencing that Smt.V.K.N has proposed/recommended for crediting TL funds to the current a/c of the borrower. In spite of preparing the debit voucher, she had not signed the same, hence her intentions behind the same need to be examined.

38. ME-7 is clearly reflecting that Smt.V.K.N has knowingly suppressed the facts of ME-3 in ME-7 too. Not only this, but also the approvals to be taken for the deviations viz, not obtaining Property tax receipt of collateral security as per legal opinion and

the irregularity pertaining to the difference between the advocate/valuers report and the collateral property documents regarding the open plot/building structure have been suppressed by Smt.V.K.N in ME7. The intentions of Smt.V.K.N behind this need to be investigated.

39. ME-7 is clearly reflecting that Smt.V.K.N has suppressed the facts about diversion/siphoning of WC funds too by not reflecting the same in ME-7

40. Smt.V.K.N and Shri.N.R.C have not responded either positively or negatively to DE-15 and DE-16 [Emails of CSO to Smt.VKN and to Shri.N.R.C respectively]. On 04-10-2013, the MW-2 has confirmed in writing that she has received DE-15. This is clearly reflecting that all the audio evidences that I have requested the Inquiring Authority to accept as evidences are true and genuine.

41. DE-13 [my letter dt.7-7-2009 to the Borrower to clear the over dues] and DE-14 [Office note dt.13-11-2010 seeking permission to file criminal action against the borrower and mortgagors] are clearly reflecting the efforts that I have made to protect the interest of our Bank after becoming Head Credmin, MSME, Hyderabad in the year 2009. Hence the charges framed against me about lack of monitoring are invalid charges.

42. Even after becoming Head, Credmin, I was not the direct dealing Credmin Officer for this SBEMPL loan case. This loan case was allocated to Smt.KRB the then AM which is clearly evident in the email dt.23-1-2009 of Shri.S.V.S the then DGM while distributing the Loan Cases by forming the Credmin Team. Hence leaving the respective dealing Credmin Officers of SBEMPL and issuing charge sheet to me is gross injustice and it is nothing but making me the scapegoat.

43. In addition to the above, I wish to inform that I have been regularly reminding my Credmin team members to undertake visits to their respective loan cases borrowers units, send reminders where ever stock statements were not received, follow-up for recovery where ever over dues were observed etc. Since I have lost

my mail data, if the same is retrieved at least from 23-1-2009, I can produce all the evidences that will witness my diligent nature of discharging duties and the recovery and follow-up efforts that were made by me. However, fortunately some mail copies I have taken print and kept with me which I could trace now are produced to IA PKK as additional evidence [DE-19].

In the beginning of the email [DE-19], I have written at point no:1 "Please recall my earlier emails on the captioned subject", this is clearly evidencing that I had been alerting and following up with my Credmin team for in turn to follow up for stock statements and conducting unit visits. These are clearly reflecting my nature of discharging the duties diligently to protect the interest of our Bank. These will prove that the charges framed against me about not undertaking unit visit and not obtaining the stock statements are invalid charges, because I had been regularly reminding the respective Credmin dealing officers to undertake visits to the borrowers units and follow up for stock statements.

Further w.r.t. visit to the subject borrower's units, I have told Smt. KRB, AM [credmin officer of this loan case] in the year 2009 several times both by email as well as orally to undertake visit to this borrower's unit. She too agreed and accepted about my reminders in our telephone discussions which are recorded by me during the year 2013 and readily available with me in the form of audio evidences which I have requested the Inquiring Authority to accept as evidences. In the mail dt.19-3-2009 (DE-19), my beginning sentence is, "please recall my earlier mails". This sentence itself is evidencing that I was vigorously following up with all my Credmin Team Officers to adhere to bank guidelines on post sanction credit matters without any negligence or delay. When the Credmin role is clearly assigned to individual dealing officers by allocating loan cases among them vide Email dt.23-1- 2009 of the then DGM-Head, CSC, Hyderabad, leaving this aspect aside and without calling for explanations from the respective Loan Case dealing Credmin Officers, making me as scapegoat is not justified. Hence the charge no: V and VI [as reproduced below] framed against me are invalid. Charge V; You failed to ensure that post disbursement visits, as envisaged in the terms of sanction, were carried out to confirm acquisition/creation of fixed assets as per the project report. Charge VI; You as Credmin Officer, failed to obtain stock and debtors statement from the company at monthly intervals and set the drawing power on the basis of such statements.

Based on the above, please find below my Charge specific presentation:

Article of Charge (i): You failed to seek clarification from the company on the observations recorded by our officials in the pre-disbursement visit conducted on Feb.23, 2008 before approving the disbursement of Cash Credit Limit

Statement of defense denying the charge (i): I have denied this charge framed against me because the disbursement note of Cash Credit Limits dated 8-3-2008 [ME-5] was not recommended by me, not approved by me and not routed through me at all. Please peruse ME-5 to confirm the same. It was recommended by Smt.V.K.N, the then Credmin Officer for SBEMPL and approved by Shri.N.R.C, the then DGM and Head, SME, Hyderabad. Whereas with respect to imputation of charges for Charge-1 noted above, I wish to inform that the then Credmin dealing officer of this SBEMPL loan case Smt.V.K.N has initiated the CC & TL disbursement notes. She was in turn one of the officers too who have conducted the pre-disbursement visit [ME-3]. In spite of her negative/adverse findings during visit [ME-3] that there was no activity, she had suppressed these facts by not bringing them to light in to the disbursements notes of CC & TL and irregularly recommended for disbursement of the same. Please peruse ME-7 TL disbursement note where in it is clearly evident that Smt.V.K.N has suppressed the facts about her adverse observations of the visit ME-3 and not reflected them in the TL disbursement note.

Where as in the Regular Hearings, she herself clearly deposed that the visit observations should be brought to the disbursement notes. In this connection, I wish to explain the circumstances under which my signature was obtained in TL disbursement note [ME-7] and its debit voucher though I was not the Credmin Officer for SBEMPL. In spite of not being aware of this loan case and not being the Credmin officer for this SBEMPL loan case, my signature is appearing in Disbursement of Term Loan of the subject loan case on 31-3-2008. It is true that I have signed that note. However it is more important to know under what kind of circumstances and instructions I have signed this note as a newly joined officer with hardly one month experience in SME, Hyderabad. During that period, SME department in our Bank was in the initial stage of formation and due to core banking software, there was no heavy manual work for SME, Hyderabad Officers regarding financial year-end work.

Hence in the evening on 31-3- 2008, as it was already 5pm, I have requested our DGM Shri.N.R.C whether I can leave for the day and Shri.N.R.C told me that I could go home. Accordingly I left the office and was proceeding to my Home. After some time of my departure, while driving my bike, I had got a phone call, then I stopped and lifted the phone and found that it was from Shri. VSV, the then DGM of ICG [who was Ex-Head of SME, Hyderabad before my joining SME in Hyderabad]. When I lifted the call, Shri. VSV has asked me whether I have reached home. Then I told him that I was still on the way, then he asked me how far away I was from the Bank and I told him that I was crossing Tank Bund [which is 2 to 3 KM away from our office], then he instructed me to come back to the office. As instructed by him immediately I returned to office. On reaching SME center, I met Shri. VSV & Shri.N.R.C (both standing together at the entrance) and they told me to wait for a while at my seat. Then within five minutes Smt. VKN came to me with a folder containing the TL disbursement note of the subject loan case and asked me to sign the same urgently as they want to disburse the TL before End of the day. Then I told her that I was not aware about the loan case and asked her to provide me the loan file and other connecting papers for my perusal, then she replied that the DGM Shri.NRC asked her to obtain my signature immediately and she has orally confirmed that all the procedure guidelines of the Bank are being followed. Then I went to the DGM Shri.N.R.C' s cabin, on my entry, sir told that there was nothing to worry to sign, since it was 31st March financial year end, they wanted to disburse it urgently and instructed me to sign the disbursement note. Further he told that the WC limits in the subject loan case were already disbursed many days back and Mrs.VKN was having more than 20years of experience in this Bank and she knows all procedure guidelines and assured that both Smt. VKN & himself will take care about adherence to procedures like payment to suppliers/vendors etc, and instructed me to sign the disbursement note without any further delay as it was late in the evening on 31-03-2008 around 6 pm. Based on my superior officer's instructions and assurances, I have signed the TL disbursement note with much reluctance. I have acted under the direction of my supervisor which is as per Rule 5 (3) of Officer's Conduct Rules and the same is further confirmed in writing as my Supervisor has also signed and approved the TL Disbursement note [ME-7]. Hence my act of signing TL disbursement note was not due to negligence. After signing the disbursement note I have told to Smt.V.K.N in the presence of Shri.NRC, DGM, not to bye-pass any procedural guidelines even due to oversight. Further they told me that after crediting the TL amount to current account, Smt.VKN & DGM would issue pay orders, Demand drafts etc to the respective suppliers/vendors. Further [i.e.,] after obtaining my signature in the TL disbursement note, Shri.N.R.C had told me that the TL proceeds would be temporarily parked in the current a/c to maintain 31st March financial year-end balances, then he had given me a debit voucher, which is already signed by him for crediting the TL disbursement amount to the Current a/c of the borrower and instructed me to sign the same too. Because I know the importance of Bankers target commitments for 31st March and as Shri.N.R.C had already signed that voucher, I too signed the same as instructed by him as he was my supervisor and as I was on probation period. Then Mr.NRC told me that I could go home. I have signed TL disbursement note and its voucher as per the instructions of my supervisor. I was not this Loan case dealing Credmin Officer and as my supervisor had assured me that they would adhere to the procedural guidelines, I have signed the TL Disbursement note on 31-03-2008. Further, as both Mrs.VKN & Shri.N.R.C, DGM having more than 20 years of experience in the Bank and as told by them that the CC limits were already disbursed by them and because it was 31st March in the year 2008 [Financial year end], thinking that, in the process of achieving year end targets, the TL must have been disbursed by parking the funds in the Current A/c of the Borrower, reluctantly I have signed the same. It is because I have trusted that they have honesty and integrity and believed in good faith that they will adhere to Bank's procedures and guidelines. My experience in SME, Hyderabad branch of this Bank as on 31-3-2008 (the date of disbursement of Term Loan to the subject borrower) was just hardly one month only because I joined SME, Hyderabad on 25-2-2008 as per officer order no: 1862 dt.15- 2-2008.

This is clearly reflecting that I was very new to the systems and procedures of this Bank. ME-3 was not provided to me on 31-3-2008 in spite of my request to provide me all the relevant files and connecting papers for signing ME-7. On perusal of ME-7, I could not find any adverse observations in ME-7. As I was not the Credmin dealing officer for this loan case, as ME-3 was not provided to me on 31-3-2008, as I was not aware about the content of ME-3 [observations made by visiting officials in ME-3], on perusing the TL disbursement note, as it had not given me any scope for suspicion, the necessity not warranted for me to seek clarification from the borrower company before signing the disbursement of TL. Hence this charge is irrelevantly framed against me, instead it should have been framed against Smt.V.K.N who has initiated and recommended both WC and TL disbursement notes by suppressing the facts about her adverse observations in ME-3 and without calling for explanation from the borrower about her own observations in ME-3.

It also gives scope to suspect that Smt.VKN and Shri.NRC must be having some vested interests in disbursing both WC and TL to this subject borrower, because, both of them are aware of ME-3 findings and both of them have signed ME-3, but still they have initiated and approved the disbursements to this subject borrower irregularly.

Further during my telephone conversations with Smt.VKN during March, 2013, she has told me that Shri.N.R.C had asked her to change the visit report ME-3 positively by removing the adverse observations. To this extent I have evidences too in the form of Audio recording of our phone conversations. I have already requested the Inquiring Authority to accept the same as Evidence to protect the interest of our Bank. Further in the same audio recordings Smt.VKN had stated that Mr.NRC has instructed her to take my signature in TL disbursement note that is why she had approached me though I had no role in this loan case. She has also stated in Telugu as follows: "mimmalni indulo irikinchadam chala anyayam", it means implicating you (LSR) in this loan case is unjustified. In the same conversation, when I have asked her about why she had not brought these adverse observations of ME-3 in to the WC & TL disbursement notes, she has replied by stating that "whether anybody will approve disbursement if we write like that?"

One can infer from the above reply of Smt.VKN that consciously she has initiated and recommended for disbursement of WC & TL by suppressing the facts of ME-3 deliberately. Hence please accept the Audio evidences too to protect the interest of our Bank.

Based on the above, the following important points would arise:

a. Smt.V.K.N and Shri.N.R.C have approved disbursement of WC on 8- 3-2008 in-spite of knowing that there was no activity at borrowers work site.

b. In-spite of knowing that the CA certificate on Book debts ME-4 is also having many drawbacks, these two officers have approved disbursement of WC.

c. There is no mention about any other work-site of the borrower in the Credit Appraisal memorandum, other than Hospet, Karnataka. Hence the other two major debtors would not arise as the works were stopped by the borrower at its work site for the past several months i.e since April, 2007 itself.

d. Why these officers have not sought for clarification from the borrower about the inconsistencies in the CA certificate ME-4 need to be examined.

e. Without seeking clarification from the company on the observations recorded by our officials in the pre-disbursement visit conducted on Feb.23, 2008, why Smt.VKN and Shri.N.R.C have approved the disbursement of Cash Credit Limit irregularly need to be paid attention.

f. Without ensuring end use of WC disbursed and without monitoring/observing the account operations in the Cash Credit account of SBEMPL, it is not correct on the part of Smt.V.K.N to initiate office note recommending disbursement of TL funds too.

g. In spite of seeing that the collateral security property documents and advocate/valuer's opinions are contradicting with each other, why Smt.V.K.N and Shri.N.R.C have suppressed this fact and irregularly disbursed WC need to be investigated.

As per Bank's Officers conduct rule no: 5. GENERAL (1) Every Officer shall, at all times, take all possible steps to ensure and protect the interest of the Bank. Hence, strictly as per rule 5[1], I have made and I am making all attempts to protect the interest of our Bank and in this process I have gathered audio evidences too. So, please accept these audio evidences and protect the interest of our Bank as per Rule: 5[1].

Article of Charge (ii): You failed to ensure that payments were made to the suppliers/vendors directly from the Term Loan amount disbursed and instead disbursed the amount by crediting the funds disbursed to the current account of the company.

I am denying this charge framed against me because after obtaining my signature in the TL disbursement note, Shri.N.R.C had told me that the TL proceeds would be temporarily parked in the current a/c to maintain 31st March financial year end balances and then he had given me a debit voucher, which is already signed by him for crediting the TL disbursement amount to the Current a/c of the borrower and instructed me to sign the same too. Because I know the importance of Bankers target commitments for 31st March and as Shri.N.R.C [my supervisor] had already signed that debit voucher, I too signed the same as instructed by Shri.N.R.C as I was on probation. After signing the disbursement note, I have told to Mrs.VKN in the presence of the DGM Shri.N.R.C not to bye-pass any procedural guidelines even due to oversight. Further they have assured me that they will issue pay orders, Demand drafts etc to the respective suppliers/vendors. Being a new employee with hardly one month experience in SME, Hyderabad, how can I suspect that my supervisor and my colleague who have put up more than 20 years of experience in the bank would not adhere to the procedural guidelines stipulated by the Bank?

As on the date of Disbursement of TL and subsequently up to 5-5-2008 I was neither having finacle ID nor finacle knowledge [DE-3 is confirming the same]. Further I was not the Credmin dealing Officer of this Loan case and all the Credmin matters pertaining to this loan case were directly dealt by Smt.V.K.N in the year 2008 and she was directly reporting to the DGM Shri.N.R.C [as deposed by DW-1 Shri.EKL on 04-10-2013 in RH]. Smt.VKN being the Credmin dealing Officer, ensuring the payments to Suppliers and vendors was her duty. Smt.VKN has prepared the voucher recommending to credit the TL proceeds to the Current a/c of the borrower and Shri.N.R.C has verified the voucher by authorizing the entry in finacle at about 06.47 pm in the late evening on 31-3-2008 [DE-12]. Please see Smt.VKN's hand writing appearing on the TL disbursement voucher. Being the Credmin dealing officer of this case, having prepared the TL voucher, what made Smt.V.K.N not to sign the voucher need to be examined. In spite of knowing that I was not the Credmin dealing officer for this Loan case and also knowing that I was neither having finacle ID nor finacle knowledge, why Smt.VKN and Shri.N.R.C have obtained my signature in the TL disbursement note and in TL debit voucher is a surprise to me. I doubt that they have decided to make somebody scapegoat and they have chosen me for this purpose.

After approving the parking of TL funds in the current a/c of the borrower, Why Smt.VKN and Shri.NRC have not taken any care either to lien mark or debit freeze the current a/c to ensure payment to Suppliers/vendors from the TL funds also need to be investigated. Though the current a/c of SBEMPL is clearly reflecting the diversion/siphoning of TL funds, by suppressing this fact, why Smt.VKN and Shri.N.R.C have recommended for re-fixation of repayment schedule of TL on 22-4-2008 also need to be investigated.

On 31-3-2008 itself, other finacle transactions like DC no: 28031, 41751 & 60422 are entered/verified by Smt.VKN pertaining to some other Loan cases where in she must have prepared the vouchers too. In additions to the above, she has prepared hundreds of vouchers while working in SME/CSC, Hyderabad. Hence I request the Inquiring Authority to examine the above vouchers pertaining to the above DC numbers and other office notes containing Smt.VKN's hand writing to confirm the handwriting of Smt.VKN on the TL debit voucher and bring to light the intentions of Smt.VKN in preparing the voucher for directly crediting the TL amounts to Current a/c and subsequently why she has cleverly not signed the voucher in spite of there is a column in the voucher about the person who has prepared the same. Knowing that I had neither finacle ID nor finacle knowledge as on those days, both Smt. VKN and Shri.N.R.C made me scapegoat by deceitfully obtaining my signature in TL disbursement note and in its debit voucher though I was not the Credmin Officer for this loan case.

Even while obtaining PDVC on 17-3-2008, Smt.VKN and Shri.N.R.C have intentionally provided some irrelevant documents to the PDVC certifying Officer and misguided her. For example, they have provided the valuation report to the PDVC officer which is not pertaining to the mortgaged properties. Further they have not provided certain relevant documents like legal opinions of the collateral properties for PDVC, thus encouraged collateral fraud. In fact the discrepancy about the collateral property [i.e] whether it is an open land or with building structures is clearly evident in both the property documents and the valuation/legal reports if they are cross checked comparatively. Hence, it is not correct to certify/consider that the PDVC as generally in order. If the PDVC officer could have been provided with correct documents, the collateral fraud could have been avoided and the loans could not have been disbursed at all, thus entire financial loss to the Bank could have been avoided.

In the above manner as how Smt.VKN and Shri.N.R.C have misguided the PDVC Officer, similarly, these two Officers have given me false assurances by saying that they will adhere to all the procedure guidelines of Bank while disbursing TL. Thus, in spite of assuring me that they will ensure payment to suppliers/vendors etc, Smt.VKN and Shri.NRC have not adhered to the procedural guidelines of the Bank and they have extended their cooperation to the Borrower for diversion and siphoning of TL funds and ultimately suppressed all these facts and recommended for re-fixation of TL repayment schedule too.

In view of the above explained, it is evident that the officers who are supposed ensure the payment to the suppliers/vendors were Smt.V.K.N & Shri.N.R.C. Hence, I humbly request you sir to recommend for withdrawing this charge framed against me and protect the interest of our Bank by catch holding the internal fraudsters if any involved in this collateral fraud.

Article of Charge (iii): You failed to ensure that from the Term Loan amount disbursed payments are made to the suppliers/vendors, which were named by the company in its project report and also failed to seek documents/proof of creation/acquisition of fixed assets from the funds lent by the Bank

Statement of defense denying the charge (iii): Smt.VKN was the Credmin dealing officer of this Loan case. While disbursing the Term Loan Mr.N.R.C and Smt.VKN have given me oral assurance that they will ensure adherence to all the procedural guidelines including payments to supplier/vendors. As she was directly dealing with this Loan case and directly reporting to the DGM Shri.N.R.C and as this loan file was in the lock and key custody of Smt.VKN, it is her duty to ensure that from the Term Loan amount disbursed, payments are made to the suppliers/ vendors, which were named by the company in its project report and seek documents in proof of creation/acquisition of fixed assets from the funds lent by the Bank. Now on perusal of the Project Report/Feasibility report [DE-17], it is evident that the details of the Vendors/Suppliers are not mentioned in the same. However, to ensure end utilization, Credmin dealing officer Smt.VKN should have taken care about the payments to Vendors/Suppliers by obtaining the list of the same from the borrower duly taking approval for he same from the competent authority. In view of the circumstances prevailing in SME ***as explained by me in the Preamble part of my reply to the charges dt.13-3-2013, and as both MW-2 Smt.VKN and Shri.N.R.C have assured me that they will follow all procedural guidelines of our Bank, the need does not arise for me to to cross-check whether Smt.VKN & Shri.NRC have ensured payments to suppliers/vendors and whether they have obtained documents/proofs of creation/acquisition of fixed assets from the funds lent by the Bank.*** The DGM Shri.N.R.C who has verified the entry in Finacle while disbursing the TL and Mrs.VKN, the then dealing credmin officer of the subject loan case who has prepared TL disbursement debit voucher should have at least lien marked the current a/c to the extent of

TL portion and should have allowed withdrawals/Transfers duly ensuring end utilization and should have followed up for documents/proof of creation/acquisition of fixed assets for the funds lent by the Bank. ***It is because Mr.NRC has told that the parking of funds in current a/c was due to financial year-end target commitments, I did not suspect the integrity of Smt.VKN and Shri.N.R.C that they will not adhere to the laid down systems and procedures of our Bank.*** Further as I was new to our Bank's systems and procedures and as I was not the Credmin dealing officer for this loan case, I have not crosschecked the end use. Mrs.VKN' s Performance Appraisal Report [PAR] for the year 2007-08 & 2008-09 can also be cross checked with our HR records to confirm that she was directly reporting to DGMs and on 04-10-2013 in the Regular Hearing the DW-1 Shri.EKL, AGM has also confirmed that Smt.VKN was the Credmin Dealing officer for this loan case and she was directly reporting to the respective DGMs in the year 2008.

Further, recently while examining the chronology of events taken place in this fraud loan case, I came to know that in ME-1 and in DE-17 there is no mention about any supplier/vendor in these documents. Hence Smt. VKN and Shri.N.R.C should have taken care in this regard by obtaining the suppliers/vendors details from the borrower before disbursement of TL to ensure end use. In this connection, please find the following question and the answer pertaining to Regular Hearing dt.17-8- 2013:

Q-6 by PO to MW-2: Please offer your comments on procedure to be followed while disbursing actual funds to the borrower. Also comment on the precautions required to be taken in case of TL funds are disbursed through current a/c maintained by the borrower with us. Please offer your comments on ME-7.

Reply of MW-2 VKN: We have to ensure all the pre-disbursement conditions as per the SL are to be complied with and approval has to be sought for the deviations if any. Pre-disbursement visit observations have to be captured in the disbursement note. As no specific guidelines were available in the sanction memorandum and SL with regard to suppliers from whom the machinery to be purchased, TL was released to current a/c as per the prevalent practice, in the absence of any specific conditions stipulated in the SL.

In the above reply, Smt.VKN [MW-2] has confirmed the following by stating that:

a. Pre-disbursement visit observations have to be captured in the disbursement note, but she had not captured ME-3 observations in the WC and TL disbursement notes initiated and recommended by her. It is reflecting that she knows the procedural guidelines but intentionally not adhered to the same.

b. Further she stated above by saying that "As no specific guidelines were available in the sanction memorandum and SL with regard to suppliers from whom the machinery to be purchased, TL was released to current a/c as per the prevalent practice, in the absence of any specific conditions stipulated in the SL. Being a newly joined officer in this Bank, I might not be knowing the prevalent practice, but she has clearly confirmed above by stating the following:

   i. no specific guidelines were available in the sanction memorandum and SL with regard to suppliers from whom the machinery to be purchased,

   ii. TL was released to current a/c as per the prevalent practice.

Based on the above confirmations given by MW-2, it is crystal clear that the above charge number: 3 is irrelevantly framed against me, because:

i. no specific guidelines were available in the sanction memorandum and SL with regard to suppliers from whom the machinery to be purchased,

ii. As per the prevalent practice, Smt.VKN and Shri.N.R.C have released TL funds to the Current a/c of the borrower.

However after releasing the TL funds to the current a/c, both of them should have taken care to see that the end use is ensured. In spite of knowing the importance of ensuring the end use, Smt.VKN and Shri.N.R.C have acted in contradiction to the procedural guidelines of our Bank.

Please find the following evidence in support of my point:

Q-7 of PO: Please also comment up on the procedure and practice followed to ensure end use of funds in case of working capital and also TL.

MW-2 VKN's Answer: The end use of funds for working capital is generally monitored through the buildup of current assets as reflected in the periodic statements [DP fixation], regular submission of stock statements etc. The end use of funds in TL is monitored through creation of the fixed assets acquired/purchased with the loan proceeds, including by way of physical inspection, collection of documentary evidence such as bills, receipts, CA certificate etc.

The above reply given by Smt.VKN is clearly reflecting that she knows how to ensure end use of funds, but she had not ensured end use of funds. That is why while recommending note for re-fixation of repayment schedule of TL [DE-2], both Smt.VKN and Shri.N.R.C have suppressed all the facts about diversion and siphoning of WC and TL funds and irregularly recommended for re-fixation of repayment schedule of TL [DE-2] too.

If I was the Credmin Officer of this Loan case, this note DE-2 should have been initiated/routed through me, but in fact my signature is not there on DE-2 as it was not initiated/ not routed through me. Why it was not routed through me was because I was not the Credmin Officer for this Loan case and Smt.VKN was independently dealing with this loan case by directly reporting to Shri.N.R.C.

Further the Draft note for TL disbursement [DE-11] was also not routed through me as I was not the Credmin Officer for this loan case. This fact is confirmed by Smt.VKN herself during the regular hearing on 4-10-2013 vide question numbers 36 & 37 of CSO to MW-2 and the answers to the same given by MW-2 Smt.VKN. Considering the above, I humbly request you sir to recommend for dropping this charge.

Article of Charge (iv): You failed to ensure that the account was closely monitored and clarifications from the company were obtained regarding transfer of funds to the individual accounts of promoters and also failed to ensure that the funds lent by the Bank are utilized for business purposes only

Statement of defense denying the charge (iv): All sorts of monitoring work in this loan case including A/C transaction monitoring through finacle was the duty of Smt.VKN as she was the Loan Case dealing Credmin Officer up to the end of January 2009. It means, after the sanction of this loan in the year 2007 up to the end of January, 2009 [almost for 15 months] Smt. VKN was independently dealing with this loan case and she was directly reporting to the SME Center Heads/ DGMs. I was not this Loan case-dealing Credmin Officer.

As per DE-3, it is evident that I was neither having finacle ID nor finacle knowledge up to 5-5-2008. The siphoning and diversion of Loan funds by this subject borrower happened during March and April 2008 itself. ***As I was not the Loan Case Credmin Officer, the question of monitoring the account transactions by me does not arise, secondly even though I have signed ME-7, without having finacle ID and finacle knowledge I can not monitor Loan a/c of the borrower in finacle. Hence it is clear that these charges are irrelevantly framed against me.***

Smt. VKN had moved a note for re-fixation of repayment schedule of TL of the subject borrower vide office note dated 22-04-2008 [DE-2]. By seeing this note as well as all other office notes pertaining to the year 2008, anybody can easily understand that Smt. VKN was the Credmin officer of the subject loan case and this is confirmed by DW-1 Shri.EKL also in his deposition in RH on 04-10- 2013. I would like to emphasize that, though I have signed the TL disbursement note as instructed by Shri. NRC, subsequent notes moved in this subject loan case were not routed through me/not recommended by me which further gives evidence that I was not the credmin dealing officer of the subject loan case.

If anybody says that I was the Credmin officer for this loan case in the year 2008, then why all these ME-3, ME-5, DE-2, DE-11 and PDVC note etc were not routed through me?

Hence, it is very clear that these notes were not routed through me as I was not the Credmin officer for this loan case and Smt. VKN was independently dealing with this loan case by directly reporting to Shri.N.R.C, that is why the Draft note for TL disbursement [DE-11] was also not routed through me as deposed/confirmed by Smt. VKN herself on 04-10-2013 in the Regular Hearing.

In the statement of imputation of charges, vide point no: iv, it is mentioned that, out of CC limits of Rs.80 lakhs disbursed during March, 2008, the company had transferred Rs.70 lakhs to the individual A/Cs of the promoter of the Company and others in the month of March 2008 itself. The said Rs.70 lakh payments made to individual a/cs of the promoters and others from the CC a/c happened before 31-3-2008 as on which ***date I was not even aware of the name of this subject borrower and not having finacle ID [please refer DE3].***

Further while moving the TL disbursement draft note DE-11, MW-2 Smt. VKN should have brought this aspect to light in DE-11, but she has suppressed these facts about diversion/siphoning in DE-11. DE-11 was prepared and put up by MW-2 Smt. VKN and she herself confirmed in writing on 4-10-2013 that the DE-11 TL disbursement draft note was not routed through CSO LSR and it was not recommended by CSO.

The facts about the conduct of the CC a/c operations as on 31-3-2008 should have been brought out and discussed by Smt. VKN in DE-11 and ME-7 the TL disbursement note. But by suppressing these facts about diversion/siphoning aspects, TL disbursement was recommended by Smt. VKN and approved by Shri.N.R.C duly giving false assurances to me about end utilization of TL funds as explained by me in this letter as well as in the my reply dt.13-3-2013 while denying the charges.

On observation of the a/c transactions in the CC a/c and Current A/C of the subject borrower, it is clearly evident that, as on 22-04-2008 the TL and CC funds were already diverted without ensuring end use, but surprisingly without highlighting these issues and duly suppressing the facts, Smt. VKN and Shri.N.R.C have recommended office note to the Head Office for refixation of repayment of TL a/c on 22-04-2008 [DE-2].

In this connection, I wish to inform that up to 31-03-2008 I was not even aware of the name of this subject borrower case. In this entire episodes of the subject borrower case [i.e.] in the sanction letter dt.02-11-2007 [ME-2], in the pre-disbursement visit dt.23-2-2008 [ME-3], in the Loan documentation on 05-03-2008 [DE-10], in the disbursement of Cash Credit Dt.08-03-2008 [ME-5], in the Pre-disbursement verification note dated 17-03-2008 [enclosure to ME-7], in the TL disbursement draft note dt.31-3-2008 [DE-11] and in the office note for restructuring of Term Loan dated 22-04-2008 [DE-2], I was nowhere in the picture as I was not the Credmin Dealing officer of this case.

My name appeared only once i.e., in ME-7 on 31-03- 2008 and the reasons for the same were already explained by me in this letter as well as in my reply to the charge sheet vide my letter dt.13-3-2013. Further I was not having either finacle ID or finacle knowledge up to 5-5-2008 [as per DE-3]. Hence I am not the right person from whom this explanation has to be sought for vide this article of Charge and I strongly deny this Article of Charge and request you sir to recommend for withdrawal of this Article of Charge.

Article of Charge (v): You failed to ensure that post disbursement visits, as envisaged in the terms of sanction, were carried out to confirm acquisition/creation of fixed assets as per the project report.

Statement of defense denying the charge (v): I was made Head Credmin, MSME, Hyderabad w.e.f.23-01-2009 and the subject loan case was allotted to Mrs.KRB w.e.f. January 23, 2009. Until then, Mrs. VKN was the subject Loan case-dealing Credmin officer and she was directly reporting to the DGMs in these matters. After I was made as the Head Credmin, we have contacted Mr.SPR, Promoter of the borrower Company over phone several times & vigorously followed up for recovery. During our recovery follow-up over phone, several times we have asked Mr.SPR to arrange/accompany for a visit to the work site, but every time the borrower avoided/postponed visit to the work site stating that "Forest department had seized the vehicles, he was making efforts to get them released and there was nothing to show even if he takes us for field visit". Further many times Mr.SPR had given unsatisfactory excuses over phone to avoid field visit stating that he is out of station etc. Several times I have advised Smt.KRB [the loan case dealing Credmin officer for this loan w.e.f.23-01-2009] to conduct field visit and submit visit report.

Further, several times we have called Mr.SPR for discussions and advised him to clear the over dues. In addition to that we have sent letters to the borrower to this extent asking to clear the over dues. All the evidences to this extent are available in the loan case files in CSC, Hyderabad.

In addition to this, in the process of our follow up, various mail correspondence were also done by Mr.SPR with CSC, Hyderabad wherein he has given many promises in the form of action plans stating that he will clear the over dues, but every time he did not fulfill his promises. As I have lost my mail data, if our Bank could retrieve my email data at least from 23-1-2009, the same can be verified/confirmed. Further, please examine DE-13 [my letter dt.7-7-2009 to the borrower reminding to clear the over dues], the content of the letter DE-13 is evidencing that I have made several telephonic discussions and correspondence with the borrower prior to July 2009 too. This is proving and evidencing that I have made vigorous efforts as Head Credmin for recovery of the dues in the process of monitoring this loan case.

In view of the non-cooperation of the borrower, we have initiated office note seeking Head Office permission to proceed under SARFAESI Act and got the approval. On getting the approval from HO, when I along with Mr.NCD, Manager, proceeded for identification of collateral property before sending demand notice under SARFAESI Act, we have identified the discrepancy/fraudulent angle in the collateral property. Subsequently we have further conducted many visits to the collateral property along with Bank's Legal team consisting Smt.SD, AGM and Sri.SL, AGM and empanelled Advocate Shri.HNR at different intervals. Further we have made discreet enquiries with Revenue, Town Survey and Municipal Corporation authorities and after getting confirmation about the discrepancies in the collateral security we have moved a note to Head Office explaining the observations and seeking HO permission to file a criminal case against the borrowers and mortgagors vide DE-14.

On perusal of DE-14 it is clearly evident that several visits were conducted by me and by my Credmin team on 22.04.2010, 26.07.2010, 23.08.2010, 02.09.2010 etc. and the same may be crosschecked by inquiring with our Legal AGMs Smt.SD and Shri.SL, our empanelled advocate Shri.HNR, our Manager Shri.NCD and our one more

Manager Shri.G.V.SR, because during every visit, at least one of them have accompanied me. In addition to this, I have audio record evidences where in Smt.KRB the Credmin officer for this SBEMPL loan case w.e.f.23-1-2009 has confirmed that I have advised her several times to undertake visit to SBEMPL work site and follow up for stock statements.

I have already requested the Inquiring authority to accept this Audio evidence as witness. DE-19 [my emails to the Credmin Team of CSC, Hyderabad] is/are one more evidence in support of my defense against this article of charge. As seen from the above, it is evident that I have made my best efforts in discharging my duties with utmost integrity, honesty, devotion and diligence to protect the interest of the Bank. However, in the post sanction period, this SBEMPL Loan case was specifically allotted to Smt.V.K.N in the year 2008 and to Smt.K.RB w.e.f. 23-1-2009. Without asking any clarification on the same from the respective dealing officers about why visits were not conducted, issuing a charge sheet to me is not justified. Hence I humbly request you sir to recommend for dropping this Article of Charge.

Article of Charge (vi): You as Credmin Officer, failed to obtain stock and debtors statement from the company at monthly intervals and set the drawing power on the basis of such statements.

Statement of defense denying the charge (vi): I was not the Credmin officer for the subject loan case. When Smt.VKN had been the dealing Credmin officer for this Loan case during the first fifteen months from the date of its Sanction, she should have followed up and ensured obtaining Stock & debtors statements. ***I am not able to understand why it is concluded and charge sheet issued to me confirming that I was the Credmin Officer for this Loan Case in spite of availability of all the evidences showing who has moved all the office notes, who has conducted pre-disbursement visit, who has conducted documentation, who has fixed drawing power in WC a/c and who has recommended for re-fixation of repayment schedule of SBEMPL etc.***

Is it because of DE-5, the purported cybercrime email of Smt.VKN or is it because of DE-7 [CSO⊠s oracle bio-data supplied by HO] that the Staff Accountability is fixed on me? If these are the bases to fix accountability, then I should say that due to oversight the accountability is wrongly fixed upon me by the Bank. It is stated in the statement of Imputation that after one stock statement dated February 29, 2008 received before disbursement of CC limits, there was nothing on record which evidences that the company had not submitted stock & debtor's statement. Since it is very important point, now I am getting a doubt that, being aware of non-receipt of stock statement, why Smt.VKN and Shri.N.R.C have recommended for re-fixing of repayment of TL on 22-04-2008 vide DE-2. It is clearly evident that the receipt of stock statement was already over-due as on DE-2 date.

After I was made as Credmin Head in January, 2009, and after this Loan case was allotted to Smt.KRB, myself and my team made best efforts to impress up on the borrower/promoters for submission of stock and debtors statements. Despite our best efforts, this borrower did not submit the same. Please see the emails sent by me to my Credmin Team [DE-19] to confirm the follow up made by me through the Credmin Team for receipt of Stock and debtor statements. The above emails [DE-19] and DE-13 [Letter to the borrower to clear the over dues] are clearly reflecting my diligent nature of discharging duties by following up with my Credmin Team as well as with the borrowers too to ensure healthy portfolio.

By the time, the Loan case came under my purview as Head Credmin, the CC a/c was already overdue and over drawn for a period of more than four months and started showing delinquency. The promoters were not cooperative for submitting stock statement and for clearance of over-dues. However, in view of our vigorous follow-up, within a span of two months [i.e.] by March 2009, we could able to bring down the CC below the sanctioned level by recovering the over-dues and from January, 2009 up to June 2010, we have recovered to a tune of Rs.14,10,000/- [Rupees fourteen lakhs and ten thousands only] from the borrower. On perusal of ME-8, the same is evident.

The other monitoring and follow-up efforts that were undertaken by me as well as by my Credmin Team have been explained in detail in my reply to the Article of Charge no: V vide my letter dt.13-3-2013. However, it is the Loan case dealing Credmin officer who should follow up for stock statement and put up note to Head Credmin seeking approval to issue reminders etc. On perusal of the office record available, it is clearly evident that either Smt.VKN or Smt.KRB have never put up any such office notes. It was always me who used to remind them to discharge their credmin duties without any negligence. Ignoring the Loan case dealing credmin officer, issuing charge sheet to me by framing this kind of charge is gross injustice. Further, I have audio record evidences where in Smt.KRB the Credmin officer for this SBEMPL loan case w.e.f.23-1-2009 has confirmed that I have advised her several times to undertake visit to SBEMPL work sites and follow up for stock statements. I have already requested the Inquiring authority to accept this audio recordings as evidence. DE-19 is one more evidence in support of my defense against this article of charge

In view of the above explained chronology of events taken place and charge specific clarifications submitted, I request the Inquiring authority to recommend for withdrawal of all the charges framed against me and avoid this unwanted mental agony to me. Further, as a responsible officer of the Bank and as per the Officers conduct rules, to protect the interest of our Bank, I feel it is my responsibility to bring the following facts to your notice based on the Inquiry proceedings held from May, 2013 to October, 2013. The details are as follows:

On 17-8-2013 during Regular Hearing [RH], Q no 23 of CSO: Can you identify the hand writing that is appearing on the TL disbursement voucher [who has prepared] i.e Annexure to ME-7. DC No: 82339 Dt.31-3-2008?

Reply by MW-2: It is not mentioned on the voucher that who has prepared the voucher.

Actual answer to Q no: 23 should be "Smt.VKN' s hand writing", because the handwriting on the voucher is Smt.VKN' s only. Smt.VKN who in turn is MW-2 must have identified her hand writing, but cleverly replied stating that "It is not mentioned on the voucher that who has prepared the voucher". Smt. VKN had prepared hundreds of vouchers in MSME, Hyderabad which are readily available on record in SME, Hyderabad branch in every file that she had dealt with. Hence, at least she should have told that it appears as if it is her hand writing only.

Please find the scanned images containing her hand writing on some other document pertaining to some other loan that I have incorporated in my overall presentation dt.30-11-2013 for your confirmation. Those two hand writings are evidencing that the hand writing on the TL debit voucher is Smt. VKN's hand writing only. If the Inquiring authority wants to see, there are many other vouchers available at Hyderabad Branch, which were prepared by Smt. VKN during the same period. On 31-3-2008 itself, other transactions like DC no: 28031, 41751 & 60422 etc are entered/verified by Smt. VKN pertaining to some other Loan cases where in she must have prepared the vouchers too. Kindly examine the same to know the hidden truth as to why Smt. VKN had intentionally avoided signing the TL disbursement voucher in spite of preparing the same.

During RH on 4-10-2013: Q no: 36 of CSO: Whether MW-2 has prepared and put up Draft TL disbursement note [D-11] to Shri.N.R.C?

MW-2's Answer: Yes, it appears from DE-11 that the same has been modified and initialed by Shri.N.R.C.

Based on the above question and answer, the important aspect that draws our attention is the MW-2 Smt. VKN who could not identify her own hand writing on the debit voucher of TL dated 31-3-2008, identified and confirmed the hand writing and initial of Shri.N.R.C pertaining to 31-3-2008. This is a clear evidence to show that the MW-2 gave true answers where ever she felt that the same would not lead for herself conversion into CSO and she has given false replies to those questions where in if she gives true reply, her role in this fraud case will come to light. Please find below many examples of such nature:

RH 17-8-2013, Q no: 5 of CSO: Whether the ME-3 observations are in line with the notings in credit appraisal memorandum about the works executed by SBEMPL?

Answer of MW-2: "The position at the time of Visit was recorded in ME-3.

My observation: During the pre-disbursement visit, the common practice is, if anything is observed in visit that is against to the recordings in Credit appraisal, those observations must be highlighted both in the visit report and in the disbursement notes. In this loan case, Smt. VKN had intentionally suppressed these facts while disbursing WC facilities and TL facilities.

RH dt.17-8-2013: Please find Q no: 10 and its answer: CSO Q no:10: As far as accepting the receivables as per ME-4 are concerned in fixing DP, do you think the Working Capital disbursing authorities have neglected the observations of ME-3 signing officers?

MW-2's Answer: ME-3 was conducted on 23-2-2008 while the release was made on 08-03-2008 based on receivables position as on that date [ME-4].

My observation: The reply given was not related to the question asked. Because the point in Q:10 is, as there was no activity since April, 2007, the book debts below 90 days would not arise, hence the MW-2 Smt VKN and Shri.N.R.C were not supposed to release the WC at all.

RH dt.17-8-2013: Please find Q no: 11 and its answer: Q no:11 of CSO: Whether the working capital disbursing officers signed in ME-5 have brought/reflected the adverse comments of ME-3 in ME-5?

MW-2's Answer: Observations of ME-3 were not reflected in ME-5 as the disbursement format does not contain the relevant column.

My observation: While replying, the MW-2 Smt. VKN correctly stated that the observation of ME-3 pre-disbursement visit report were not reflected in the WC disbursement note, but she tried to give some unsolicited explanation stating that the format does not contain the relevant column. In this connection, please find the scanned image of the WC disbursement note ME-5 reproduced in my overall presentation dt.30-11-2013: On examination of the ME-5 office note format that was adopted by MW-2 and Shri.N.R.C, it is evident that it is an open sheet without any tabular format, without any specified sub headings or specified columns. As it is entirely an open sheet with open option to mention all the facts descriptively, it is easily possible that Smt. VKN should have brought her observations of Unit visit ME-3 in to the WC Disbursement note ME-5 but she did not do so. It means she has intentionally suppressed the facts while recommending WC & TL disbursements that there was no activity at the work sites of SBEMPL for the past several months.

In this connection, please find the following pertaining to RH dt.4-10-2013: CSO:32: ***Before disbursement of Working Capital, whether Shri.N.R.C has asked MW-2 to change the visit report ME-3 positively?***

MW-2 Answer: I do not remember any such thing. ME-3 indicates the status of work at Hospet at the time of visit.

My comment: The above reply given by MW-2 is a false reply. I have audio record evidence where in the MW-2 during March, 2013 clearly told me over phone that in March 2008 before disbursing WC facilities, Shri.N.R.C has asked her to change the visit report positively. I have already requested the Inquiring Authority to accept this audio record evidence as evidences.

Please find the following pertaining to RH dt.17-8-2013, CSO's Q no:7: Whether ME-3 signing officers have made any attempt to visit the work sites of SBEMPL where in the works pertaining to Singan Projects were undertaken?

Answer of MW-2 Smt. VKN: As per Report, the visiting Officers have not visited any other site except the site of Noble Mining Company, Hospet.

On observation of ME-4 CA certificate on Book Debts, it is evident that there are total three debtors from whom the Receivables are due. The details are as follows: 1. Noble mining company were Rs.16,38,400/- 2. Receivable from Lakshmi Aruna Minerals, Bellary were Rs.34,92,800/- 3. And Receivables from Singan Projects was amounting to Rs.94,55,550/- It is clearly evident that, as per ME-3 the activity/works of SBEMPL pertaining to debtor-1 were already stopped long back. Then the ME-3 officers should have enquired about other work sites of SBEMPL where in the activity is going on, but as per the answer to Q no: 7, they have not visited any other work site. They have not checked whether there are any other work orders at all available with SBEMPL. In fact either in ME-1 or in DE-17 there was no mention at all about Debtors number 2 & 3 noted above.

Hence, as there was no activity, disbursing the WC is the first mistake and without confirming the genuineness of Debtor no: 2 & 3 i.e. without visiting the work sites of SBEMPL pertaining to Debtor no: 2 & 3, disbursing WC is the second mistake and suppressing this fact in the WC disbursement note that there was no activity for the past several months and releasing the WC facility is the biggest mistake.

CSO's Q no: 9 [RH dt.17-8-2013"]; Receivables considered for arriving DP includes the receivables of subsequent date of ME-4 position date. Do you agree with this?

Answer by MW-2 Smt. VKN: Yes, however the DP was released on 8-3-2008 while the statement included the book debts of 4-3-2008 amounting to Rs.34.92 lakhs. Hence the same might not have been excluded.

On examination of the above question no: 9 and its answer, one can easily understand that the ME-4 dated 29-2-2008 should never contain anything that is subsequent to 29-2-2008, but it is containing book debt dt.4-3-2008 which may be an irregularity or a typographical mistake. Whatever it may be, the ME-5 officers without asking any clarification from the CA or from the borrower, considering the book debt dt.4-3-2008 for fixing DP is the first mistake and without accepting this, the MW-2 Smt. VKN replied stating that the DP was released on 8-3-2008 hence they have not excluded that book debt. This reply is confirming that she was intentionally trying to cover the irregularity taken place while releasing WC.

Further on 17-8-2013: CSO: Q 13: Whether Loan documentation and collateral security mortgage documentation happened at a time in one sitting:

MW-2: Cannot comment based on the available exhibits.

My comment: Why can't she comment, because MW-2 herself had conducted the documentation? She could have well stated the truth, but she did not. In fact, the truth is that she had not conducted mortgage documentation in the Hyderabad branch premises but given these mortgage documents to somebody else for conducting execution by the mortgagors in some Hotel.

This can be confirmed from Shri.G.V.S.R, the then Manager of this Bank. I have already requested the Inquiring Authority to accept the witness of Shri.G.V.S.R, because the reason for the financial loss to our Bank is the collateral security fraud taken place in this loan a/c.

RH dt.17-8-2013 CSO Q no: 14: Whether the officers who have disbursed working capital limits have obtained PDVC before recommending working capital disbursement?

MW-2 Answer: PDVC was obtained on 17-3-2008 while working capital was released on 08-03-2008.

The answer to the above question is reflecting that the PDVC was not done before disbursement of Working Capital loan which is also an irregularity and it is against to the Bank's circular guidelines as on that date.

CSO Q NO: 15: Whether the officers who have initiated the note to obtain PDVC have provided all the correct and relevant documents to the PDVC Certifying Officer?

MW2 Answer: The PDVC indicates the details of documents submitted to the officer in the report dated 17-03-2008.

The above answer is escaping in nature, because MW-2 Smt.VKN had not provided the correct and relevant documents to the PDVC certifying Officer and misguided the PDVC certifying Officer. Please find the following example:

CSO: Q16: As per PDVC dt.17-3-2008, the item no: XIII, valuation report dt.30-10- 2007 provided by the SME officers to the PDVC certifying officer. Whether it pertains to the collateral securities on which the mortgage was already created on 05-03-2008.

MW2 Answer: Cannot comment as per available records.

My comment: In fact the above valuation report furnished to the PDVC Officer is not pertaining to the collateral securities on which security is already created. MW-2 Smt.VKN had provided some irrelevant valuation report to the PDVC certifying Officer purely to misguide.

CSO: 17: Whether the legal opinions were obtained on the collateral securities before recommending WC disbursement?

MW2 Answer: Yes as per Annexure-II, Page 5, item no: 18 of exhibit ME-5.

CSO: Q 19: Whether the WC disbursing officers have provided legal opinion reports on collateral security already mortgaged, to the PDVC certifying Officer

MW-2 Answer: Can not confirm based on the PDVC certificate [Annexure to ME-7]

My comment: In fact MW-2 Smt.VKN has not provided the Legal opinion reports to the PDVC certifying Officer because MW-2 VKN might be knowing that it is a fraudulent collateral security which is non-existing. Further the discrepancies are clearly visible when comparatively cross checked with property documents and Legal and valuation reports, because in the legal and valuation reports it is mentioned as open plot, but in the property documents it is mentioned as House property with a colour photograph too in each collateral property document. Also the discrepancy pertaining to not obtaining of 'Property Tax Receipt' would have been highlighted by the PDVC officer if the legal opinions are produced for PDVC.

In view of the above, it can be inferred that Smt.VKN [MW-2] had misguided the PDVC officer. The PDVC is clearly evidencing that the Legal opinion reports are not produced for PDVC. However, a special investigation is required to be done to bring to light the facts pertaining to the co-operation extended by Smt.V.K.N. and Shri.N.R.C to this fraudulent borrower and mortgagors in successfully committing the fraud.

CSO: Q 24: on verification of CC a/c statement [ME-8], whether any diversion/siphoning has taken place between 8-3-2008 to 31-3-2008 out of WC disbursement amount?

MW-2 Answer: ME-8 indicated cash out go to individual accounts of different persons.

My comment: The answer to the above question given by the MW-2 is correct, but without reflecting the same in TL disbursement note, knowing that I was not having finacle ID and finacle knowledge hence I could not cross check, she had irregularly recommended for disbursement of TL by suppressing these facts and by putting pressure on me saying that it is an urgent disbursement to be done as it was financial year end on 31-3-2008.

CSO: Q 25: Your observation to the above question No: 24, while preparing ME-7, whether the officer who has prepared the TL disbursement note has brought it to light in the TL disbursement note?

MW-2 Answer: Not reflected in the TL disbursement note [ME-7].

My descriptive comments against question number 24 are proved correct if the Inquiring Authority examines the Q no: 25 and its answer given by MW-2 reflected above. MW-2 Smt.VKN has prepared the TL disbursement note and the draft note for TL disbursement by suppressing all the adverse facts and irregularly recommended/disbursed bank funds to this fraudulent borrower and by keeping me in dark about TL draft disbursement note [DE-11], deceitfully by hiding facts obtained my signature in ME-7.

CSO: Q 26: While disbursing the working capital limits whether the officers recommended for disbursement have commented anything about visit to the collateral securities in ME-5?

MW-2 Answer: No

By seeing Q no: 26 and its answer given by MW-2, it is evident that how grave the irregularity committed by WC disbursing officers while disbursing CC limits was.

It is the primary responsibility of MW-2 Smt.VKN who is the actual credmin dealing officer to confirm the physical existence of the collateral securities too and their adequacy as well as marketability. Neglecting this aspect and by suppressing all the adverse observations, she has irregularly recommended/disbursed WC loan in this case against to the circular guidelines of our Bank.

CSO: Q 28: Whether TL disbursement funds are diverted/siphoned between 31- 3-2008 to 22-4-2008, please comment based on current a/c statement [ME9] of SBEMPL?

MW-2 answer: Based on the statement, an amount of Rs.6 lakh has gone to individual name.

My comment: So, in-spite of identification of the diversion and siphoning in TL funds by the MW-2 VKN, she had irregularly recommended for re-fixation of repayment schedule in TL on 22-4-2008. Thus misguided the Regional Head as well as Country Head of SME department vide office note 22-4-2008 [DE-2].

Please find few more questions and answers of 04-10-2013 during Regular Hearing and my comments on the same:

CSO: Q 36: Whether MW-2 has prepared and put up draft TL disbursement note D-11 to Shri.N.R.C?

MW-2 Answer: Yes, it appears from DE-11 that the same has been modified and initialed by Shri.N.R.C.

CSO: Q38: In DE-11[TL draft disbursement note], whether the margin money brought in was already confirmed by Shri.N.R.C?

MW-2 Answer: Yes

CSO: Q37: Whether DE-11 was routed through CSO [LSR]

MW-2 Answer: NO as per DE-11

The above answers of MW-2 VKN are true. What was modified by Shri.N.R.C in DE11 was confirmation about the margin brought in by the borrower and recommendation to disburse the entire TL in one go.

Few important points draw our attention from the above three questions and answers are as follows:

1. As per the SAC minutes it is mentioned that LSR has not confirmed the margin brought in by the borrower, that is why staff accountability was fixed on LSR, but in fact the margin brought in by the borrower was already confirmed by Shri.N.R.C in DE-11 itself which is prior to ME-7 [TL disbursement note].

2. The MW-2 VKN who intern was the credmin officer for this loan case has correctly identified the initial of Shri.N.R.C in DE-11
3. DE-11 which is prior to ME-7 was not routed through CSO LSR. It is because CSO LSR was not the Credmin Officer for this SBEMPL loan case as alleged in the Charge sheet.

Please find the following:

Q No: 39: Whether MW-2 had initiated note for re-fixation of repayment schedule of TL [DE-2]?

MW-2 answer: Yes as per DE-2

CSO: Q40: Whether MW-2 can comment about why DE-2 is not routed through CSO LSR?

MW-2 Answer: Cannot comment based on the exhibits available. However though approval has been obtained, to my knowledge the same has not been affected in finacle.

The above Q no:39 & 40 asked by me and answers given by the MW-2 Smt.VKN are further confirming that the MW-2 Smt.VKN has initiated the office note for refixation of repayment schedule [DE-2] and this DE-2 was not routed through CSO LSR as LSR was not the Credmin Officer for this Loan case. Further the MW-2 Smt VKN is confirming that this approved note is not implemented in finacle for re-fixing the repayment schedule. ***She knows this fact because she was the Credmin dealing officer for this loan case during the year 2008.***

Q no: 41: In the opinion of MW-2, whether all the facts about utilization of WC and TL funds should be commented in DE-2?

MW-2 answer: Not captured as per DE-2.

The above question and answer are reflecting the following: Normally whenever an office note is moved to Head Office seeking approval for re-fixation of repayment schedule, the dealing officer should reflect all the facts pertaining to

a. The end utilization of loans already disbursed,

b. The nature of conducting the operations in the CC a/c,

c. A brief about the activities at the borrowers unit along with the comments about the adequacy of the value of the securities charged and their physical existence.

Whereas on examination of DE-2, it is evident that the MW-2 Smt. VKN being the Credmin Officer of this loan case has misguided the higher authorities of our Bank by suppressing all the adverse facts about SBEMPL by not commenting anything on the above points a, b & c in the DE-2.

CSO: 42: In the charge sheet dated February 27-28, 2013 issued to the CSO, it is mentioned that out of Rs.80 lakh WC funds, Rs.70 lakh was transferred to individual accounts of promoter etc during March 2008 itself. Whether this fact was captured in DE-2?

MW-2: Not captured as per DE-2

CSO: 43: Whether Officers signing DE-2 have intentionally suppressed these facts?

MW-2 answer: DE-2 was prepared for re-fixation of repayment schedule of TL. However the same has not been given effect in finacle

It is evident from the above Q no: 42 & 43 of CSO and its answers given by MW-2 VKN that the MW-2 Smt.VKN who was the Credmin officer of this loan case and who was supposed to closely monitor the loan a/c by seeking clarifications from the company regarding transfer of funds to the individual accounts of promoters to ensure that the funds lent by the Bank are utilized for business purposes only has failed to ensure the same. The CSO LSR was neither having finacle ID nor having Finacle knowledge as on those dates and it is already proved that the CSO was not the Credmin Officer for this Loan Case. Hence the Article of Charge no:(iv) [You failed to ensure that the account was closely monitored and clarifications from the company were obtained regarding transfer of funds to the individual accounts of promoters and also failed to ensure that the funds lent by the Bank are utilized for business purposes only] framed against me is invalid.

CSO Q no: 44: Whether Shri.GG, AGM had alerted MW-2 VKN about SBEMPL stating that it was a problematic case [while both of them visiting Steadfast Apparels Pvt Ltd]?

MW-2 Answer: I do not remember any such thing.

My comment: The answer given by MW-2 for Q no: 44 is a lie. I have telephone conversation audio record evidence to this extent with me. During March, 2013, while speaking to MW-2 Smt.VKN, she has told me that Shri.GG, AGM had alerted her about SBEMPL stating that it is a problematic case [while both of them visiting SAP Ltd]. Hence MW-2 Smt.VKN has told lie during RH on 4-10-2013.

Further, we can draw the following points from the above question and answer if comparatively crosschecked with the Audio Evidences I have:

a. Shri.GG, AGM has worked in SME, Hyderabad during the year 2007 and in the beginning of the year 2008 [i.e. before disbursement of WC facilities to SBEMPL]

b. Shri.GG and Smt.VKN jointly undertaken visit to SAP Ltd loan case before the disbursement of WC facilities to SBEMPL

c. Shri.GG, AGM had alerted MW-2 Smt.VKN about SBEMPL stating that it was a problematic case while both of them were visiting SAP Ltd [i.e. before disbursement of WC facilities to SBEMPL]

d. That means, before the disbursement of WC facilities itself to SBEMPL, Smt.VKN [MW-2] knows that it is a problematic loan case and during the pre-disbursement visit, she personally found and observed that there was no activity at the SBEMPL works site. In spite of this, she disbursed WC facilities to SBEMPL irregularly on 8-3-2008. The intentions or the vested interests of the MW-2 VKN in this regard need to be investigated to protect the interest of our Bank.

e. Hence I request you sir to accept the audio record evidences I have offered as additional evidence and make use of them to protect the interest of our Bank.

CSO Q no: 45: While preparing WC disbursement note [ME-5], whether MW-2 and Shri.N.R.C discussed that though it was a problematic loan case, they were unnecessarily pressurized to disburse it?

MW-2 answer: I dont remember any such thing. However the note was prepared at the instructions of my superior official.

My comment: The above answer of Smt.VKN is one more lie. In fact Shri.N.R.C has clearly told me the same over phone (in the year 2013) by saying that Smt.VKN and Shri.N.R.C have discussed several times that though it is a problematic loan case, they were unnecessarily pressurized by Shri. VSV to disburse it. The audio record evidence for the same is readily available with me. The fact told by Shri.N.R.C was already told by Smt.VKN too many times in the year 2010 after I have detected this fraud. To that extent one more audio record evidence as stated by Smt. VKN which is almost in line with what Shri.N.R.C stated is also available with me. Hence I request you sir to accept these audio record evidences to protect the interest of our Bank.

CSO: Q 46: On 31-3-2008 evening, whether MW-2 had asked Shri. EKL, AGM to sign TL disbursement note [ME-7]?

MW-2 Answer: I do not remember after a lapse of 5 years, but to my knowledge Shri.EKL was in pre-sanction team and not in credmin team during that period.

My comment: Again this is also a lie answer given by MW-2. To that extent a confirmation deposition was already given by Shri.EKL before the Inquiring Authority on 04-10-2013 while answering the first question of CSO, he stated that Smt.V.K.N, the then Manager has requested him to sign the disbursement note of TL of SBEMPL. Subsequently how I was trapped to sign the TL disbursement note by Smt.V.K.N Shri.N.R.C and Shri. VSV were in detail explained by me in my reply to the Charge sheet dt.13-3-2013 as well as in this letter too.

CSO: Q50: Whether MW-2 has received DE-15 [CSO's email dt.13-3-2013 addressed to MW-2]?

MW-2 answer: It appears from DE-15 that it has been received by MW-2.

My comment: The MW-2 is none other than Smt.VKN. The content of DE-15 is as follows: "I recall your attention to our tel cons during the first week of this month. In this connection during our phone discussion you have told me that it is very unjustified to see that I [LSR] was dragged in to this loan case. Thank you very much madam for your appreciating the fact. Further, on the next day I have requested you whether you can give the same in writing, what you have orally stated to me on the previous day, as you had dealt with all matters pertaining to this loan case. Then you have asked me whether you can give like that in writing and on my attempt to convince you, you have told me that you will speak to your higher authorities and revert back to me. Hence I once again request you to give the same fact in writing for which act of kindness I would be very grateful to you madam." Surprisingly, the MW-2 VKN did not revert back to me nor she has objected/condemned the content in the above mail. This is confirming two things:

a. All the telephonic conversations I had with Smt.VKN which are available with me and offered to accept as evidences are true and genuine.

b. Smt.VKN had dealt with all matters pertaining to this loan case in the post sanction period during the year 2008.

If these points are wrong, the MW-2 VKN would have immediately reverted back by questioning me for sending such email. The reason for the silence of MW-2 Smt.VKN is because all that reflected in DE-15 are truths only.

Based on the detailed facts presented by me in this letter, please find my observations on the illogical, baseless and blind conclusions drawn by the Presenting Officer in his written brief dt.18-11-2013:

The conclusions drawn by the Presenting Officer are not giving correct definition to the concept of 'Loan case handling Credmin officer'. He has ignored many facts and exhibits and blindly given an illogical report. His written brief is evidencing that it is very much against to protect the interest of our Bank but to safeguard the internal fraudsters.

However, I recall your attention to the Audio Record evidences that I have requested you to accept as evidences, because these evidences are clearly proving that I was not the Credmin Officer for this Loan case and I have signed that ME-7 at the instructions of my supervisor only. Please find certain parts of content these audio evidences are containing:

- *In these audio evidences, Shri.N.R.C has stated that LSR has no assigned role in this loan case, further he stated that he is ready to tell the same before any committee or inquiring authority.*
- *Secondly Smt. V.K.N has also stated during our phone conversation that just because Shri.N.R.C has instructed her to obtain my signature in TL disbursement note [ME-7], she has approached me, otherwise she would not have approached me. She further stated that "implicating LSR in this loan case is not justified". Hence I once again request you sir to accept all the audio evidences to protect the interest of our Bank.*

From the day one of inquiry proceedings regular hearings I have been mentioning in writing as well as orally stating that I have these Audio record evidences of phone conversations I have gathered in the month of March, 2013 while talking to Shri.N.R.C and with Smt.V.K.N and the same is brought on record in the RH proceedings dt.3-5-2013 too.

It is already proved in the RH dt.17-8-2013 that Smt.VKN in the capacity of Management witness gave witness against the Management Evidence ME-1? Please refer question no: 1 of CSO and the answer given by MW-2 Smt.VKN. Over and above the same there are many other instances/examples where in I have found Smt. VKN while she was telling lies. I have audio record evidences to this extent wherein she has stated something in the Regular Hearing and against to the same, she has already stated something else to me during our phone conversation and her both statements are contradicting. As a Presenting Officer on behalf of the Bank, I believe that the PO must have perused all the papers, notes, reports and security documents pertaining to this loan case. If he has really examined the entire file and all the security documents, I draw PO's attention to the following points: If the PO has seen the legal opinion reports of the collateral securities obtained from the empanelled advocate:

a. It is clearly visible that the advocate has clearly mentioned in these legal opinion reports that these are vacant plots? Whether PO is acting blind to see the same?

b. Also it is clearly visible in the collateral property documents [gift deeds] that these plots are having each one building [the photograph of the building property is also part of the original gift deeds mortgaged with our Bank, each property document i.e. gift deed no: 301/2008 and gift deed No:302/2008 executed by Shri. BJ in favor of Shri.RJ and Shri.AJ respectively have these color Photographs].

c. Hence, it is an irregularity on the part of Smt.VKN and Shri.N.R.C for not seeking clarification about this difference/ discrepancy between the property documents and the Legal opinions [regarding whether they are open plots or plots with buildings?].

d. One more blunder and irregularity on the part of Smt.VKN is not conducting visit to collaterals to establish the fact about whether the collaterals are open plots or plots with building/s. Hence it is against to circular no: Ref.No.HO.PSD/2006-07/198 Dt. December 22, 2006 guidelines issued by the Bank Further it is mentioned in these legal opinion reports that the mortgagors" names are not mutated in the revenue records. In this connection it is very important to take approval for this deviation before recommending WC disbursement? But Smt.VKN and Shri.N.R.C have not obtained any approval for this deviation.

e. It is clearly mentioned in these legal opinion reports that 'Property tax receipts' should also be obtained as one of the documents to be deposited during equitable mortgage? but, Smt.VKN and Shri.NRC have not collected the Property Tax receipts while conducting Equitable Mortgage as prescribed by the empanelled advocate vide serial no:16 of the list of title deeds to be deposited? This is one more glaring irregularity on the part of Smt.VKN and Shri.N.R.C for not obtaining the approval for the deviation for not collecting the 'Property Tax Receipt' before conducting documentation and accepting property for mortgage before disbursing WC. This act of Smt.VKN and Shri.N.R.C made the job of fraudsters easy and thus caused financial loss to our Bank.

Hence all these irregularities taken place while conducting Equitable Mortgage are giving scope to suspect the involvement of Smt. VKN and Shri.N.R.C in extending their cooperation to the fraudulent borrower and mortgagors for cheating our Bank.

All the above points are establishing the fact that the reason for financial loss to our Bank is the collateral security fraud knowingly committed by the borrower and the mortgagors? Hence it is not proper to attribute the reason for the financial loss to our Bank is lack of monitoring, if anyone draws such conclusion, then that is not correct because the fate of this loan case was pre-decided in pre sanction and pre-disbursement stages itself. The borrower has approached our bank with an intention to cheat and with the cooperation extended by Smt. VKN and Shri.N.R.C the fraudulent borrower and mortgagors have successfully cheated our bank

f. Further it is clearly visible in the valuation report too that these properties are vacant plots. The valuer has not given any valuation for the building structures. In the valuation reports in Part B, against the valuation of Building, the valuer has clearly mentioned that it is "Not Applicable". Hence this is one more irregularity on the part of Smt. VKN and Shri.N.R.C to ignore this naked truth before disbursing WC facilities.

g. The dates in the colour photographs of both the property documents are clearly reflecting that the building photo snap shots were taken on 07-02-2008 whereas the valuation report is dated 16-2-2008. Then how come the buildings suddenly disappeared in the legal opinions and valuation reports and why Smt. VKN has suppressed these naked facts while disbursing WC facilities and why Bank does not want to investigate in this regard?

Without paying attention at all to all these important points noted above, the Presenting Officer has blindly concluded by saying that the CSO has recommended for WC disbursement too.

In fact I have not recommended for WC disbursement [ME-5] and my signature is not there on ME-5 at all. Without examining the MEs and DEs properly, the Presenting Officer should not have made such blind conclusions that will misguide both the Inquiring Authority and the Disciplinary Authority.

h. It is one more irregularity on the part of Smt. VKN and Shri.N.R.C to misguide the PDVC Officer by providing irrelevant valuation report [not pertaining to this collaterals]. Hence it is important to know whether Smt. VKN and Shri.N.R.C had any mala fide intentions in resorting to all these irregularities by extending cooperation to the fraudulent borrower and mortgagors and in misguiding the PDVC officer.

Investigating all these aspects thoroughly and bringing the facts to light is very important to protect the interest of our Bank.

i. It is also important to find out the actual fact behind whether Shri. VSV has conducted pre-sanction visit. If so what were his visit findings and whether he has submitted the visit report. If submitted, whether that record was tampered.

j. Further it is more important to know how this loan is irregularly sanctioned in contradiction to Bank's circular guidelines without obtaining Credit Rating approval from Risk department.

As all these points are proving that the reason for the financial loss to our Bank is due to collateral fraud, it is not correct to say that the financial loss happened as the Credmin Officer has not monitored the loan case.

k. In spite of seeing the DE-3 too [Proof of date on which finacle ID was provided to me], it is not correct on the part of PO to conclude illogically by saying that all the charges are established.

In view of the above, it is clear that the conclusions drawn by the PO are not correct and they are illogical? All the questions that I have asked the MW-1 & MW-3 are only to highlight the irregularities committed by Smt. VKN and Shri.N.R.C. Hence all the conclusions drawn by the PO in his written brief as well as my questions to MW-1 & MW-3 and their answers given by MW-1 & MW-3 are clearly establishing the irregularities committed by Smt. VKN and Shri.N.R.C.

Overall Conclusion (of my over all presentation):

1. The reason for the financial loss to our Bank in this loan case is the collateral security fraud committed by the Borrower/ mortgagors and the cooperation extended to these fraudsters by Smt.V.K.N and Shri.N.R.C

2. If signing in one office note under the official instructions of supervisor without giving scope and time for verifying/ vetting of back papers is the reason for framing charges against me, then what is the right course of action to be taken on the officer who has conducted pre-disbursement visit, conducted documentation, accepted the documents of fake property for mortgage, recommended WC disbursement, Fixed DP in WC, recommended PDVC note, misguided the PDVC Officer, Initiated TL draft note for disbursement, recommended for TL disbursement, recommended for re-fixation of repayment schedule of TL and by generating a fake email misguided Head Office too.

3. As per the documentary evidences viz., ME-3, DE-10, ME-5, WC DP fixation excel sheet [attachment to ME-5], the PDVC office note to request Smt. RE to conduct PDVC, DE-11, DE-2, DE-5, DE-15 and DE-16 it is established that the Credmin dealing officer for this Loan Case up to January 2009 was Smt. VKN and subsequently w.e.f.23-1-2009 it was Smt.KRB. Hence Issuing Charge sheet to me is gross injustice.

4. The witness given by Shri.EKL has further confirmed that the Credmin dealing officer for this SBEMPL Loan Case from the date of its sanction to till January 2009 was Smt. VKN and subsequently w.e.f. 23-1-2009 it was Smt.KRB.

5. ***As I have been repeatedly saying that I have left for the day from office on 31-3- 2008 after taking permission from Shri.N.R.C, if I was the Credmin officer for this loan case and when the TL disbursement is planned for the day, he would not have given me permission at all to leave the Office at 5 pm. This is clearly establishing that I was not the Loan Case dealing Credmin Officer for SBEMPL as he has permitted me to go home. However, subsequently after my departure, why they have***

decided to make me scapegoat by calling me back to office [with Shri. VSV***'s phone call] is not known to me.***

6. It is important that the Bank has to establish that the SBEMPL Loan case is allocated to me. Without providing any evidence to this extent, initiating major penalty proceedings against me is gross injustice. Further my service in SME, Hyderabad as on 31-3-2008 i.e., as on the date of TL disbursement was hardly one month. This is clearly establishing the fact that I was very new to the systems and procedures of our Bank and to obey the instructions of my supervisor I have signed the ME-7 but not as a Credmin Officer of SBEMPL.

7. In the audio record evidences of phone conversations I had with Shri.N.R.C, Smt. VKN and Smt.KRB separately in the year 2013, every one of them have clearly confirmed that I was not the loan case dealing Credmin Officer for this SBEMPL Loan case. Hence I once again request the Inquiring Authority to accept the same as evidences.

8. After becoming Head, Credmin w.e.f. 23-1-2009, the efforts made by me to protect the interest of our Bank are already explained in detail both in this letter as well as in my reply to the Charge sheet on 13-3-2013.

Hence it is proved that I have never reflected negligence in discharging my duties. In fact, as a prudent Banker, it is me who has detected this fraud in the year 2010 and reported to the higher authorities. Hence, I deserve appreciation in this regard, but not the Charge sheet. Based on the above, I humbly request you sir to recommend for withdrawal of all the charges.

Chapter 5

The Inquiry Report and the Major Penalty Order

The IA PKK has expressed the following in his report:

After careful perusal of all the exhibits and going through the depositions of witnesses as also the written briefs of the PO and CSO, the following two issues emerge:

- Whether the lapses/irregularities as mentioned in the charges 'i' to 'vi' have been established
- If so whether the lapses / irregularities are attributable to CSO

The CSO has not made any attempts to deny the lapses/irregularities as mentioned in the imputation of charges. In fact he has furnished more evidences and arguments thus bringing more information / submissions to substantiate the charges as also alleging more irregularities in this case. Since the purpose of the present inquiry is to find out tenability or otherwise the charges levelled by the Bank's management against CSO, submissions/allegations of the CSO not directly connected with the charges against him have not been discussed/deliberated in this report.

As regards CSO's request for submission of audio records/evidences, it is pertinent to mention that the inquiry process is general followed through exhibits and oral evidences. Further such audio records/evidences may need forensic examination to prove authenticity of the voice/s of the concerned person/s which may not be within the purview of this inquiry process. CSO was therefore advised to produce the witnesses in person during the inquiry proceedings.

From all the exhibits, oral evidences and written briefs the IA is of the view that the lapses / irregularities as mentioned in the charges levelled by the management from charge i to vi have generally been established. However the following facts need to be considered:

- PO BMM has not been able to produce sufficient evidence (except the TL disbursement note and its voucher DT 31-03-2008) showing the involvement of the CSO in this case. All other exhibits both produced by the management as also by the defence show that the credmin related notes were originated by Smt VKN and put up directly to the DGM NRC.
- Even on perusal of Smt VKN's employee bio-data, the same is established as she was directly reporting to the DGM NRC during 28-12-2007 till 01-07-2008 and thereafter to DGM SVS as officer SME, Credmin. She reported to CSO only from 01-07-2009. This is in line with the depositions made by DW-1 EKL who was the then credit officer, SME, Hyderabad.
- There is discrepancy in employee bio-data of CSO LSR furnished by HRD. While it shows CSO's posting at SME, Hyderabad from 29-12-2007 (i.e., his date of joining Bank's service), he was actually posted to Kakinada branch during 29-12-2007 till 23-02-2008 when he was relieved for reporting at SME, Hyderabad as per DE-18.
- Thus the incidence of his signing TL disbursement note /voucher dt.31-3-2008 (the evidence based on which charges have been levelled against him) occurred within five weeks of reporting to a new canter and three months from his joining to the Bank's service.
- CSO LSR has repeatedly explained the circumstances under which he had signed the TL disbursement note/voucher on 31-03-2008. His explanation is also supported by DE-11 and deposition of Smt.VKN (MW-2 and initiator of TL disbursement note) that the draft of TL disbursement note dt.31-03-2008 was not routed through the CSO LSR. A responsible officer, however is expected to put his signature on official

papers/documents only after perusing/examining all the relevant papers / documents.

- None of the management witnesses has deposed affirmatively on the involvement of the CSO LSR vis-a-vis the charges levelled against him.

IA PKK Conclusion: From the available exhibits and the depositions in the RHs, it appears that the CSO was not entrusted with the responsibility of handling credmin functions of SBEMPL loan case during the relevant period. After examining all the evidences, deliberations and submissions and keeping in view the observations as mentioned above, I am of the view that while the charge number i, iv, v & vi levelled against the CSO LSR are not proved, the charge number ii & iii are partly proved as the officer did not appear to have exercised proper due diligence before signing the TL disbursement note and voucher both dated 31-03-2008.

The Major Penalty Order: After more than a year from the date of receipt of PKK's inquiry report DT. 24-12-2013, the Disciplinary Authority (DA) of the Bank vide order DT. 09th March 2015 informed as follows and imposed Major Penalty upon the CSO LSR:

DA's comment:

Although you have submitted that you have joined the Bank newly at the time of incidence, it cannot be ignored that you were directly recruited as AGM and were also carrying experience of over 10 years of working with Banks before joining this bank and had also worked as Chief Manager of a branch. Thus you had sufficient experience, in banking to take / arrive at the decisions. Therefore your contention that you were asked to sign on voucher by your supervisor can not be accepted.

CSO LSR's comment on the above observation of the DA: The CSO's past experience in other Banks has no relation in the present context of this fraudulent loan where in the internal officers VKN and NRC have colluded with the external fraudsters (the borrower and the mortgagors) and already committed fraud as on 08-03-2008 itself. Despite the CSO asking for back papers for perusal before signing TL disbursement note and its voucher, both VKN and NRC refused to provide the same to CSO LSR. In fact they did not want to provide the same even to the DW-1 EKL also as deposed by him in the RHs. Further without even listening to the audio record evidences offered by CSO LSR where in it is very clearly proved that both VKN and NRC separately confirmed that, only at the instructions of NRC, VKN asked CSO LSR to sign the TL disbursement note and NRC also accepted and told that he is ready to tell before any authority or committee that CSO LSR has no assigned role in this case. Further as pointed by DA, though the CSO has more than ten year experience in other Bank's where he had worked, but his supervisors and senior colleagues were not fraudsters like in this present case how VKN and NRC colluded with the external fraudsters and exposed the Bank to financial loss. It can be easily understood that it is only to dilute the adverse effect upon VKN and NRC, both of them wanted to obtain some newly joined AGM signature at least in one disbursement note of SBEMPL and if the the fraud comes to light in future, they can say that they have not colluded in this fraud. That is why they have first tried to obtain DW-1 EKL's signature and subsequently thought that EKL may find out the irregularities already happened in this case if the back papers are provided to him as he is still peacefully sitting in the branch, hence decided to call back CSO LSR as he had already departed from office to go to his home, they thought that hurriedly they can obtain his signature by putting pressure considering the context and circumstances prevailing on 31-3-2008 in the Hyderabad branch premises.

In view of the above the decision of the DA is illogical, illegitimate and it is expressed without seeing/listening to all the evidences offered by CSO LSR.

DA's comment:

You were assigned the role of credmin officer and since you had signed the TL disbursement note and voucher, it was your responsibility before signing that the facts/figures are properly analyzed and its veracity is ascertained /verified and incorporated in the note. Any officer while performing any role, may be even for the time being / temporarily assumes the responsibility attached to the role he is performing. You being the part of credmin, the duties and responsibilities attached there to should have been carried out properly before recommending disbursement. Thus your contention that you had merely signed the sanction note at the behest of your supervisor lacks merit for consideration.

CSO LSR's comment on the above observation of the DA: The DA is ignoring the responsibilities and accountability of an officer on probation. She wants to act blind at the fraud already done by VKN. Instead of making VKN as CSO by resubmitting to SAC for refixation of staff accountability, the DA very illogically trying to defend the illegitimate penalty imposed upon the CSO LSR. Before justifying her stand in the above comment, DA must answer why VKN was excluded from disciplinary proceedings and how she was made a Management Winess-2? Further it is also clear from the above comment that the DA did not even read the content in full what she is signing by imposing major penalty upon a scapegoat. It was not the sanction note that the CSO LSR signed, but TL disbursement note. That is how various officers like DA, AA etc functioned in the Bank by merely signing whatever is put up by the HRD officials. DA's above comment lacks merit and rather it is a false justification given by her for punishing LSR by keeping silent on the role played by VKN. This major penalty order imposed upon LSR is a very clear example for how the officers pertaining to downtrodden sections of society have been targeted and made scape goat to protect the internal fraudsters of the so call upper caste officers in the bank.

Bank cannot escape from its responsibility by merely showing to vigilance department that some body is punished. It must identify the real reasons for the NPA of SBEMPL, find out the role played by the internal fraudsters and punish the guilty by adhering to RBI guidelines and by filing compliant with CBI. The false justifications given by DA is nothing but fraudsters' protective policy adopted by Bank's HRD and it amounts to suppression of facts by misguiding the Staff Accountability Committee of the Bank to save certain internal fraudsters.

Thus irregularly and illegitimately to protect the internal and external fraudsters, CSO LSR was imposed with Major penalty as noted below: 'Reduction by one stage in the time scale of pay for a period of one year without cumulative effect with further direction that LSR shall not earn increment of pay during the period of such reduction'.

The above mentioned penalty appears to be small in terms of the financial loss caused to the CSO LSR, but in terms of his profession, he has been completely stopped from further promotions in career ladder. This is unwritten in the penalty order but understood and implemented by the respective promotion selection committees every year as they were given access to view in their respective computer systems all that disciplinary actions initiated as well as concluded upon all the promotion aspirants. Thus the CSO LSR has been always eliminated from the selection list in every promotion process conducted up to the year 2022 and now all his promotion attempts exhausted. As a result LSR remained as AGM throughout his service tenure in this Bank without even a single promotion despite having merit, honesty and unblemished banking history.

As very much agitated with the above mentioned illegitimate penalty imposed upon him, LSR started appealing to Bank's internal authorities as well as other statutory authorities of government of India viz honorable President of India, Finance Ministry, RBI, Human Right Commission, State and National SC/ST commissions, Central Vigilance Commissioner etc.

Chapter-6

The Appeals

From the year 2015 to 2020 the CSO LSR made several appeals to the Bank's Executive Director, MD & CEO and other statutory authorities like Honorable President of India, Finance Ministry, Reserve Bank of India etc. the essence gist of the his appeals is as follows:

His appeals have been submitted in the larger interest to recover crores of public money looted by fraudsters/promoters of SBEMPL (the borrower) by colluding with few officials (internal fraudsters) of the Bank. They are not mere representations for redressal of LSR's professional grievance, but to recover public money too. To put the detailed content of the appeals in the words of CSO LSR:-

This SBEMPL NPA loan case has many angles like corruption, conspiracy, fraud, cybercrime, money laundering etc, The external and internal fraudsters in this case have so for successfully escaped from law enforcement agencies like Central Bureau of Investigation (CBI) since the year 2010 by bypassing RBI and Bank guidelines on Frauds.

Since I have detected this fraud and reported in the year 2010, certain interested parties in the Bank have colluded with internal and external fraudsters, wanted to make me scapegoat by diverting the attention from fraud angle and illegitimately imposed Major Penalty upon me in the year 2015 so as to save the internal fraudsters involved in this case including those who are presently in higher grades of the Bank. Thus, giving a message to lower grade officers like me in the Bank not to detect / report frauds committed by higher grade officers. Hence to expose the internal fraudsters who are in higher grades and as this loan case complies with the eligibility norms for the compliant to be filed with CBI; I request your highness (President of India) to order for CBI inquiry so as to recover public money by catch holding internal and external fraudsters.

Please find below few examples for my diligent nature of discharging duties in the Bank:

a. I have detected the Fraud in the account of "SBEMPL" Loan case and reported the same in the year 2010 (more than Rs.3.50 crore public money involved) while working at Bank's SME/CSC branch, Hyderabad.

b. I have resisted the irregular disbursement of SEFASU Loan to "JSL" in the year 2014 (more than 6.50 Cr public money involved and it is an NPA with more than Rs.125.00 crore of Principal dues) while working at Saidapet branch, Chennai. This loan was disbursed by violating the Delegation of Powers (DoP) in contradiction to sanction terms stipulated by Executive Committee of the Bank and despite my strong objection, this was irregularly disbursed to please some higher authorities in the Bank.

c. I have insisted for initiation of legal action against "TSL" and its promoters after the consortium of bankers declared the CDR in TSL as failure (it is a fraud loan case where more than Rs.500.00 crore public money of our Bank was lost) and stood firmly against the proposed additional funding of Rs.80.00 crore even after declaring its CDR as failure. Indian Banking industry had lost around Rs.7000 crore public money due to this fraudulent borrower. These loans were subsequently sold at a very cheap cost of Rs.50 crore to ARC at a deep discount of around 10% of principal amount, out of which 15% of cash was paid to our Bank and for remaining 85% of the assignment amount, SRs were issued despite diversion / siphoning of funds was indicated in the Special Investigative / Forensic Audit Report. The news clipping also appeared in The Economic Times DT. May 13, 2018 where in the Resolution Professional informed NCLT that the promoters of TSL siphoned off funds.

d. Despite pressure from my higher-ups, I have refused to accept/ entertain a Collateral security (fake documents) in a proposal by name "PS Hotels" for which Rs.40.00 Crore in-principle sanction approval was available. Thus I had saved huge amount to this Bank by avoiding entry to this Fraud Loan.

e. I have reported several times to our Bank about Mr.N.R.C (the then DGM) committing other frauds at Rajahmundry branch and remitting Rs.50.00 lakh in to this "SBEMPL" fraud loan account on 10-7-2012 to delay the inquiry proceedings against him and

f. I have protested in many other issues that are unlawful and detrimental to the interests of the Bank since the Bankers are the custodians of public money.

In view of the above, certain influential interested parties in the Bank who have felt that my above acts were detrimental to their personal vested interests, have been influencing and stopping my professional career growth. I have joined as AGM in this Bank in the year 2007 and still as on this date I remained as AGM only and all my promotion attempts have exhausted. Thus the interested parties in this Bank are still protecting the internal and external fraudsters (promoters and mortgagors) of SBEMPL fraud loan case by acting in contradiction to RBI and Bank's guidelines on frauds and against to the principles of natural justice.

Despite knowing that RBI guidelines were bye-passed in the year 2011 itself by the then DGM, now CGM VSV who was instrumental in bringing this fraud loan to this Bank and ensured its disbursement irregularly in the year 2008 itself, Bank has not initiated any action against him. As the interested parties in the Bank have disrupted conducting fair trail / fair investigation, I request your good selves to order for CBI inquiry in the SBEMPL matter stated above.

On examination of all the documentary and audio evidences, it can be understood that the interested parties in the Bank had framed irrelevant charges against me and imposed penalty illegitimately. In fact, those charges were supposed to have been framed against Smt.V.K.N being the then Credmin Officer for this SBEMPL fraud loan case in the year 2008 who had extended support to the external fraudsters. ***The punishment imposed upon me by Shri.S.K.V. (Ex-Executive Director of the Bank) in the form of Major Penalty order was part of conspiracy to suppress me and to stop my professional career growth as I have detected and reported this fraud in the year 2010. Shri.S.K.V. was subsequently arrested by CBI in another fraud loan case. The actions of the Bank authorities suppressing my professional career growth by supporting this conspiracy are unconstitutional and against to the principles of natural justice.***

To mention in a nutshell about the illegitimate penalty imposed upon me, the factual information is as follows:

On 31-3-2008 I, along with Smt.V.K.N and Shri.NRC signed Term Loan disbursement note and its voucher pertaining to SBEMPL. Accordingly the Term Loan funds were parked by Sri.N.R.C in the current account of the borrower SBEMPL as per the prevalent practice as well as due to the financial year end date 31-3-2008 targets. ***It is not at all a mistake, because Term Loan is a non-operative account and making payments to the suppliers and vendors by directly debiting the Term Loan account is not possible.*** Hence the Term Loan funds must be parked in some operative account. Accordingly Shri.N.R.C the then DGM had parked the funds in current account as per the then prevalent practice in the Bank (as confirmed by its Management Witness-2 during the inquiry proceedings).

Once such parking of funds is done, ***as per Bank's Circular guidelines***, the respective Credmin dealing officer of the loan case has to ensure end use by making payments to the suppliers/vendors and until then that operative account is to be either lien marked or the operations in the same should be kept under control of the Credmin officer until making payments to suppliers/vendors. Bank's Inquiry officer Shri.P.K.K vide his reports dt.24-12-2013 and 18-01-2014 confirmed that Smt.V.K.N was the loan case dealing Credmin Officer during the relevant period i.e., year 2008.

However since Smt.V.K.N and Shri.N.R.C have already colluded with the fraudulent borrower SBEMPL and irregularly disbursed Cash Credit limits on 08-3-2008 itself and encouraged its siphoning, in the similar way they have allowed/encouraged siphoning of Term Loan funds also during April 2008 itself and by suppressing all these facts, irregularly recommended for rescheduling TL repayment schedule too. As proved in the inquiry proceedings, I was neither Credmin officer for this loan case during the year 2008 nor having Finacle User ID up to 05-05-2008 (being a newly joined officer).

Over and above all, basically this is a fraud loan wherein collateral security is (land/building) non-existing. I have detected this fraud in the year 2010 and reported for initiating criminal action. As a result all internal and external fraudsters colluded with the interested parties at Bank's HO, misguided the Staff Accountability Committee and imposed illegitimate penalty upon me duly suppressing fraud angle in this loan case and bye-passing RBI guidelines on frauds. All that representations, appeals etc made by me in this regard since the year 2013 have been paid deaf year to protect the fraudsters.

Hence I have the following direct questions to the concerned officers in the Bank:

1. ***Whether I was punished only because I had signed TL disbursement note and its voucher on 31-3-2008?***

   If the answer is yes, then the penalty imposed on me by the Bank is 100% illegitimate, because TL account is not operative account and parking TL funds in the current account was the prevalent practice in this Bank as confirmed by its Management Witness in RHs.

2. ***Whether I was punished only because I had not ensured end use of funds, not made payments to suppliers/vendors?***

   If the answer is yes, again the penalty imposed by the Bank is 100% illegitimate, because as per Bank's circular guidelines, ensuring end use of TL funds is the duty of the Loan case dealing Credmin Officer. Inquiry officer Shri.P.K.K vide

his reports dt.24-12-2013 and 18-01-2014 confirmed that Smt.V.K.N was the loan case dealing Credmin Officer during the relevant period i.e., year 2008.

3. ***Whether I was punished only because I had detected and reported this fraud in the year 2010 and as this is not liked by the interested parties in the Bank's HO? The answer must be 'Yes' for this question.***

4. ***Whether I was punished only because I belong to SC category, so that I can be easily made scapegoat by threatening with the weapon of disciplinary action? The answer must be 'Yes' for this question.***

5. ***Whether I was punished because Bank's authorities have not seen all the documentary evidences viz ME-5 [Cash Credit disbursement note], ME-3 [pre-disbursement visit report], DP fixation [excel sheet] in Cash Credit, Note for identifying the officer to conduct PDVC, DE-2 [Re-fixation of repayment schedule in TL], ME-2 [Loan Sanction Letter], Draft note of TL disbursement [DE-11] and DE-10 [Transaction sheet for conducting Loan Documentation] and Inquiry officer Shri.P.K.K reports dt.24-12-2013 and 18-01-2014 which are confirming that Smt.V.K.N was the Credmin dealing Officer for the SBEMPL loan case during the relevant period (i.e., year 2008) and my role was nowhere in the above. In such case Bank's authorities mut be acting blind.***

6. ***Whether I was punished only to protect the internal fraudsters like Smt.V.K.N? The answer must be 'Yes' to this question.***

7. ***Whether I was punished only to protect other officers, who were instrumental in bringing this fraud loan proposal to Bank in the year 2008, ensured its irregular disbursement and by-passed RBI guidelines on frauds by not filing the criminal complaint with CBI in the year 2011 despite having the approval in the year 2010 itself? The answer must be 'Yes' to this question.***

In addition to the above, while responding to the reminder letter dt.15-11-2019 of Ministry of Finance, DFS written to the Bank, Bank has submitted an incorrect, misguiding and irrelevant information to MoF, DFS, and Government of India vide its letter dt.10-03-2020. The details pertaining to the same are mentioned in this appeal. These illegitimate actions of the Bank in SBEMPL loan case have been ultimately resulted in leaving the internal and external fraudsters scot-free, thus encouraging and giving scope to them to commit more frauds by looting public money.

Further, as it is a clear case of suppression and discrimination against me so as to safeguard the internal fraudsters and as the Bank authorities have caused unexplainable mental agony and irreparable professional career loss to me, I request you sir to advise/instruct by issuing orders to the Bank to avoid further delay and respond positively by taking immediate steps to safe guard public money and to avoid further career loss to me.

Based on my representation dt.08-07-2019, honorable authorities at President's Secretariat and Ministry of Finance, GOI, DFS have advised the Managing Director of the Bank to examine the issues raised by me in my representation for appropriate necessary action as per rules, but Bank without examining any of the issues raised by me in my letter dt.08-7-2019 and without giving any justification, provided a misguiding and irrelevant reply to the honorable authorities at President's Secretariat and MOF-GOI-DFS.

Subsequently based on my further representation dt.14-10-2019, honorable authorities at MOF-GOI-DFS have reminded Bank to examine the contents of my representations for appropriate necessary action. In response to the same, Bank vide its letter dt.11-03-2020 has provided a reply letter.

In this connection, on perusal of Bank's reply letter dt.11-03-2020, it is observed that the same is containing;

i. certain incorrect information,

ii. certain misguiding information,

iii. certain irrelevant information and

iv. the majority of points mentioned in my representation are simply left unaddressed despite reminder from MOF-GOI-DFS.

Thus the bank has been defending the illegitimate penalty order imposed upon me so as to protect the internal fraudsters and continuing their discriminatory practices against me so that no lower level officer will come forward to expose corruption/frauds in the Bank. Please find the details noted below:

(i) Certain incorrect information mentioned in Bank's reply letter dt.11-03-2020:

Incorrect information in Bank's reply letter dt.11-03-2020 is pertaining to the Action taken by the Bank with regard to the case being reported as fraud. As per RBI Master Circular dated July 01, 2010, a criminal case should be filed with CBI (Central Bureau of Investigation) against the internal and external fraudsters involved in this SBEMPL fraud loan, but in reality, the interested parties in the Bank have bypassed both internal and regulatory guidelines, delayed for more than a year after obtaining the approval and filed a case with Local Police at Abc Police Station, Hyderabad vide FIR No: 375/2011 dt.17-11-2011, instead of filing case with CBI, thus protected the internal fraudsters/higher officials involved there in. Approval for filing criminal case with CBI against the fraudsters was obtained by me in the year 2010 itself.

So far there is no action taken against those interested parties in the Bank who intentionally bye-passed RBI guidelines in this regard. Subsequently at end of the year 2012 CBI did not accept the compliant in this regard is altogether a different story and rejection of the case by CBI in the year 2012 was due to the acts committed by the interested parties in the Bank in the year 2011 itself in the form of local police compliant filed by them.

I have detected this collateral security fraud, reported to Bank's HO on 13-11-2010 itself and obtained permission to file criminal complaint with CBI as per the existing guidelines. Immediately upon selection as faculty, I was transferred and relieved from Bank's SME Center, Hyderabad during first week of December, 2010. Though it is almost twelve years since I have detected and reported this fraud and obtained approval for filing criminal case, the interested parties in the Bank are successfully managing everything by protecting internal and external fraudsters, thus causing loss to public money;

a. Ideally Criminal complaint was supposed to be filed with CBI, but due to the vested interests, RBI guidelines were bypassed and FIR was filed with local police under the guidance of one interested party who was instrumental for happening of this fraud in the Bank in the year 2007-08.

b. Despite knowing this irregularity, Bank did not take any action against him, but elevated him in the hierarchy by way of promotions.

c. Subsequent to his departure to Bank's HO on promotion at the end of year 2011, the then officers present at SME, Hyderabad tried to file compliant with CBI, during October-November, 2012, but it was refused by CBI with a reason that a compliant with local police filed a year back is existing.

d. It has come to my notice that, subsequently that complaint lodged with local police is also not investigated as managed by the interested parties thus protecting all the fraudsters till date.

e. Filing local police compliant instead of CBI compliant was a planned strategy of the internal fraudsters so as to escape themselves and to commit more frauds.

Hence Bank's statement at page no: 4 of its letter dt.11-3-2020 that, 'The Bank has initiated due action in conformity with applicable internal/ regulatory guidelines in respect of cases where fraud is reported/detected' is incorrect information.

Secondly, With regard to the action against the officials who had dealt with this SBEMPL loan case, the Staff Accountability Committee was also provided with incorrect information in the year 2012;

i. about who was the Credmin officer for this SBEMPL loan case during the year 2008

ii. about my date of joining at the Bank's SME department, Hyderabad and

iii. About who has disbursed Cash Credit limits to SBEMPL loan case on 08-03-2008.

In view of the above, in the charge sheet references No: HRD No:8637/ Staff/ER/1135 dt.28-2-2013, Bank's HRD Officials have incorrectly addressed me as the dealing credmin officer for this SBEMPL loan case and also mentioned incorrect information about my tenure at SME, Hyderabad.

Further, despite my written requests, Bank authorities have not provided me the copies of replies/explanations submitted by Smt.V.K.N in the year 2012 and the copies of the internal office notes submitted to the Staff Accountability Committee. If these copies are provided to me, I might have found much more incorrect information mentioned there in.

Bank's internal Inquiry officer has rightly declared in his reports that Smt.V.K.N was the dealing Credmin Officer for this SBEMPL Loan case during the relevant period, whereas, Charges were framed against me instead of framing against Smt.V.K.N and illegitimate penalty was imposed upon me in contradiction to the findings of the Inquiry Officer and by wrongly projecting me as the loan case dealing Credmin Officer for this SBEMPL Loan case during the year 2008. Even after the truth and facts coming to light vide Bank's internal Inquiry officer's reports DT. 24-12-2013 and 18-01-2014 confirming that Smt.V.K.N was the loan case dealing Credmin Officer during the relevant period, ideally the concerned authorities at Bank HRD were supposed to resubmit for revising Staff Accountability. This has not happened due to the influence of the interested parties supporting the internal fraudsters. Hence, it can be said that the Staff Accountability process was not followed correctly in my case and Bank's letter dt.11-03-2020 is containing incorrect information in this regard.

The audio record evidences offered by me as additional evidences during the inquiry proceedings were never accepted for examination. Hence the disciplinary action imposed upon me was illegitimate, because it is imposed without even accepting the evidence (audio record evidences) for examination. Hence the penalty imposed upon me was in contradiction to the Bank's D & A Rules and principles of natural justice.

In response to my letter dt.04-05-2013 addressed to the Shri.P.K.K, Internal Inquiry Officer seeking some additional documents, I have received a statement duly signed by Shri.B.M.M, the Presenting Officer, wherein he has provided me a statement containing the list of documents sought for by me, out of which what are provided to me and what are not provided to me with reasons thereof. On perusal of this statement, it is observed as follows:

a. I have asked for the copies of replies submitted by Smt.V.K.N along with the copies of explanations called for from her by Bank's HRD in the year 2012 & 2013 in connection with SBEMPL Loan case.

b. The purpose of seeking the above information/copies is to realize the false information if any provided by Smt.V.K.N therein and to know how she could manage to get appointed as Management Witness despite being the Credmin Officer for this SBEMPL fraud loan during the relevant period.

c. Shri.B.M.M, the Presenting Officer has refused to provide me the copies of explanations called for and replies submitted by Smt.V.K.N duly commenting that the information requested by me is not relevant to the charges framed against me.

d. The above comment of Shri.B.M.M is irresponsible and illogical, because all that charges framed against me were actually supposed to have been framed against Smt.V.K.N being the Credmin Officer for this SBEMPL loan during the relevant period. Bank's inquiry officer also declared her as the loan case dealing Credmin Officer for this SBEMPL loan during the relevant period. Hence obviously I am supposed to find out the false information submitted by her so as to get eliminated herself from the status of charge sheeted officer.

e. Thus by not providing me the relevant and important information, the interested parties at Bank's HO acted against to Bank's D & A Rules to protect the internal fraudsters including those who are presently in higher levels.

f. My above guess about false information submitted by Smt.V.K.N in her replies was proved correct by observing the Document no: B-9 provided by Bank's HRD. Please peruse the same. Actually I have asked for the documentary evidence if any allocating loan cases among the Credmin Officers of CSC Hyderabad in the year 2008, but Shri.B.M.M, the Presenting Officer has provided me the works allocation order issued in the year 2009.

g. On perusal of this 'B-9' document, it is observed that Smt.V.K.N had taken print of the same by manipulating / changing her computer system date to the year 2008 and submitted that 'B-9' document hard copy to Bank's HRD.

h. Bank's officials simply provided the same to me by highlighting the 'fake and manipulated date 22-6-2008' mentioned there in and falsely believing that the work distribution order was as if issued in the year 2008.

i. This is 100% negligence of duty (knowingly) on the part of dealing officials at Bank's Head Office who have assisted in Staff Accountability fixation matters.

Thus many irregularities, false beliefs, incorrect information and wrong conclusions have been stuffed at all stages at Bank's HO starting from fixing staff accountability upon me to till date, in imposing as well as in defending the illegitimate penalty order.

In view of the above, one can easily understand that the Bank's letter dt.11-3-2020 is containing incorrect information about adhering to Bank's D & A Rules

(ii) Certain misguiding information:

Bank in its letter dt.11-3-2020 provided certain misguiding information at page number 3, in second para under the heading 'Illegitimate *Internal Proceedings*'. They have mentioned there in that 'the charges against LSR were concluded as partially proved in the report of findings by the Inquiring Authority'. This is misguiding information. Please find the Inquiry officer's report dt.24-12-2013.

The gist of his findings as mentioned in his report's concluding para are as follows:

a. LSR was not entrusted with the responsibility of handling credmin functions of SBEMPL Loan case during the relevant period.

b. In view of the above, out of Six charges framed against him, Four charges were declared as NOT PROVED

c. With regard to the remaining two charges, the Inquiry Officer has declared them as PARTLY PROVED as the inquiry officer **felt** that 'LSR did not appear to have exercised proper due diligence before signing TL disbursement note and its voucher both dt.31-3-2008'.

This opinion or **feeling** of the Inquiry officer expressed at point no: 'C' above is 100% wrong, irrational, illogical and it is contradicting to his own findings in his report, because all that charges framed against me were pertaining to the Credmin Officer's duties and he had confirmed in his report that Smt.V.K.N was the dealing Credmin Officer for this loan case during the relevant period.

Further, any inquiry officer shall draw his conclusions based on the documentary and other evidences. With regard to these two charges, the documentary evidences are clearly reflecting that these two charges (charge number 2 & 3) are not proved against me at all.

Details in this regard are noted below:

As per the inquiry proceedings vide Regular Hearing held on 17-8-2013 between Presenting Officer (PO) and MW-2, vide Question NO:4 (page 5 of 14) the Management Witness-2 has confirmed that 'there were no specific directions available in the Sanction memorandum and sanction letter with regard to the suppliers from whom the machinery has to be purchased. Hence the disbursement of Term Loan was released to the current account of the borrower as per the prevalent practice in the Bank'.

Ensuring end use of funds by making payments to the suppliers/ vendors and obtaining proofs/bills etc was the responsibility of the loan case dealing Credmin Officer as per Bank's circular guidelines.

Smt.V.K.N being the loan case dealing Credmin officer during the relevant period as confirmed by Inquiry officer in his reports dt.24-12-2013 and 18-01-2014, should confirm end use of funds and obtain documents/proofs in this regard. Further in the capacity of Management Witness-2, she has given written statement that the disbursement of Term Loan was released to the current account of the borrower as per the prevalent practice in the Bank.

In view of the above, charge number ii & iii mentioned as partly proved against me are actually NOT PROVED as per the documentary evidences. Hence the conclusion of the Inquiry Officer about the two charges as partly proved against me is incorrect and illogical and it is in contradiction with documentary and other evidences. In view of the above, all the charges framed against me are NOT PROVED. In view of the above, it can be confirmed that the Bank vide its letter dt.11-03-2020 has provided certain misguiding information.

Further in the same page number 3 of Bank's letter dt.11-3-2020, it is mentioned that they have obtained Bank's CVO's advise before imposing penalty on me. Yes, this may be a true statement, but while seeking CVO's advise, Officials must have put up some office note to the CVO. I have been repeatedly requesting Bank to provide me a copy of this office note, but Bank has not yet responded positively in this regard.

My purpose of seeking the copy of this office note is to find out the incorrect and misguiding information, if any, mentioned there in this office note put up to CVO. In fact it is not a confidential note at all and being the illegitimately affected party, I have every right to peruse this office note. Since most of the papers dealt-with in this illegitimate disciplinary proceedings against me are stuffed with false information about my role, my date of joining etc., I strongly suspect that this office note put up to Bank's CVO must also be containing similar false and misguiding information.

(iii) Certain irrelevant information:

Bank's letter dated 11-03-2020 containing the data of SC/ST officers promoted since the year 2011 to 2020. Being a public sector Bank and fully owned Government of India undertaking until recent times, adhering to SC/ST reservations is obviously a statutory norm to be complied with by the Bank and there is nothing great or special in it. Further this data has no relevance to the caste based discrimination shown against me in the internal promotion process since the year 2011 so as to protect the internal and external fraudsters.

This caste based discrimination against me actually started when I have detected this fraud during the year 2010 and this discrimination has become more aggravated especially after seeing the conclusion part of my letter dt.13-03-2013 while submitting the replies to the charges framed against me. Since I belong to SC category, the interested parties at Bank's HO thought that I will simply keep quite because of the fear of illegitimate disciplinary action proceedings. The interested parties at Bank's HO wanted to protect Smt.V.K.N (the internal fraudster). Hence they behaved and acted as if they are blind towards all the documentary evidences proving that she was 100% involved and colluded with internal and external fraudsters. Please find some of the documentary evidences where in Smt.V.K.N' s role is clearly evident viz., ME-5 [WC disbursement note], DP fixation [excel sheet] in Cash Credit, Note for identifying officer to conduct PDVC, DE-2 [Re-fixation of repayment schedule in TL], ME-2 [Loan Sanction Letter], Draft note of TL disbursement [DE-11] and DE-10 [Transaction sheet for conducting Loan Documentation] etc,. The interested parties at Bank's HO were silent about collateral security fraud while framing charges against me and behaved as if they are blind to look at the above documents where in her role is clearly evident as the credmin officer for SBEMPL loan case in encouraging the fraud to take place.

Being an officer belonging to SC category, they took me for granted and made me scapegoat so as to protect Smt.V.K.N. Further, if I am allowed to grow in career ladder, they thought that definitely I will get the opportunity to bring all the truths to light. Hence they have been suppressing me in the internal promotion process. Even while imposing illegitimate penalty upon me, they have further continued their discriminatory practice by mentioning as 'Minor Penalty' in the order issued to Smt. KVD as she belong to the so called upper caste and mentioned it as 'Major Penalty' in the order issued to me as I belong to

SC category, though the actual penalty is 'one increment cut without cumulative effect' for both of us.

Further the general practice in the Bank is that those who are imposed with major penalty will be never promoted in the internal promotion process and the respective selection committees would take special care by giving least qualifying marks in the interview thus automatically eliminate them from selected list. Accordingly since major penalty was imposed upon me illegitimately, I have been not promoted.

In addition to the above, there are many more important points raised by me that were left unaddressed by Bank in its letter dt.11-03-2020 viz., Cyber Crime Angle, Money Laundering angle, Corruption angle, Conspiracy angle, Vigilance angle, Cheating angle, By-passing RBI guidelines angle (not punishing the persons involved in it) and Fraud angle etc,.

Further Bank has confirmed in its letter dt.11-03-2020 that it is not in a position to consider my representation with regard to the disciplinary proceedings already happened as there is no provision for further review in terms of Officers' (Discipline & Appeal) Rules 2006. In this connection, it is also important to note that Officers' (Discipline & Appeal) Rules 2006 do not encourage protection to internal fraudsters, do not accept caste based discrimination, do not agree for bypassing regulatory and internal guidelines and do not safeguard those who have bypassed internal and regulatory guidelines. Then how come Bank is doing all this non sense.

In view of the above, I am submitting the following points in detail with evidences and justifications for your examination sir with a request to issue suitable instructions to the Bank.

Evidences:

1. Evidence number:1 - The WC Cash Credit Disbursement note dt.08-03-2008(ME-5) and
2. Evidence number 2: Pre-disbursement visit report (ME-3) dt.26-02-2008:

If the WC Cash Credit Disbursement note dt.08-03-2008 (ME-5) is examined jointly along with the pre-disbursement visit report (ME-3) dt.26-02-2008 and the Audio record evidence of Smt.V.K.N. we can easily draw the following conclusions:

a. Smt.V.K.N along with Smt.KRB have conducted visit to the Borrowers work place at Hospet in Karnataka state on 23-02-2008 and submitted their visit report on 26-02-2008 to the then DGM Shri.N.R.C.

b. Shri.N.R.C has perused the visit report and agreed with the observations/comments mentioned in this visit report by signing the same.

c. One of the important observations in the visit report is that there is no activity at Borrowers works site for the past one year.

d. If there is no work activity for longer time, WC limits should not be disbursed.

e. In contradiction to her own negative observations vide visit report dt.26-02-2008, Smt.V.K.N had irregularly disbursed Cash Credit limits vide ME-5 (CC disbursement note) on 08-03-2008 duly colluding with Shri.N.R.C and with the external fraudsters.

f. Smt.V.K.N had not captured the negative observations of her visit in the Cash Credit limits Disbursement note.

g. Smt.V.K.N and Shri.N.R.C have disbursed Cash Credit limits on 08-03-2008 to this SBEMPL fraud loan borrower without involving me.

h. Except at Hospet, Karnataka, there were no other work sites for this SBEMPL fraud borrower.

i. Based on the debtors statement and CA certificate dt.29-2-2008 on debtors (ME-4), SBEMPL WC Cash Credit Drawing power was fixed by Smt.V.K.N and Shri.N.R.C.

j. This drawing power fixed by Smt.V.K.N and Shri.N.R.C in Cash Credit disbursement is also irregular. Out of the total three debtors of SBEMPL, the Singan Projects and Laxmi Aruna Minerals are the two high value debtors as per ME-4 [CA certificate dt.29-2-2008 on debtors. Entire drawing power of SBEMPL was derived from these two high value debtors only, but, in ME-1 [credit appraisal memorandum and in DE-17 [project report/feasibility report, there is no mention at all about these two high value debtors]. In spite of no activity at the borrowers works site since April 2007, these two new and high value fake/cooked debtors are appearing in ME-4 under within 90 days receivables category and without calling for explanation about the same from the borrower, Smt.V.K.N and Shri.N.R.C had disbursed WC limits irregularly by fixing Drawing Power on 8-3-2008 vide ME-5.

k. Thus by disbursing Working Capital Cash Credit limits to SBEMPL, both Smt.V.K.N and Shri.N.R.C have extended cooperation to the fraudulent borrower and paved way for this fraud to take place in the Bank.

l. Further, as disclosed by Smt.V.K.N during our phone conversation, Shri.N.R.C had asked Smt.V.K.N to change the visit report positively before disbursing Cash Credit limits itself. Evidence for the same is available in the form of audio recordings.

m. These four evidences i.e., 1) Pre-disbursement visit report (ME-3) dt.26-02-2008, 2) The Cash Credit Disbursement note dt.08-03-2008(ME-5) 3) CA certificate dt.29-2-2008 on debtors (ME-4) and 4) audio recordings of Smt.V.K.N conversations with me are enough to fix staff accountability against Smt.V.K.N in this SBEMPL fraud loan case.

n. Based on the above, instead of fixing staff accountability on Smt.V.K.N, the interested parties at Bank's Head Office have targeted and irregularly fixed accountability upon me by leaving the internal fraudster scot-free.

o. In view of the above, Bank has to clarify whether it is because I belong to Scheduled Caste or is it only to protect the internal fraudster Smt.V.K.N, they have irregularly fixed accountability up on me. Bank's response is silent on this point in its reply letter dt.11-3-2020 submitted to MoF, DFS and Government of India.

3. Evidence number 3:Transaction sheet/attendance sheet for conducting Loan Documentation (DE-10):

   a. Transaction sheet/attendance sheet for conducting Loan Documentation (DE-10) was prepared by Smt.V.K.N for this SBEMPL loan case and she only had conducted documentation on 05-03-2008 at Hyderabad branch premises.

   b. This attendance sheet is partly typed and partly hand written

   c. Generally the loan case dealing credmin officer conducts documentation and he/she would be aware of the persons supposed to visit branch premises for execution of loan/security documents.

   d. The mortgagors of SBEMPL loan case had not visited Bank on 05-08-2008 for execution of mortgage security documents

   e. Smt.V.K.N and Shri.N.R.C had handed over the attendance sheet along with duly prepared mortgage documents to the fraudulent borrower Shri.SPR for obtaining the signatures of mortgagors in respective Equitable Mortgage documents. This is an irregular practice.

   f. Smt.V.K.N had never seen mortgagors until the year 2010. She had first time met one of the mortgagors, only after this fraud was detected by me in the year 2010 and when one of the mortgagors had visited Bank's SME canter in this context. During this context, when I asked her whether she knows that person, she said that she had never seen him. This happened in front of the officers present in the then CSC, Hyderabad.

g. Handing over Equitable mortgage documents (to be executed) to the borrower for obtaining the signatures of the mortgagors is a grave irregularity and amounts to gross negligence of duty. Both

Smt.V.K.N and Shri.N.R.C should be jointly held responsible for the same as this SBEMPL is basically has fraud aspect in immovable property Collateral Security and this is the root cause for this loan account becoming NPA.

4. Evidence number 4: The PDVC certification Report:

   a. As per Bank's Circular No.97 / CBSD – 24 / 2006-07 dt.28-10-2006 guidelines existing as on the year 2008, PDVC (pre-disbursement verification of documents by an officer not dealing with the loan case) was supposed to be conducted prior to 08-03-2008 i.e., before disbursing Cash Credit in SBEMPL Loan case.

   b. However though the PDVC was conducted on 17-3-2008, the dealing team consisting of Smt.V.K.N and Shri.N.R.C have provided an irrelevant and unrelated valuation report of collateral security to PDVC certifying officer for verification.

   c. The Legal opinion/Title investigation reports obtained from the empanelled advocate on the collateral securities were not provided at all to the PDVC certifying officer by Smt.V.K.N and Shri.N.R.C for verification.

   d. If these reports would have been provided to the PDVC certifying officer, the irregularities/fraudulent aspects in the collateral security must have come to light before disbursement of TL itself.

   e. For example, the title deeds are reflecting the collateral security as land and building where as the Valuation report is reflecting it as open land.

   f. Further the property tax receipt is not obtained by Smt.V.K.N and Shri.N.R.C as stipulated in the title investigation report.

   g. Smt.V.K.N and Shri.N.R.C did not obtain any approval for not obtaining property tax receipt.

   h. Thus Smt.V.K.N and Shri.N.R.C have avoided many aspects to come to the notice of PDVC certifying officer by not providing Title Investigation Reports for PDVC.

i. Hence, the PDVC is not in order and Smt.V.K.N and Shri.N.R.C have misguided the PDVC certifying officer by providing irrelevant documents for scrutiny as they have already disbursed Cash Credit limits to this SBEMPL borrower on 08-03-2008 itself by extending cooperation to the external fraudsters.

j. Thus they have suppressed the fraud angle coming to light both by not conducting PDVC in CC pre-disbursement stage as well as by providing irrelevant valuation report to PDVC Certifying Officer.

k. Though I have highlighted this aspect in my overall presentation DT. 30-11-2013 itself (submitted to Inquiry Officer Shri.P.K.K, Bank had not ordered for any inquiry to catch hold the internal fraudsters. Thus the internal fraudsters are protected and encouraged by the interested parties at Bank's HRD/HO.

l. The above mentioned is true and factual and the same may be cross-checked by comparatively perusing the Valuation reports, Title investigation reports and the Certification given by the PDVC officer. This matter was highlighted by me in my various replies and representations submitted to Bank's HO.

m. Despite the above irregularity brought to the notice of Bank by me in the year 2013 itself, the interested parties at Bank's HO colluded with the fraudsters and did not take any action against them.

n. The internal office note for identifying the PDVC officer was moved and approved by Smt.V.K.N and Sri.N.R.C.

5. Evidence number 5: Draft note of TL disbursement [DE-11]:

   a. Smt.V.K.N and Shri.N.R.C were the parties involved in preparation and finalization of Draft note of TL disbursement [DE-11].

   b. Though I was available in the office on 31-03-2008 throughout the office hours from 10 am to 5 pm, this Draft note of TL disbursement [DE-11] was neither moved through me nor was I aware about SBEMPL loan case proposed disbursement.

c. During the inquiry proceedings regular hearing held on dt.04-10-2013, while answering question no: 37, Smt.V.K.N had confirmed that she had not routed this Draft note of TL disbursement [DE-11] through me.

d. As confirmed by Smt.V.K.N, the hand writing at manual corrections appearing in this Draft note of TL disbursement [DE-11] is of Shri.N.R.C, the then DGM and he had confirmed therein the margin brought in by the promoters of SBEMPL (borrower)

e. Shri.N.R.C had also increased TL loan amount to be disbursed by making corrections in this Draft note of TL disbursement [DE-11], thus disbursed the entire TL in one go.

f. Staff Accountability Committee vide its minutes dt.16-08-2012, fixed accountability on me for not confirming the margin brought in by the borrower. Actually as per the circular guidelines dated February 11, 2008 the loan case dealing credmin officer Smt.V.K.N should confirm the margin brought in by the borrower. However Shri.N.R.C being the then DGM, had already confirmed the margin brought in, in the Draft note of TL disbursement [DE-11] itself. Hence, leaving both Smt.V.K.N and Shri.N.R.C, fixing accountability on me is irregular as well as illegitimate.

g. Thus the staff accountability committee was misguided by the interested parties at Bank's HO

6. Evidence number 6: ME-7 - TL Disbursement note and its voucher:

   On 31-3-2008 I, along with Smt.V.K.N and Shri.N.R.C signed Term Loan Disbursement note and its voucher pertaining to SBEMPL. Accordingly the Term Loan funds were parked by Sri.N.R.C in the current account of the borrower SBEMPL as per the prevalent practice as well as due to the financial year end date 31-3-2008 targets. ***It is not at all a mistake, because Term Loan is a non-operative account and making payments to the suppliers and vendors by directly debiting the Term Loan account is not possible. Hence the Term Loan funds must be parked in some operative account.***

Accordingly Shri.N.R.C the then DGM had parked the funds in current account as per the then prevalent practice in the Bank (as confirmed by its Management Witness-2 during the inquiry proceedings).

Once such parking of funds is done, as per Bank's Circular guidelines, the respective Credmin dealing officer of the loan case has to ensure end use by making payments to the suppliers/vendors and until then that operative account is to be either lien marked to the extent of TL funds or the operations in the same should be kept under control of the Credmin officer until making payments to suppliers/vendors. Inquiry officer Shri.P.K.K vide his reports dt.24-12-2013 and 18-01-2014 confirmed that Smt.V.K.N was the loan case dealing Credmin Officer during the relevant period i.e., year 2008.

However since Smt.V.K.N and Shri.N.R.C have already colluded with the fraudulent borrower SBEMPL and irregularly disbursed Cash Credit limits on 08-3-2008 itself and encouraged its siphoning, in the similar way they have allowed/encouraged siphoning of Term Loan funds also during April 2008 itself and by suppressing all these facts, irregularly recommended for rescheduling TL repayment schedule too. As proved in the inquiry proceedings, I was neither Credmin officer for this loan case during the year 2008 nor having Finacle User ID up to 05-05-2008 (being a newly joined officer).

Over and above all, basically this is a fraud loan wherein collateral security is (land/building) non-existing. I have detected this fraud in the year 2010 and reported for Initiating criminal action. As a result all internal and external fraudsters colluded with the interested parties at Bank's HO, misguided the staff

Accountability Committee and imposed illegitimate penalty upon me duly suppressing fraud angle and bye-passing RBI Guidelines on frauds. All that representations, appeals etc made by me in this regard since the year 2013 have been paid deaf year to protect the fraudsters.

Further, all the documentary evidences viz ME-5 [Cash Credit disbursement note], ME-3 [pre-disbursement visit report], DP fixation [excel sheet] in Cash Credit, Note for identifying the officer to conduct PDVC, DE-2 [Re-fixation of repayment schedule in TL], ME-2 [Loan Sanction Letter], Draft note of TL disbursement [DE-11] and DE-10 [Transaction sheet for conducting Loan Documentation] etc., including the TL Disbursement note ME-7 are confirming that Smt.V.K.N was the Credmin dealing Officer for the SBEMPL loan case during the relevant period (i.e., year 2008)

The Audio recording evidences of Smt.V.K.N and Shri.N.R.C are also confirming that Smt.V.K.N was the Credmin dealing Officer for the SBEMPL loan case during the relevant period i.e., year 2008 and

The depositions given by Shri.EKL, GM (the then AGM/ DW-1) during the regular hearing conducted on 4-10-2013 are also confirming that Smt.V.K.N was the Credmin dealing Officer for the SBEMPL loan case during the relevant period (i.e., year 2008)

DE-3 is confirming that, as on the date of Disbursement of TL i.e., 31-3-2008 and subsequently up to 5-5-2008, I was neither having Core Banking Finacle ID nor Finacle knowledge. In fact up to 05-05-2008, I had never worked in core banking software as my previous banks were not running on core banking platform as on year 2008. Hence fixing accountability upon me was irregular.

As deposed by DW-1 Shri.EKL on 04-10-2013 in Regular Hearing, all the Credmin matters pertaining to this SBEMPL loan case were directly dealt by Smt.V.K.N in the year 2008 and she was directly reporting to the then DGM Shri.N.R.C.

In addition to all the above, vide my reply dt.13-3-2013 while denying the charges, I have already explained in detail the circumstances under which my signature was deceitfully obtained by Smt.V.K.N and Shri.N.R.C in the TL Disbursement note -ME-7 and its voucher. ***However signing the TL disbursement note and its voucher is not at all a misconduct.***

Though I was available in the office on 31-03-2008 throughout the office hours from 10 am to 5 pm, the Draft note of TL disbursement [DE-11] was not routed through me. During the inquiry proceeding regular hearing held on dt.04-10-2013, while answering question no: 37 Smt.V.K.N had confirmed that she had not moved this Draft note of TL disbursement [DE-11] through me.

Based on all the above points, it is very simple to understand that, Shri.N.R.C and Smt.V.K.N have deceitfully obtained my signature in TL disbursement note and its voucher so as to dilute the negative impact on them if this fraud comes to light in future and this act is a part of their planned conspiracy.

If they would have moved Draft note of TL disbursement [DE-11] through me, definitely I would have insisted for and checked all the back papers and brought all the facts black and white before finalizing TL disbursement note despite not being the dealing Credmin officer and signing TL Disbursement note ME-7 in good faith would not have aroused and TL would not have disbursed at all.

Being a newly joined officer at SME department of Hyderabad branch with hardly two weeks of experience, not being the loan case dealing Credmin Officer, having assured by Smt.V.K.N, Shri.N.R.C and Shri. VSV that everything is in order and all the disbursement procedures of the Bank were adhered to and Cash Credit limits were already disbursed by them three weeks back and over and above all, that day/date being the 31-3-2008 financial year end date and as it was late in the evening, it is impossible to suspect the conspiracy involved in obtaining my signature in TL disbursement note. ***Further, as I was not supposed to disobey my supervisor Shri.N.R.C's oral instruction, I have acted under the directions of my then supervisor Shri.N.R.C which is as per Rule 5 (3) of Officer's Conduct Rules. Hence my signing of TL disbursement note shall not be attributed as misconduct on my part.***

In view of the above, fixing staff accountability on me just by looking at my signature in TL Disbursement note-ME-7 and its voucher is irregular and illegitimate. The interested parties at Bank's HO have deceitfully projected me as the Loan case dealing Credmin Officer before Staff Accountability Committee by suppressing all the above facts.

To defend their actions, the interested parties at Bank's HO have provided wrong information in the office notes submitted to Staff Accountability committee. They took date of DE-5 [fraudulently purported and manipulated email of Smt.V.K.N dt.22-6-2008] as the main basis and falsely exposed me as the loan case dealing Credmin officer for this SBEMPL Loan case. Thus misguided the staff accountability committee by providing false information in the office notes submitted to Staff Accountability Committee.

Further they have provided additional wrong information about my date of joining Bank's SME department at Hyderabad as 29-12-2007, but subsequently it was proved as wrong information during the inquiry proceedings. Inquiry Officer report dt. 24-12-2013 may please be referred in this regard.

In view of such false information provided to Staff Accountability committee, a major penalty charge sheet was issued to me containing the charges pertaining to the duties and functions of Credmin officer. This is 100% irregular and illegitimate.

We may also refer to Charge number 'vi' framed against me in the charge sheet dt.27/28 February, 2013, where in Bank authorities have addressed me as follows: "You as Credmin officer failed to obtain………". This is the best example to confirm that, the office note submitted to Staff Accountability Committee was mostly cooked with false information by projecting me as the Credmin officer to this SBEMPL loan case during the year 2008.

If Bank feels that my above point is wrong, I once again request the concerned authorities at Bank to provide me a copy of the office note submitted to Staff Accountability Committee.

Though, as a whole the inquiry officer Shri.P.K.K had taken utmost care in conducting inquiry proceedings transparently, the following drawbacks are still persisting in his report:

i. Though all the charges are not proved at all against me, he had declared only four charges out of Six as NOT PROVED. Regarding the remaining two charges he has declared them as partly proved, but this is a wrong conclusion. In his opinion I did not exercise proper due diligence before signing TL disbursement note and its voucher dt.31-3-2008, hence, he had concluded that Charge no: ii & iii are partly proved.

ii. While commenting that I did not exercise proper due diligence before signing TL disbursement note and its voucher dt.31-3-2008, he had forgotten the conspiracy angle involved in obtaining my signature and he has not given justification in his report as to how my act of signing TL disbursement note and its voucher amounts to misconduct to frame charges against me by simply leaving the dealing Credmin officer Smt.V.K.N.

iii. I have already explained in detail, in my replies to the charge sheet dt.13-03-2013 and in my overall presentation dt.30-11-2013 submitted to the Inquiry Officer as how my signature appeared in TL disbursement note and its voucher dt.31-3-2008. Hence what is mentioned as partly proved is actually not proved at all against me.

iv. He only declared in his inquiry findings/reports that Smt.V.K.N was the actual Credmin Officer for this SBEMPL Loan case during the relevant period. He was well aware that Smt.V.K.N should have ensured payments to the suppliers/vendors directly from the Term Loan amount disbursed, instead disbursing the amount by crediting the funds disbursed to the current account of the company. He is also aware that she should have ensured that, from the term loan amount disbursed, payments are made to the suppliers/vendors and should have obtained documents/ proof of creation/acquisition of fixed assets from the funds lent by the Bank.

Despite knowing all these, finding fault on my part by mentioning that this charge is partly proved against me is irregular and illegitimate. There might have been some pressure upon him too from the interested parties at Bank's HO for making me scapegoat as conspired by them.

In view of the above, my signature in TL disbursement note and its voucher should not be considered as basis for imposing an illegitimate punishment upon me by leaving the internal fraudster Smt.V.K.N who had extended full cooperation to the external fraudsters.

In fact Shri. N.R.C has verified the voucher by authorizing the entry in finacle at about 06.47 pm in the late evening on 31-3-2008 [DE-12]. Please see Smt.V.K.N's hand writing appearing on the TL disbursement voucher. Being the Credmin dealing officer of this case, having prepared the TL voucher, what made Smt.V.K.N not to sign the voucher was not examined. Shri.P.K.K being the Inquiry Officer had missed out all these points and as a result given a wrong conclusion about the two charges as partly proved against me.

After approving the parking of TL funds in the current a/c of the borrower, Smt.V.K.N and Shri.N.R.C have not taken any care either to lien mark or debit freeze the current a/c to the extent of TL funds to ensure payments to Suppliers/vendors from the TL funds. This is because they have colluded with the external fraudsters.

On 31-3-2008 itself, other finacle transactions like DC no: 28031, 41751 & 60422 pertaining to some other Loan cases were entered / verified by Smt.V.K.N wherein she had prepared the vouchers too. In additions to the above, she has prepared hundreds of vouchers while working in SME/CSC, Hyderabad. Hence I have requested to examine the above vouchers pertaining to the above DC numbers and other office notes containing Smt.V.K.N's hand writing to confirm the handwriting of Smt.V.K.N on the TL debit voucher and bring to light the intentions of Smt.V.K.N in preparing the voucher for directly crediting the TL amount to the Current a/c and subsequently why she has cleverly not signed the voucher in spite of a column available in the voucher about the person who has prepared the same. Knowing that I had neither Finacle ID nor Finacle knowledge as on those days, both Smt.V.K.N and Shri.N.R.C made me scapegoat by deceitfully obtaining my signature in TL disbursement note and in its debit voucher though I was not the Credmin Officer for this loan case.

Further, as how Smt.V.K.N and Shri.N.R.C have misguided the PDVC certifying officer, similarly they have given me false assurances by saying that they will adhere to all the procedure guidelines of the Bank while disbursing TL.

Thus, in spite of assuring me that they will ensure payment to suppliers/vendors, Smt.V.K.N and Shri.N.R.C have not adhered to the procedural guidelines of the Bank and they have extended their cooperation to the Borrower for diversion and siphoning of TL funds and ultimately suppressed all these facts and recommended for re-fixation of TL repayment schedule too by further cheating Bank.

Hence, it is proved that the officers who are supposed ensure the payments to the suppliers/vendors were Smt.V.K.N & Shri.N.R.C. In view of the above, the major penalty imposed upon me in the year 2015 was irregular, illogical and illegitimate and it amounts to safeguarding internal fraudsters.

7. Evidence number 7: Explanations submitted by Smt.V.K.N to Bank's Head Office in the year 2011 and 2012 in connection with SBEMPL Fraud Loan case:

   a. Smt.V.K.N was the loan case dealing Credmin Officer for this SBEMPL fraud loan case during the relevant period i.e., year

2008. The same was proved and confirmed by the internal inquiry officer Shri.P.K.K in his reports dt. 24-12-2013 and 18-01-2014.

b. In addition to the above, the following list of documents are also confirming that Smt.V.K.N was the Credmin dealing officer for this SBEMPL fraud loan case in the year 2008:

   i. ME-3 [pre-disbursement visit report], ME-5 [WC disbursement note], DP fixation [excel sheet] in Cash Credit, Note for identifying officer to conduct PDVC, DE-2 [Re-fixation of repayment schedule in TL], Draft note of TL disbursement [DE-11] and DE-10 [Transaction sheet for conducting Loan Documentation] etc.,

c. ***Despite 'a' and 'b' points noted above, based on the explanations submitted by Smt.V.K.N to the Bank HRD in the year 2011, she was excluded from staff accountability by projecting her as if she had no role at all in this fraud loan case. This is a big blunder took place at Bank's HO due to the conspiracy implemented by interested parties.***

d. Hence it is important to see the explanations submitted by Smt.V.K.N to Bank's HRD in connection with the explanations called for by them from Smt.V.K.N in the year 2011-12 so as to realize all that false points she had mentioned there in defending herself for excluding her from staff accountability and to understand the role played by internal interested parties at Bank's Head office to protect her.

e. In view of the above, on examination of the Explanations submitted by Smt.V.K.N to Bank's Head Office in the year 2011-12 in connection with SBEMPL Fraud Loan, it can be proved that she had submitted false information to Bank and Staff Accountability Committee was also provided with false and misguiding information by the interested parties at Bank's HO. Bank is still hiding this explanations submitted by Smt.V.K.N and not providing a copy of the same to me despite several requests/reminders made by me in this regard. This amounts to protecting the fraudsters.

f. ***Since Bank had framed Credmin related charges against me, the utmost important question that arises here is whether Bank does not want to consider the findings of its own inquiry officer concluding Smt. V.K.N as the Credmin dealing officer for SBEMPL loan case during the relevant period?***

g. ***And whether Bank does not want to look at the documents mentioned at point 'b' above that are confirming that she was the dealing credmin officer for SBEMPL loan case and I was in no way connected to this SBEMPL loan case during the year 2008.***

8. Evidence number 8:- Smt.V.K.N's cybercrime Email with fake/ manipulated date.22-6-2008:

    a. In response to my letter dt.04-05-2013 written to Bank's Internal Inquiry Officer Shri.P.K.K, he had provided me a copy of this fraudulently purported email with fake/manipulated date 22-6-2008 of Smt.V.K.N.

    b. This email is actually dated 23-01-2009 and it is pertaining to the Works distribution/ allocation order issued in Bank's SME department, Hyderabad in the year 2009. Its date was purportedly/fraudulently manipulated as dt.22-6-2008 by Smt.V.K.N and submitted to Bank's HO with a mala-fide intension to save her skin. Instead of looking at the correct date i.e., 23-01-2009 in the same email copy, the officer/s at Bank's HRD have wrongly presumed this email date as 22-6-2008 and provided me this email copy through the Internal Inquiry Officer and Bank's Presenting Officer duly highlighting the email date 22-6-2008 and giving number 'B-9' to this document.

    c. Based on this email copy, the officers at Bank's HO have falsely believed that I was the Credmin dealing officer for this SBEMPL fraud loan case during the year 2008.

    d. As a result, they have falsely projected me as the Credmin dealing officer in the internal office notes submitted to the Staff Accountability Committee/s and to other higher authorities.

e. Accordingly, Bank's HRD had wrongly concluded and declared me as the credmin dealing officer for this SBEMPL Loan case during the year 2008 and framed Credmin related charges upon me duly adding additional false information about my date of joining at Bank's Hyderabad branch and about SBEMPL Cash Credit disbursement etc., in the charge sheet dt.27/28-Feb, 2013.

f. Hence this primary document based on which I was considered by Bank's HRD as the loan case dealing Credmin officer for this SBEMPL loan case is a false and fraudulent evidence.

g. As per Information Technology Act, this email is a Cyber Crime committed by Smt.V.K.N to misguide Bank's HO.

h. ***The discrimination and suppression against me in this Bank has penetrated so deep and strong that even after seeing the inquiry officer's reports dt. 24-12-2013 and 18-01-2014 confirming Smt.V.K.N as the dealing Credmin officer during the relevant period and even after realizing that this email date.22-06-2008 was fraudulently purported and manipulated one, the then higher ups at Bank's HRD had not resubmitted the facts to the Staff Accountability Committee/s. Thus by misguiding the staff accountability committee/s, they have ensured suppression and discrimination against me. I strongly believe that this is because I belong to SC category.***

i. In fact if we see the 'B-9' document received from Bank's Internal Inquiry Officer Shri.P.K.K, we can understand that this is a work distribution order issued on 23-01-2009 and it was not related to the fraud happened period i.e., October 2007 to April 30 2008.

j. I strongly believe that the Date 22-6-2008 highlighted by HRD while providing B-9 document to me is definitely a conspiracy and it is not due to error. Basically, this B-9 document is an irrelevant document for fixing accountability upon me.

k. In view of the above, if Bank's authorities still wants to say that there is no caste based discrimination against me, then they should tell the reasons as to why the staff accountability committee was misguided even after receipt of inquiry officer's reports dt. 24-12-2013 and 18-01-2014 confirming Smt.V.K.N as the dealing Credmin officer during the relevant period.

l. In view of the above, the accountability fixed upon me is not tenable and penalty imposed upon me is illegitimate.

9. Evidence number 9: Bank's HO Internal Office note/s put up to Staff Accountability Committee for fixing accountability upon me:

   a. Based on the false explanations received from Smt.V.K.N in the year 2011-12 and due to the fraudulently purported and manipulated email, certain officers at Bank's Head Office have submitted internal office note/s to the Staff Accountability committee/s duly exposing my name as the dealing Credmin officer for this SBEMPL fraud loan case in the year 2008.

   b. This internal office note is containing false information about my date of joining at Bank's SME, Hyderabad. My actual date of joining was 25-2-2008 at SME, Hyderabad where as it was wrongly mentioned there in the internal office note as 29-12-2007.

   c. This internal office note must have wrongly projected me as the loan case dealing Credmin officer before SAC.

   d. They must have wrongly projected my name as if WC-CC was also disbursed by me (because the charge sheet framed against me is containing this false charge also)

   e. Whereas, in both the reports of internal inquiry officer, he has rightly found and declared Smt.V.K.N as the Credmin dealing officer for this SBEMPL loan case during the relevant period.

   f. This internal office note/s must be containing much more false information and until I see them, those false points mentioned there in would not come to light.

g. I have been requesting Bank to provide me a copy of this internal office note/s, but there is no response from Bank.

h. Based on the DE-6- SAC minutes and B-9, I can conclude that this internal office note was cooked with false information by projecting me as the dealing Credmin officer for this SBEMPL loan case so as to protect the internal fraudsters.

i. Hence I once again request Bank to provide me a copy of this internal office note/s put up to Staff Accountability Committee recommending for fixing staff accountability on me.

10. Evidence number 10: Staff Accountability Committee Minutes (DE-6:SAC minutes):

a. The following wordings reproduced below are mentioned in the Staff Accountability Committee Minutes dt.16-8-2012 (DE-6) ***'Accountability was attributed to Shri.LSR for not confirming the margin money brought in and end use of funds at the time of disbursement'***

b. The margin confirmation and end utilization confirmation are the duties of the loan case dealing credmin officer as per Bank's Guideline Ref. No. H.O.SME /2007-08/597 Dt. February 11, 2008 issued vide Circular No. 211/ SME - 60/ 2007-08 (Credmin Officer Job description)

c. In view of point number 'b' above, Smt.V.K.N's name should have appeared in Staff Accountability Committee Minutes dt.16-8-2012 (DE-6) instead of my name as the internal inquiry officer Shri.P.K.K in his reports DT. 24-12-2013 and 18-01-2014 has confirmed that Smt.V.K.N was the Credmin Officer for this SBEMPL loan case during the relevant period.

d. In fact Term Loan margin brought in was already confirmed by Shri.N.R.C in DE-11 (draft note for TL disbursement) and the same was proved in the inquiry proceedings regular hearing dt.04-10-2013 as per the answer given by MW-2 to the question number: 38 asked by me.

e. After perusing DE-11 (draft note for TL disbursement) along with the above mentioned points, it can be concluded that the concerned officers at Bank's HO had given false/wrong inputs to Staff Accountability Committee and as a result my name (LSR) was wrongly mentioned in DE-6- SAC minutes.

f. However, at least after receiving internal inquiry officer Shri.P.K.K's reports dt. 24-12-2013 and 18-01-2014, the concerned officers at Bank's HO dealing with SAC matters should have resubmitted to staff accountability committee for excluding my name from accountability.

g. Point number 'f' mentioned above did not happen because the interested parties at Bank's HO had intentionally made me scapegoat by ensuring my name in DE-6-SAC minutes.

h. For doing this irregular activity noted at point number 'g' above, the concerned officers dealing with staff accountability matters at Bank's HO had intentionally ignored DE-10 [Transaction sheet for conducting Loan Documentation], ME-5 [WC disbursement note], DP fixation [excel sheet] in Cash Credit, ME-3 [pre-disbursement visit report], Note for identifying officer to conduct PDVC, DE-2 [Office note for Re-fixation of repayment schedule in TL], Draft note of TL disbursement [DE-11] an many more other documents which are 100% confirming that Smt.V.K.N as the dealing Credmin Officer for this SBEMPL fraud loan case during the year 2008.

i. Hence it is 100% a conspiracy to protect the internal fraudster Smt.V.K.N by making me scapegoat.

11. Evidence number 11: Charges framed against me vide Bank's letter dt.27/28 February, 2013 (Charge Sheet):

    a. This charge sheet letter DT. 27/28 February, 2013 of the Bank is containing many false allegations against me that are lies.

    b. One of the best examples for the lies/false allegation is that they have gone to the extent of alleging that I have irregularly disbursed working capital limits. My signature is nowhere in

Working capital CC disbursement note and it was not routed through me at all.

c. Hence it can be easily understood that the interested parties at Bank's HO were over enthusiastic to make me scapegoat so as to protect the internal fraudsters.

d. In fact all the charges framed against me were the points related to Credmin Officer's duties and responsibilities and it was confirmed by the Internal Inquiry Officer in his reports dt.24-12-2013 and 18-01-2014 that Smt.V.K.N was the dealing Credmin officer for this SBEMPL fraud loan case during the relevant period. Hence the Charges framed against me vide Bank's letter DT. 27/28 February, 2013 are baseless, illegitimate and not tenable.

e. ***It appears that the interested parties in Bank do not have anything to prove against me, hence Bank's Head Office has mentioned in its letter dt.11-03-2020 that I, LSR had more than ten year of experience in Banking prior to joining this Bank, hence I deserve punishment. What a horrible point it is? Yes, it is true that I had more than ten year of experience in Banking but whether that is a crime to make me eligible for receiving punishment? The truth is that, upon joining the Bank, unfortunately I had worked with two internal fraudsters i.e., my immediate supervisor Shri.N.R.C and my colleague Smt.V.K.N. It was due to their hidden conspiracy, I was made a scapegoat. The audio evidences that I have been offering as additional evidences would clearly prove the same. Without even accepting the audio recording evidences for examination, Bank is still trying to defend its actions with regard to illegitimate punishment imposed upon me. In fact, I have acted under the directions of my supervisor which is as per Rule 5 (3) of Officer's Conduct Rules. How can I, being a newly joined officer with less than one month experience in the Bank at Hyderabad SME department, doubt the intentions and integrity of my immediate supervisor Shri.N.R.C and my colleague Smt.V.K.N?***

f. Since there is nothing left to prove against me, the internal Inquiry officer in his report dt.24-12-2013 declared charge no: i, iv, v & iv as not proved against me and with regard to the remaining two charges (ii & iii) he has mentioned that they are partly proved against me as I did not appear to have exercised proper due diligence before signing TL Disbursement note and its voucher both dated 31-3-2008.

g. How can I, being a newly joined officer with less than one month experience in the Bank at Hyderabad SME department doubt the intentions and integrity of my immediate supervisor Shri.N.R.C and my colleague Smt.V.K.N? My immediate bosses and colleagues who have worked with me in other Banks were never did any conspiracy and they were never involved in any fraudulent activities. Further these two internal fraudsters have told me that the working capital limits to this SBEMPL borrower were already disbursed long back (without involving me). Hence, no doubt, obtaining my signature in TL disbursement note is a planned conspiracy committed by Shri.N.R.C and Smt.V.K.N so as to dilute the negative impact on them if this fraud comes to light in future.

h. Now I wish to mention below how each charge was framed against me in an unpleasant way to make me scapegoat. However out of Six Charges, Internal Inquiry officer had declared Four Charges as Not Proved and regarding the remaining two charges, he had expressed his opinion that they are partly proved. Hear I wish to explain as to how all the charges framed against me are irrelevant and illegitimate.

(i) Charge-1:"You failed to seek clarification from the company on the observations recorded by our officials in the pre-disbursement visit conducted on 23-2-2008 before approving the disbursement of cash credit limit."

My comments:

A. *Those who have framed this charge against me must be either blind or adamant to look at the facts in the cash credit limit disbursement note (ME-5). In fact they must have colluded with the internal fraudsters and framed this false charge.*

B. Framing this charge against me amounts to negligence of duty on the part of the officers who have mentioned this false information as article of charge (i).

(ii) Charge-2: "You failed to ensure that payments were made to the suppliers/vendors directly from the Term Loan amount disbursed and instead disbursing the amount by crediting the funds disbursed to the current account of the company."

My comments:

A. As proved in the inquiry proceedings vide Regular Hearing dt.17-08-2013, crediting the Term Loan funds to the current account of the borrower was the then regular practice in the Bank in the year 2008 (As per the reply given by MW-2 to the Q No:4 asked by PO).

B. Crediting the Term Loan funds to the current account of SBEMPL was a conscious decision taken by Smt.V.K.N (MW-2) and Shri.N.R.C. DGM with mala-fide intentions,

C. The core banking Finacle screen shot confirming that Shri.N.R.C had verified the entry in Finacle duly crediting the funds to the current account of SBEMPL.

D. The hand writing on the voucher crediting the funds to the Current account proving that it was prepared by Smt.V.K.N, but she cleverly escaped by not signing the same at relevant space in the voucher with mala-fide intention.

E. Hence leaving Smt.V.K.N and framing this charge against me in the year 2013 was irregular and illegitimate

F. Fully knowing that I was a newly joined officer at SME, Hyderabad with hardly two weeks of experience and neither having core Banking Finacle software operating user Id nor its knowledge, the interested parties at Bank's HO have framed this charge against me only to make me scapegoat.

G. Despite all the above points, the inquiry officer has mentioned that this charge is partly proved against me but, this conclusion is irrational and irregular and it is in contradiction with his own inquiry findings wherein he had confirmed that Smt.V.K.N was the dealing credmin officer for SBEMPL during the relevant period. Further his conclusion is in contradiction to the documentary evidences.

(iii) Charge-3:"You have failed to ensure that from the term loan amount disbursed, payments are made to the supplier/vendors, which were named by the company in its project report and also failed to seek documents/proof of creation/acquisition of fixed assets from the funds lent by the Bank."

My comments:

a. This charge is nothing but repetition of second charge noted above just by jumbling the words. The interested parties at Bank's HO wanted to show that more number of charges are framed against me, hence continued their attempts by framing this third charge which is nothing but repetition of second charge noted above.

b. Ensuring disbursement to suppliers/vendors and obtaining vouchers/documents/proofs to this extent after disbursement is the duty of loan case dealing Credmin officer as per the internal circular guidelines issued by Bank vide Guideline Ref. No. H.O.SME /2007-08/597 Dt. February 11, 2008 issued vide Circular No. 211/ SME - 60/ 2007-08 (Credmin Officer Job description)

c. Bank's internal inquiry officer Shri.P.K.K had confirmed vide his reports dt.24-12-2013 and 18-01-2014 that Smt.V.K.N was the loan case dealing credmin officer for this SBEMPL loan case during the relevant period. Hence, she should have obtained documents/proof of creation/ acquisition of fixed assets for the funds lent by the Bank.

d. In fact, as observed, there are no names of the vendors/ suppliers to whom the term loan proceeds are to be disbursed. Hence this SBEMPL loan appraisal and sanction itself is irregular. Bank has to clarify whether it had taken any action against the loan sanctioning committee members.

e. Hence this charge is not tenable and baseless. It is illegitimately framed against me only to make me scapegoat by showing more number of charges against me irregularly.

f. However, in contradiction to his own findings vide his reports dt.24-12-2013 and 18-01-2014 confirming that Smt.V.K.N was the Credmin Officer, the inquiry officer has mentioned that this charge is partly proved against me, but, his conclusion is irrational and irregular, because ensuring end used and obtaining documents/proof was the duty of Smt.V.K.N being the SBEMPL dealing Credmin officer during the relevant period.

(iv) Charge-4: You failed to ensure that the account was closely monitored and clarifications from the company were obtained regarding transfer of funds to the individual accounts of promoters and also failed to ensure that the funds lent by the Bank are utilized for business purpose only.

My comments:

a. This charge is about monitoring the transactions in the Loan and other operative accounts. This charge is declared as NOT proved against me by the inquiry officer in his report DT. 24-12-2013

(v) Charge- 5:"You failed to ensure that post disbursement visits as envisaged in the terms of sanction, were carried out to confirm acquisition/creation of fixed assets as per the project report".

A. This charge is declared as NOT PROVED against me by the inquiry officer in his report DT. 24-12-2013.

B. It seems the interested parties at Bank's HO were more enthusiastic to frame more number of charges against me by simply acting blind at all the documents confirming Smt.V.K.N as the Credmin dealing officer for this SBEMPL loan case.

C. Further those officers must have colluded with internal fraudsters.

(vi) Charge- 6: "You as credmin officer failed to obtain stock and debtors statement from the company at monthly intervals and set the drawing power on the basis of such statements"

A. This charge is declared as NOT PROVED against me by the inquiry officer in his report DT. 24-12-2013

B. As has been rightly pointed out by me since the year 2013, it is an open truth that the interested parties at Bank's HO must have wrongly projected me as the Credmin officer for this SBEMPL loan case in all the internal office notes put up to Staff Accountability Committees and to the CVO of the Bank.

C. Bank's authorities may be aware that there must be transparency in disclosing all the evidences before punishing any officer, but unfortunately the interested parties have irregularly imposed illegitimate punishment upon me by neither providing the documents sought for by me nor accepting the audio recording evidences offered by me for examination.

The heights of irregularity in this entire episode of imposing illegitimate punishment upon me is appointing the internal fraudster Smt.V.K.N as the Management Witness-2' for the inquiry proceedings.

12. Evidence number: 12 - Bank's Guideline Ref. No. H.O.SME /2007-08/597 Dt. February 11, 2008 issued vide Circular No. 211/ SME - 60/ 2007-08 (Credmin Officer Job description). This circular speaks about Job Description of Key Functionaries in SME Vertical along with the Credmin Officer duties.

Some important duties envisaged in this circular that were discharged/paid deaf year by Smt.V.K.N in SBEMPL loan case in the capacity of Credmin Officer are as follows:

- Issue of sanction letter to the borrower as per the sanctioned terms and conditions of the proposal. (Yes issued by Smt.V.K.N)
- Co-ordinate with Bank's approved valuer for carrying out valuation of security offered by the borrower (Yes coordinated by Smt.V.K.N)
- Execution of documentation and maintain the documents at the CSC under joint safe custody with Head CSC (Partially yes, Loan documents execution was conducted by Smt.V.K.N but, mortgage documents execution happened in her absence because she has colluded with the external fraudsters and handed over the same to Mr.SPR for conducting execution by the mortgagors)
- Responsible for all documents stored at the Security Locker at CSC (Yes).
- Monitors, conducts and ensures that the inspections/ plant visits are carried out as per the prescribed schedule. (Except pre-disbursement visit to the work site of SBEMPL on 23-2-2008 conducted by Smt.V.K.N, she had paid deaf year to the remaining periodical visits and she had not at all inspected the collateral security either before disbursement of cash credit limits or after)
- Ensure that adequate insurance cover is in place for all the secured advances and that the policy has the requisite endorsement in the Banks favour. (No, not ensured by Smt.V.K.N)
- Ensure that all the terms of sanction are complied with prior to disbursement of the limits and that all documents are live and that revival letters are taken at the appropriate time. (No, only partly complied by Smt.V.K.N)

- Follow-up with CPU for opening of account.(Yes, the loan accounts were opened by Smt.V.K.N)
- From scrutiny of various operations in the account the officials ensure that the funds are used for the purpose intended at the time of sanction and that there is no diversion of funds. (No, WC Cash Credit disbursement was done irregularly by Smt.V.K.N and its end use was not ensured by Smt.V.K.N. In addition to the above, TL funds diversion and siphoning was also encouraged by Smt.V.K.N)
- Stock statement and QIS submitted by the customers are scrutinized / analysed carefully to monitor the movements in NWC / security value on ongoing basis.
- (No, drawing power was fixed irregularly in Cash Credit limits by Smt.V.K.N)
- EODs (Even of Defaults) stipulated at the time of the sanction are monitored / analysed periodically & reports submitted to the competent authority in case of any deviations/ triggers. (NO not monitored by Smt.V.K.N)

13. Evidence number13: Approved office note appointing Smt.V.K.N as Management Witness-2:

    a. HO officials must have suppressed the information about Smt.V.K.N's role in all the documents viz., ME-5 [WC disbursement note],ME-3 [pre-disbursement visit report], DP fixation [excel sheet] in Cash Credit, Note for identifying the officer to conduct PDVC, DE-2 [Re-fixation of repayment schedule in TL], ME-2 [Loan Sanction Letter], Draft note of TL disbursement [DE-11] and DE-10 [Transaction sheet for conducting Loan Documentation] etc.,. In fact these are all evidencing that Smt.V.K.N was the Credmin Dealing officer for this SBEMPL loan case during the year 2008.

    b. Thus by resorting to irregular means, both by providing wrong information and by suppressing the factual information, the interested parties at Bank's HO appointed Smt.V.K.N as Management Witness-2 in SBEMPL fraud loan inquiry proceedings.

c. One should not forget that this is a collateral security fraud case and Smt.V.K.N had fully extending her cooperation to the fraudsters.

d. When such grave irregularities in the form of fraud encouraged by Smt.V.K.N are clearly visible, appointing Smt.V.K.N as the Management Witness is nothing but further colluding with the fraudsters.

e. Until and unless Bank's authorities provide a copy of this office note to me, the actual facts would not come to light. I have requested for copy of the same several times, but it seems Bank's authorities do not want to provide the same to me.

14. Evidence number 14: Inquiry Officer Shri.P.K.K's Report dt.24-12-2013:

I bring the following plus and minus points in the Inquiry Officer Shri.P.K.K's Report dt.24-12-2013:

a. All the charges framed against me were pertaining to the duties and functions of Loan case dealing Credmin Officer and the Inquiry Officer has rightly mentioned at the conclusion part of his report dt.24-12-2013 as follows: "from the available exhibits and the depositions in the regular hearings it appears that the CSO LSR was not entrusted with the responsibility of handling Credmin functions of SBEMPL loan case during the relevant period".

b. Based on the above conclusion, though all the charges framed against me are not proved in reality, the Inquiry officer had declared only 4 out of 6 charges as NOT PROVED against me. Regarding the remaining two charges he has mentioned that they are partly proved and reason for such conclusion mentioned by him in the conclusion part of his report (last three lines) was, 'I should have exercised proper due diligence before signing TL disbursement note'.

c. This is an irregular and illogical conclusion and his statement saying that the two charges are partly proved is 100% irrelevant in the context of SBEMPL TL disbursement, because it had the conspiracy angle of the internal fraudsters and they have obtained my signature in TL disbursement note and its voucher only to dilute the negative impact upon them in case the fraud comes to light in future.

d. Though Shri.P.K.K was the GM as on those days and was appointed as the Inquiry officer in this SBEMPL loan case, one should not forget that he was also an internal officer of the Bank. Hence obviously he had obeyed the instructions of Bank's HRD interested parties as ordered/instructed to him.

e. That is why he had not provided many of the documents sought for by me vide my letter dt.04-05-2013 sent to him

f. Secondly he is well aware that all the charges framed against me were pertaining to the duties of Credmin officer and he has declared in his report that Smt.V.K.N was the Credmin officer for this loan case during the relevant period. Hence, instead of recommending for re-examination of staff accountability, declaring two charges as partly proved against me is senseless. Duly ignoring this aspect, imposing major penalty upon me by Bank's authorities is 100% illegitimate.

g. Further, his inquiry proceedings and the conclusions drawn by the inquiry officer in his report have certain irregularities:

   i. He had not provided me certain important documents sought for by me vide my letter dt.04-5-2013 and

   ii. He has not even agreed to receive the audio recording evidences offered by me for examination as additional evidences

   Based on the above two irregularities, we can understand that he was more influenced by Bank's HRD's oral instructions rather than acting independently and transparently in a justified manner.

h. Hence the penalty imposed upon me is illegitimate and irregular and it was only to protect the internal fraudster Smt.V.K.N.

15. Evidence number 15: Ref.No.HO.PSD/2006-07/198 dt.December 22, 2006 containing the check list of points advised vide circular No. 139/PSD- 12/2006-07 before sanctioning loan proposals. Please find some of the points mentioned there in along with my observations on the non-compliances to it:

    Request letter on Company / Firm Letter Head (Loan application):

    - In the Loan application "Basic Information Sheet", it is confirmed by the borrower that Shri. VSV [the then Head, SME, Hyderabad] now CGM has undertaken visit to the work site of the applicant.
    - The credit proposal appraising officers have not examined this visit report nor made any comments about Shri. VSV's visit observations in the credit appraisal memorandum [ME-1].
    - In fact the visit report of Shri. VSV is not available on record in the Loan files.
    - Whether Shri. VSV had not submitted the report, or had not conducted the visit or anybody has tampered this report was not established.
    - This is a very important aspect, because as per ME-3, activity at the borrowers unit was stopped since April, 2007 itself but the loan proposal was sourced during September/October-2007, hence entertaining the loan proposal itself is irregular when there was no activity at all since April, 2007.

    Site visit report duly signed by the visiting officer Annexure II -

    - Not available on record

      Net worth certificates of the Promoters/borrower-

    - Net worth certificates of the Promoters not obtained but net worth was mentioned as 225 lakh

- Net worth details are not available as to how it was arrived and
- Net worth was not obtained as per Annexure-V of the circular

Market Inquiries about the borrower were not done prior to sanction.

- ME-1 is silent on the same.

Proofs of approvals/permissions for undertaking mining activity were not obtained.

- As per the Basic Information sheet attached to the loan application which is supposed to be filled in by SME officers, important aspects like Proofs of approvals/permissions for undertaking mining activity were not obtained.

Detailed Project Report in case of Term Loan / Working Capital for new set-up

Or expansion-

- The Project Report/feasibility report [DE-17] is not containing the details of the vendors/suppliers to whom the TL is to be disbursed.

Before sending this loan proposal for sanction, as per DE-1 [HO circular] Credit Rating has to be approved by the Risk department, Head Office:

- Credit rating approved by Risk department is not available.
- ME-1 is reflecting that the DE-1 guidelines are not adhered to by the Appraisal team of SME, Hyderabad.
- Hence the sanction of this SBEMPL loan case itself is not complying with the circular guidelines of the Bank.
- Whereas, for another loan proposal [i.e.], "SD Agencies" submitted by SME, Hyderabad to the same sanctioning Committee on the same day, Risk department approval was obtained as per DE-1, but not obtained/not available for SBEMPL.

- Further, in ME-1, it is clearly mentioned that the rating is initiated by Shri. VSV in the subject loan proposal. Hence, it is important to know how the sanctioning committee was misguided and how the loan was sanctioned without complying with the circular guidelines of the Bank and without Risk department approval.
- Whether there was any deliberate act to bye-pass Bank's Risk department, HO and misguide ZCC was not investigated.
- The main reason for the financial loss to Bank was non-compliance to the guidelines of the Circular Ref.No.HO. PSD/2006-07/198 Dt. December 22, 2006 before sanctioning the Loan
- Despite the above, Bank has not fixed accountability on the Loan sanctioning committee members for their negligence of duty in ensuring compliance to Bank's policy and circular guidelines before sanctioning the Loan to SBEMPL,
- ***In the Inquiry report dt.18-01-2014, a false excuse was accepted i.e., due to heavy work load (weekly two proposals), the dealing team could not adhere to the stipulated circular guidelines. There are few things to be observed here i) The actual work load was very low, because there were hardly three to five loan proposals entertained in that entire quarter i.e., from 01-10-2007 to 31-12-2007 by Hyderabad SME department (old records may please be checked), ii) Whether Bank can simply and leniently accept false excuses for not adhering to Bank's circular guidelines? i.e., nonadherence to Bank's Circular no: Ref.No.HO.PSD/2006-07/198 Dt. December 22, 2006 guidelines mentioned above***
- Many of the irregularities observed in the pre-sanction and pre-disbursement stages including the above were taken so casually by the interested parties at Bank's Head Office and simply excused. One of the reasons shown for excusing the involved officers was the work load. Bank may please be advised to provide the list/number of the loan cases sanctioned and

disbursed from October 2007 to March, 2008 pertaining to Bank's SME, Hyderabad. By looking at the number of loan cases sanctioned and disbursed vis-à-vis the number of officers present at SME, Hyderabad during the same period would really disclose the true picture that the non-compliance to the prescribed internal guidelines was not due to the heavy work load.

16. Minor Penalty order issued to Smt. KVD in the same SBEMPL fraud loan case:

    a. Is it true that Bank has given same punishment to Smt. KVD and to me/LSR i.e., one increment cut without cumulative effect, but in the punishment order, Bank has mentioned it as Major Penalty in the penalty order issued to me and mentioned as Minor Penalty in the penalty order issued to Smt. KVD.

    b. Actually the severity of the irregularities happened was more in the appraisal and sanction process, but the punishment given to Smt. KVD is Minor Penalty and despite no fault from my side at all, just to protect the real internal fraudster Smt.V.K.N, it was mentioned as Major penalty in the illegitimate penalty order imposed upon me.

    c. Please refer Bank's Ref.No.HO.PSD/2006-07/198 dt.December 22, 2006 containing the check list of points advised vide circular No. 139/PSD- 12/2006-07 before sanctioning loan proposals. The main reason for the financial loss to Bank was non-compliance to the guidelines of the Circular Ref.No.HO.PSD/2006-07/198 Dt. December 22, 2006 by the appraisal team.

    d. It is a simple truth that when an SC category officer gets Major penalty, that would be a full stop to his career growth. Hence, this punishment is 100% cast based discrimination to ruin my professional career growth and to avoid SC/STs climbing the career ladder despite being meritorious, performing and honest.

17. Additional evidences confirming the irregularities committed by internal officers:

    i. Internal office notes put up to the Disciplinary Authority for imposing Major Penalty upon me; and

    ii. Internal office notes put up to the Appellate Authority for confirming Major Penalty imposed upon me; and

    iii. Internal office notes put up to the CVO of the Bank for imposing Major Penalty upon me

        a. Copies of all the three office notes noted above were sought for by me are not yet provided by the concerned authorities at Bank's HO.

        b. These three office notes must have wrongly exposed me as the loan case dealing Credmin officer for this SBEMPL Loan case

        c. In these three Office notes, they must not have reflected the factual information about the need for re-examination of staff accountability based on the findings of the inquiry officer as to the role of Smt.V.K.N as the dealing Credmin officer during the relevant period

        d. In these three Office notes, they must have suppressed the facts about all that charges not proved against me (crediting TL funds to the current account of the borrower was the then practice in the Bank as deposed by the Management Witness-2 and ensuring end use by obtaining the documents/proofs from suppliers/vendors was the responsibility of Smt.V.K.N being the Credmin Officer during the relevant period) as per Inquiry Officers reports.

        e. They must not have correctly disclosed the factual information about my date of joining SME department at Hyderabad

        f. They must not have correctly disclosed the factual information about the date of providing Finacle user ID to me

g. The facts about Smt.V.K.N's reporting structure in the year 2008 must have been suppressed there in

h. The information about WC Cash Credit Limits disbursement which happened without my involvement on 08-3-2008 itself must have been either suppressed there in or some false information might have been provided there in showing as if I have done the same.

i. Presentation about the findings of the Inquiry Officer submitted vide his report DT. 24-12-2013 must not have been properly reflected in these three internal office notes or might have been reflected with false information.

j. About the false basis for fixing staff accountability on me (i.e., fraudulently purported and manipulated email dt.22-6-2008) must have been simply omitted there in these office notes

k. Based on the fraudulently purported/manipulated email dt.22-6-2008 of Smt.V.K.N, the wrong assumptions made and the mistake committed by the officers by wrongly projecting me as the Credmin officer before the staff accountability committee must not have been brought into these office notes

l. The audio evidences offered by me as additional evidence and non-acceptance of the same at all even for listening/examination by the Inquiry officer must not have been brought in to these office notes

m. The conspiracy angel involved and the cooperation extended by the internal fraudsters as explained in my overall presentation and as proved in the Regular Hearings must not have been brought into these office notes.

n. The facts about DE-11 (draft note for TL disbursement) must not have been captured at all in these three office notes.

o. Some other documents sought for by me from the inquiry officer vide my letter dt.04-05-2013 and the fact about it that the same were not provided in full to me must not have been captured in these three notes submitted to the DA, AA and CVO.

p. False content captured in the office note while appointing Smt.V.K.N as the Management Witness must not have been brought to the notice of DA, AA & CVO in these three respective office notes

In view of all the above, the Major penalty imposed upon me in the year 2015 is 100% illegitimate. Until I see the copies of these three office notes along with the office notes put up to the SAC, the facts about what was supposed to be captured but was not captured there in would not come to light. Bank is yet to provide copies of these four office notes to me.

18. FIR filed with Local Police- FIR No: 375/2011 dt.17-11-2011 registered with Abc Police Station, Hyderabad.

a. In the year 2010, after detection of collateral security fraud in SBEMPL loan case vide DE-14 (Office note dt.13-11-2010) the collateral security fraud was immediately reported by me to Bank's Head office and approval obtained on 15-11-2010 itself for filing criminal case against the fraudsters. During the same time period, I was selected as Faculty, relieved from SME department and joined Bank's Staff Trailing College as Faculty during first week of December 2010. During the same time period Shri. VSV the then DGM now CGM was transferred from ICG, Hyderabad to SME Hyderabad as DGM.

b. Shri. VSV continued his tenure as DGM, SME approximately for a year from November 2010 to August 2011. Initially when this SBEMPL fraud loan happened in the year 2007-2008, he was heading SME, Hyderabad. As per the Inquiry Officer Report dt.18-01-2014, the initial Credit appraisal, unit visit and Rating initiation etc were done by Shri. VSV in this SBEMPL Loan case. However all the three viz initial credit appraisal memorandum, his visit report and Risk department approved rating are not available in the SBEMPL loan files.

c. Though I have obtained approval on 15-11-2010 itself for filing criminal case against SBEMPL fraudster, but during the entire 2nd tenure of Shri. VSV at SME Hyderabad, he had not filed criminal case with CBI as per Reserve Bank of India's Master Circular dated July 01, 2010.

d. Just before getting relieved from SME Hyderabad during August, 2011, Shri. VSV had instructed his subordinates to file compliant with local police against SBEMPL fraudster. This action is in contradiction to Reserve Bank of India's Master Circular dated July 01, 2010 and Bank's Internal guidelines on Frauds issued based on the above RBI Master Circular.

e. As a result, Bank's SME AGM issued letter dt.16-8-2011 to Shri.K.P.S (Bank's Empanelled Advocate) requesting him to file case with concerned police station in Hyderabad and accordingly FIR No:375/2011 dt.17-11-2011 was registered with Abc Police Station, Hyderabad against SBEMPL Fraudsters.

f. This action of filing compliant with Local Police instead of filing compliant with CBI is quite against to the RBI Guidelines as well as Bank's internal guidelines on frauds.

g. Despite being fully aware of RBI and Bank's guidelines on Frauds, deaf ear was paid to them by not filing compliant with CBI and no disciplinary action was initiated by bank against these individual/s who deliberately bypassed regulatory guidelines on frauds.

h. I have another audio record evidence to confirm that Shri VSV had intentionally by-passed RBI & Bank's internal guidelines on frauds by not filing compliant with CBI. This is because, he (Shri. VSV) was instrumental in bringing this fraud loan case to Bank during the year 2007-08 and he personally ensured irregular disbursement to this SBEMPL borrower as confirmed by Smt.V.K.N and Shri.N.R.C in other audio record evidences that I have been requesting Bank to accept for examination.

i. Ultimately to my surprise, recently I came to know that this local police case FIR No: 375/2011 dt.17-11-2011 registered with Abc Police Station, Hyderabad has also disappeared. Thus there is neither CBI Compliant nor Police Compliant available against the internal and external fraudsters.

j. On 25-10-2012 during the tenure of Shri.VSG as GM, SME, a compliant was submitted to CBI against to SBEMPL, but the same was rejected by CBI as the FIR No: 375/2011 dt.17-11-2011 was already registered with local Abc Police Station, Hyderabad by Bank. Further CBI, EOW, Chennai vide its letter dt.08-11-2012 informed to the Bank as follows: 'It is seen that the bank had already lodged a complaint in the said matter with Abc police Station, Hyderabad, vide FIR No:375/2011 dt.17-11-2011 and the same is pending with them. As the subject matter is already being dealt by local police for nearly a year, this CBI branch cannot take up the said compliant, which has already been taken cognizance by police. Hence the original compliant along with all the enclosures as received was returned to the Bank for pursuing the pending investigation at your end'.

k. Subsequent to rejection and return of compliant by CBI, there was no action initiated by Bank on the individuals responsible for filing compliant with Abc (local) police vide FIR No:375/2011 dt.17-11-2011.

l. The main reason for filing FIR No:375/2011 dt.17-11-2011 with Abc Police duly avoiding CBI compliant was due to the fear that the truths would come to light and the real internal fraudsters would also be caught hold by CBI.

m. ***In view of the above, Bank's authorities may please refer its letter dt.11-03-2020 written to Finance Ministry under copy to me and think once again about their false justification as to compliance to regulatory and internal guidelines on frauds in respect of this SBEMPL fraud loan case.***

n. It is due to the fear that all the facts would come to light including his involvement in this SBEMPL fraud loan case,

Shri. VSV has avoided filing the case with CBI and gave compliant to local police for suppressing his involvement coming to light in this fraud. Subsequently that local police compliant was also appears to have been disappeared as managed by the interested him. Thus he has acted against to the internal and regulatory guidelines on Frauds. Hence as of now, there is neither CBI case nor Police case in this fraud loan case.

o. Thus there is a non-compliance to internal and regulatory norms on Frauds. If Bank tries to defend by saying that CBI complaint was filed in this SBEMPL loan case, a copy of FIR of CBI may please be called for.

p. Further, Bank has not initiated any inquiry to find out the involvement of internal officers if any, in this fraud loan case.

q. In the year 2013 itself, while submitting the replies to the charges framed against me, I have highlighted about involvement of Shri. VSV in this fraud cum conspiracy in SBEMPL loan case, but no steps initiated by Bank to bring the facts to light nor any action initiated against him for bye-passing internal and regulatory guidelines on frauds.

r. The audio record evidences offered by me as additional evidences may also be referred to find out how Shri. VSV used to cheat/pressurize his subordinates in the fraud loan cases organized/brought by him.

19. Bank's letter ref no: HRD/ERS/2019-20/7726 dt.11-03-2020 sent to the Under Secretary to the Government of India, DFS, Ministry of Finance:

    a. In this letter Bank has responded on three points i.e., (i) caste based discrimination, (ii) illegitimate internal proceeding while imposing Major Penalty order upon me and (iii) action by the Bank with regard to the case being reported as fraud as well as with regard to the other dealing officials.

    b. Against the point 'Caste based discrimination' Bank's authorities broadly concluded that there was no caste based discrimination and in support of the same they have provided the data of promoted SC/ST officer since the year 2011-12 to 2019-20.

c. But their reply dt.11-03-2020 does not contain the responses to the following points raised by me:

   i. SC/ST officers, if punished with Major Penalty in the Bank, then Bank strictly follows an unwritten but strict rule, (i.e.,) at any cost that SC/ST Officers will not be promoted in the internal promotion process ***irrespective of whether that penalty imposed up on them is illegitimate or not.*** As per my knowledge, for the past 10 years and above, none of the SC/ST officers in AGM cadre imposed with Major penalty were promoted to DGM cadre. Bank's response is silent to this point in its letter dt.11-03-2020.

   ii. Since my date of joining the Bank, I have never seen any officer of SC/ST categories imposed with Major penalty promoted from AGM to DGM cadre. The internal promotion selection committees deliberately give least marks to SC/ST officers' performance in interviews and automatically eliminate them from selection list. I am the true and best example in this regard. Bank's authorities have not disclosed the marks awarded to me in the interview by the selection committees since the year 2011. What are the minimum qualifying marks in interview vis a vis what were the marks allotted to me since the year 2011 to 2020 were not mentioned in their letters addressed to honourable DFS Authorities. Bank's response is silent to this point in its letter dt.11-03-2020.

   iii. At Bank's Head office level, the caste based discrimination started against me right from the date of initiating office notes that were put up to the Staff Accountability Committee against me.

   iv. To protect the internal fraudster Smt.V.K.N who had colluded with the borrower and mortgagors of SBEMPL loan case, I was chosen as scapegoat to impose penalty illegitimately by the then interested parties at Bank's Head Office as I belong to Scheduled Caste.

v. That is why, the cybercrime Email copy dt.22-6-2008 created by Smt.V.K.N was considered and accepted as one of the basis for fixing staff accountability upon me. Her computer system date was fraudulently changed by Smt.V.K.N in forward option while taking print of the actual email dated 23-01-2009. HRD officials must have provided wrong information to Staff Accountability Committee for fixing accountability against me by wrongly mentioning the work distribution order date as 22-6-2008, but actually works allocation was done on 23-01-2009. Please recall the context under which this email printed copy was provided to me by the Bank's Internal Inquiry Officer/presenting officer. In support of the same I am reproducing the statement signed by Bank's Presenting officer Shri.B.M.M where in it is evident that I have asked for the works distribution order if any issued in the year 2008, whereas Bank's Presenting officer Shri.B.M.M provided me the works distribution order dt.23-01-2009 duly highlighting the fake/manipulated date 22-06-2008 appearing on the top of the sheet reflecting the emails details. Bank's response is silent on this point in its reply letter dt.11-3-2020 submitted to MoF, DFS.

vi. The copies of Bank's HO Internal Office notes put up to Staff Accountability Committee for fixing accountability on me are not yet provided to me despite several reminders. On perusal of the same by me, the true picture of factual and false submissions incorporated there in would come to light. Bank's response is silent on this point in its reply letter dt.11-3-2020 submitted to MoF, DFS.

vii. Primarily the interested parties at Bank's HO must have intentionally projected me as the Credmin Officer for this SBEMPL fraud loan case in the office note put up to Staff Accountability. That is why in the SAC minutes dt.16-08-2012, Staff Accountability was fixed on me for not confirming margin money brought in and end use of funds at the time of disbursement. In fact, as per DE-11, Shri.N.R.C has already confirmed the margin money brought in and it is evident there in that the amount recommended by Smt.V.K.N for TL disbursement was Rs.195 lakh only, whereas Shri.N.R.C has corrected the amount and recommended for full TL disbursement of Rs.274 lakh in one go at a time. Mr.N.R.C has put his initial also for the above modification/ recommendation. DE-11 may please be perused to establish the same. Further, on 4-10-2013 during the regular hearing, the MW-2 has confirmed in writing that the hand writing and the initial appearing in DE-11 is of Shri.N.R.C. This is clearly evidencing that Shri.N.R.C has recommended for full and final disbursement of TL in one go on 31-3-2013 and he has confirmed the Margin money too brought in by the Borrower in DE-11 itself [as witnessed by MW-2 on 4-10-2013 RH]. Accordingly Smt.V.K.N has proposed and Shri.N.R.C has approved ME-7.. Despite proving all these facts during inquiry proceedings regular hearings and despite presenting the same in my overall presentation dt.30-11-2013 and despite Inquiry Officer Shri.P.K.K having agreed to the above facts and having declared that Smt.V.K.N as the Credmin officer for this loan case during the relevant period, the concerned authorities at Bank's HRD/HO have never felt the need to resubmit the facts to the Staff Accountability Committee and just gone ahead by imposing illegitimate major penalty order upon me.

viii. The false replies received by Bank's HRD from Smt.V.K.N must also had been another basis for projecting my name as Credmin officer for this SBEMPL Loan case. While inquiry proceedings were going on, vide. my letter dt.4-5-2013 addressed to the Inquiry Officer Shri.P.K.K, I have already sought for the copies of the replies submitted by Smt.V.K.N to Bank's HRD, but the same were not provided to me. ***This is also due to caste based discrimination and as they have already decided to protect Smt. V.K.N, they did not provide the copies of replies received from Smt. V.K.N.***

ix. In fact this act of not providing the documents sought for by me vide my letter dt. 4-5-2013 amounts to not keeping up to the promises/assurance given by Disciplinary Authority while conducting the disciplinary proceedings/inquiry proceedings in a transparent manner.

x. Further, vide Charge no: 'vi' framed against me in imputation of charges letter dt.27/28-2-2013 of the Bank, it is mentioned as follows:

"You as Credmin officer failed to obtain........" This is the best example to confirm that, the office note submitted to Staff Accountability Committee was mostly stuffed with false information by projecting me as the Credmin officer to this SBEMPL loan case during the year 2008. This is 100% due to caste based discrimination, as they want to protect Smt.V.K.N, they must have provided false information in the internal notes put up to SAC.

xi. However even after receiving the inquiry officer report dt.24-12-2013, where in it was proved that the dealing Credmin officer for this SBEMPL loan case was Smt.V.K.N, the interested parties at Bank's HO did not put up for revising the staff accountability. This is 100% due to the caste based discrimination against me and to save Smt.V.K.N.

xii. In its letter dt.11-03-2020 at page no:3, Bank authorities have mentioned that '*the charges levelled against me were concluded as partly proved in the report of findings by the Inquiry Authority*'. Basically this is a wrong statement. Actually the Inquiry Authority has concluded that four charges out of six charges are not proved.

Regarding the remaining two charges, as per ***the opinion*** expressed by inquiry officer 'I LSR did not appear to have exercised proper due diligence before signing TL disbursement note and its voucher both dated 31-3-2008' hence he has felt that and expressed ***his opinion*** in his report that remaining two charges are partly proved.

This ***opinion or feeling*** of the Inquiry officer is 100% wrong, irrational and irregular. Any inquiry officer shall draw his conclusions based on the factual documentary and other evidences. With regard to these two charges mentioned as partly proved against me, the documentary evidences are clearly reflecting that these two charges (charge number 2 & 3) are not proved against me at all. Please see the charges and factual evidences along with two charges reproduced below:

Charge-2: "You failed to ensure that payments were made to the suppliers/vendors directly from the Term Loan amount disbursed and instead disbursing the amount by crediting the funds disbursed to the current account of the company."

Charge-3:"You have failed to ensure that from the term loan amount disbursed, payments are made to the supplier/vendors, which were named by the company in its project report and also failed to seek documents/proof of creation/acquisition of fixed assets from the funds lent by the Bank."

In a nutshell, the allegations in these two charges (Charge-2 & 3) are about;

i. Crediting the Term Loan funds to Current account of the borrower;

ii. From the Term Loan account, ensuring payments directly to the suppliers and vendors which were named by the company in its project report; and

iii. Obtaining the documents in proof of creation/acquisition of fixed assets from the funds lent by the Bank.

I bring the following factual and documentary evidences to confirm that above three points in these two charges are also not proved against me:

a. As per the inquiry proceedings vide Regular Hearing held on 17-8-2013 between Presenting Officer (PO) and MW-2, vide Question NO:4 (page 5 of 14) the Management Witness-2 has confirmed that 'there were no specific directions available in the Sanction memorandum and sanction letter with regard to the suppliers from whom the machinery has to be purchased. Hence the disbursement of Term Loan was released to the current account of the borrower as per the prevalent practice in the Bank'.

b. Based on point 'a' above (confirmation given by MW-2), we can easily understand that the crediting of Term Loan disbursement funds to the current account of SBEMPL was a conscious decision taken by Smt.V.K.N and Shri.N.R.C, DGM as disclosed by Smt.V.K.N at 'a' above in the capacity of MW-2.

c. The core banking 'Finacle screen shot' is confirming that Shri.N.R.C had verified the entry in Finacle duly crediting the funds to the current account of SBEMPL account at about 6.47pm on 31-3-2008.

d. The hand writing on the voucher dt.31-3-2008 crediting the TL funds to the Current account is evidencing that it was prepared by Smt.V.K.N being the loan case dealing Credmin officer.

e. Ensuring the payments to suppliers/vendors from the Term Loan proceeds is the responsibility of Smt.V.K.N being the loan case dealing Credmin officer during the relevant period (as confirmed by the Inquiry officer in his report dt.24-12-2013).

f. As on those days of TL disbursement (31-3-2008), I was not aware of the systems and procedures followed in the Bank. I joined SME at Hyderabad on 25-2-2008. Hence my experience at SME, Hyderabad as on 31-3-2008 (date of TL Disbursement) was very short and I was not even having a table and chair to sit and discharge my office duties.

g. In fact by the time I joined the Bank, my previous banks where I had worked earlier were not running on core banking software platform at all. Hence up to June-2008 my knowledge in dealing with the computers was very poor and my Finacle software operating knowledge was NIL.

h. Bank has provided me core banking Finacle operating user ID on 05-05-2008 as confirmed vide its email dt.13-6-2013 (i.e., document no: B-4 provided to me by the inquiry officer on my written request) by Zintech.

i. Fully knowing that I was neither having core Banking Finacle software operating user ID nor its knowledge, both Smt.V.K.N and Shri.N.R.C have deceitfully obtained my signature in TL disbursement note by giving false assurance to me that they will adhere to all the systems and procedures of the Bank and they had already disbursed Cash Credit Limits on 8-3-2008 itself.

j. The purpose for deceitfully obtaining my signature in TL disbursement note and its voucher dt.31-3-208 by Smt.V.K.N and Shri.N.R.C was only to get diluted the negative impact on them in case if this fraud coming to light

k. Smt.V.K.N and Shri.N.R.C were having more than 20 years of experience in the Bank as on those days of TL disbursement, hence Smt.V.K.N being the loan case Credmin Officer along with Shri.N.R.C should have taken care to lien mark the current account to the extent of Term Loan disbursement portion and should have released payments directly to the vendors and suppliers from the current account of SBEMPL to confirm end use of funds and should have obtained the documents in proof of creation/acquisition of fixed assets from the funds lent by the Bank.

l. AS per the regular hearing dt.17-8-2013 between Presenting Officer (PO) and MW-2, vide Question NO:4 (page 5 of 14) the Management Witness-2 has confirmed that 'there were no specific directions available in the Sanction memorandum and sanction letter with regard to the suppliers from whom the machinery has to be purchased. In such case, Smt.V.K.N and Shri.N.R.C should have obtained the list of supplier and vendors in writing from the Borrower along with the quotations/estimations of the respective suppliers/vendors and after exercising due diligence w.r.t. to the genunity of the same, they should have ensured end use of funds by making payments directly to the vendors/suppliers from current account and should have obtained the documents in proof of creation/ acquisition of fixed assets from the funds lent by the Bank.

m. Despite all the above factual points with documentary evidences, Shri.P.K.K expressing his opinion as if this charge is 'partly proved' against me is 100% irrational and irregular. Ensuring end use of funds, obtaining documents in proof of creation/ acquisition of fixed assets from the funds lent by the Bank was the responsibility of Smt.V.K.N being the Loan case dealing Credmin Officer as per the circular guidelines of the Bank.

n. Any inquiry officer shall draw his conclusions and findings based on the documentary and other evidences, but Shri.P.K.K, being the internal Inquiry officer unfortunately ignored the documentary and other evidences and also his own findings in his report as to who was the Credmin officer and mentioned that the charge no: ii & iii are partly proved against me as *I did not appear to have exercised proper due diligence before signing TL disbursement note and its voucher on 31-3-2008.*

o. In continuation to the above noted point number 'n', it is also important to highlight here another point mentioned by the Bank officials in its letter dt.11-3-2020 at page 3 in italics i.e., *'although Shri.LSR had submitted that he had joined the Bank newly at the time of incidence, it cannot be ignored that he was directly recruited as AGM and was also carrying experience of over 10 years of working with Banks before joining this Bank and also worked as Chief Manager of a Branch. Thus he had sufficient experience in banking to take/arrive at the decisions and hence his contention that he had merely signed the documents at the behest of his supervisor was not considered'.*

p. Both, i.e. (i) the opinion of the Inquiry officer expressed at point number 'n' above and (ii) the justification of Bank's

Officials mentioned in its letter dt.11-3-2020, reproduced at point number 'o' above are incorrect. Please find the justifications noted below:

- My previous experience in other banks before joining this Bank has definitely benefitted this Bank in the form of my qualitative lectures at Bank's apex staff College as Faculty and contributed in imparting qualitative knowledge about maintaining Healthy Credit Portfolio.
- Because of my previous experience I could do proper monitoring of loan cases handled by me thus ensured healthy credit portfolio
- By discharging my duties diligently, I have avoided slippage of many accounts into NPAs in this Bank.
- Due to my diligent nature of discharging duties certain fraud loans tried to enter this Bank were stopped by me (example: PS Hotel proposal for Rs.40.00 Crore)
- Even from the Bad and Loss Assets where in 100% provision is created, I have been able to recover substantial amounts in the capacity of Recovery Officer in this Bank
- I can proudly say that I have been always protecting Bank's interest as a sincere and loyal officer.
- In fact, because of my previous experience, I could able to detect the fraud angle in this present SBEMPL Loan case and reported to HO. Entire credit comes to me in bringing this fraud to light.
- Unlike Shri.N.R.C who is involved in many Fraud Loan cases of Agri Business Group including this SBEMPL, my immediate bosses in my previous Banks were neither fraudulent nor corrupt.
- Unlike Smt.V.K.N, my senior colleagues in my previous Banks were not lacking integrity and were never colluded with the fraudsters.

- ***Instead of concentrating in justifying the illegitimate penalty order imposed on me, the concerned authorities in this Bank should have focused on catch holding and punishing the internal fraudsters who have colluded with the external fraudsters in SBEMPL Loan case.***
- The only reason for this SBEMPL Loan account becoming NPA is the fraud in Collateral Security. Borrower has come to the Bank with the intention to cheat the Bank and evade the loan repayment. Instead of accepting this truth, trying to focus on monitoring angle is 100% illogical and irregular.
- The concerned authorities in the Bank made mistakes by:
    i. Leaving the internal and external fraudsters scot-free
    ii. Ignoring the collateral security fraud aspect
    iii. Not filing the criminal compliant with CBI
    iv. Not initiating action against those who have intentionally avoided filing compliant with CBI
    v. Not accepting the audio record evidences offered by me
    vi. Accepting fraudulently purported/manipulated documents provided by Smt.V.K.N as the basis for fixing accountability upon me irregularly
    vii. Acting blind at all the documentary evidences that are confirming Smt.V.K.N having fully extended her cooperation to the fraudsters by:
        A. disbursing WC Cash Credit in contradiction to her own observation during the pre-disbursement visit conducted by her to borrowers work site,
        B. Fixing drawing power based on fake debtors
        C. Misguiding PDVC Officer
        D. Suppressing the facts in WC and TL disbursement notes

E. Encouraging diversion and siphoning of both WC & TL loan funds and

F. Irregularly recommending for re-fixation of repayment schedule of TL

viii. Ignoring Money Laundering angle (remittance of Rs.50 lakh by cash by Shri.N.R.C at Rajahmundry branch in to this SBEMPL Loan out of some other Agri fraud Loan disbursement proceeds) and

ix. Focusing more attention on imposing illegitimate penalty upon me rather than genuinely finding the facts.

Important reasons to suspect the involvement of Smt.V.K.N and Shri.N.R.C in this fraud:

a. Smt.V.K.N and Shri.N.R.C have not conducted mortgage documents execution in the the Bank branch premises

b. Smt.V.K.N and Shri.N.R.C have approved Working capital Cash Credit disbursement on dt.08-03-2008 (as per ME-5) irregularly by not bringing the negative observations of pre-disbursement visit report (ME-3) dt.26-02-2008 into WC Cash Credit disbursement note (ME-5).

c. Smt.V.K.N and Shri.N.R.C fixed WC Cash Credit drawing power irregularly despite knowing that the debtors mentioned in CA certificate dt.29-2-2008 (ME-4) are fake and cooked debtors.

d. Smt.V.K.N and Shri.N.R.C audio recording evidences wherein they have confirmed that the credit facilities to this SBEMPL fraud borrower were disbursed by them due to pressure from Shri. VSV, the then DGM now CGM.

e. Smt.V.K.N not complying with the Bank's Guidelines issued vide Ref. No. H.O.SME /2007-08/597 Dt.February 11, 2008 Circular No. 211/ SME - 60/ 2007-08

f. Smt.V.K.N and Shri.N.R.C not moving Draft note of TL disbursement [DE-11] through me but, deceitfully obtaining my signature in TL disbursement note (ME-7) hurriedly in the late evening on 31-03-2008.

g. Smt.V.K.N and Shri.N.R.C suppressing the WC diversion and siphoning aspect in TL disbursement note (ME-7)

h. Smt.V.K.N and Shri.N.R.C have recommended DE-2 [office note for re-fixation of TL repayment schedule] to the Vertical Head/ED, SME duly suppressing the diversion/siphoning aspect of WC & TL funds in the same (DE-2).

i. Smt.V.K.N and Shri.N.R.C misguiding the PDVC Certifying Officer by providing irrelevant documents for verification and by hiding the actual documents that would bring the collateral fraud angle to light and

j. Last but not the least i.e., Smt.V.K.N's Email cybercrime with manipulated date.22-6-2008 which misguided Bank's HRD and Staff Accountability committee to exclude her from the accountability. It is impossible to forward a future date email with past date unless that person resorts to cybercrime with mala-fide intentions.

In addition to the above, please find the below mentioned comparative statements given by Smt.V.K.N in the telephone discussions had with me vis a vis the written statements in the Regular Hearings during the Inquiry Process:

Few Contradictory Statements of Smt.V.K.N	
During the Telephonic discussion in the year 2013 (Audio recording available)	**Written statement during the Inquiry Process Regular Hearings (RH) dt.17-08-2013**
Shri.N.R.C asked me to change the visit report positively before disbursement of WC, it was good that I did not agree to his request.	RH October 4, 2013: CSO Q No: 32: Before disbursement of working capital, whether N.R.C has asked MW-2 to change the visit report ME-3 positively? MW-2: I don't remember any such thing.

Shri.G.G AGM had alerted me about SBEMPL stating that it was a problematic case	CSO Q no.43: Whether Shri.G.G AGM had alerted MW-2 about SBEMPL stating that it was a problematic case MW-2: I don't remember any such thing
Shri.N.R.C and Shri. VSV both are DGMs, can't he say to Shri. VSV asking not to put pressure upon him for disbursing loans to SBEMPL. Myself and NRC have discussed several times that Shri. VSV is putting unnecessary pressure upon us to do this irregular disbursement.	CSO Q No.45: While preparing WC disbursement note ME-5, whether MW-2 and Shri.N.R.C discussed that, though it was a problematic loan case, they were unnecessarily pressurized to disburse it. MW-2: I don't remember any such thing

On perusal/examination of the above points and evidences, it can be easily understood that the then interested parties at Bank's Head Office wanted to protect the internal fraudster Smt.V.K.N. In the process of protecting her, I was chosen as scapegoat to impose penalty as I belong to Scheduled Caste and to show to Vigilance department that somebody is punished.

Based on the above, it is proved that the charges framed against me were irrelevant and illegitimate. They were supposed to have been framed against Smt.V.K.N being the then Credmin Officer for this fraud loan case. The punishment imposed on me by AA Shri.S.K.V in the form of Major Penalty order was illegitimate and it was part of conspiracy to suppress me and to stop my professional career growth as I have detected and reported this fraud. The actions of the Bank's authorities suppressing my professional career growth by supporting this conspiracy are unconstitutional and against to the principles of natural justice.

In view of the above, as it is a clear case of suppression and discrimination against me to safeguard the internal fraudsters and as the Bank's authorities have caused unexplainable mental agony and irreparable professional career loss to me, I request

you sir to advise/instruct by issuing orders to the Bank to avoid further delay and respond positively by taking immediate steps to avoid further loss to my career. The solutions to patch up the loss happened to me are: Withdrawing the illegitimate penalty order imposed upon me in the year 2015and Passing necessary orders for my thribble Promotion. Over and above all, Bank should take immediate steps to file FIR with CBI to catch hold the fraudsters in SBEMPL fraud loan case to protect Bank's interest and to punish the internal and external fraudsters and advise CBI (Central Bureau of Investigation) to accept the Compliant to be filed by the Bank in SBEMPL Loan case.

Chapter-7

The Writ Petition-Counter and Rejoinder

Since bank does not want to respond proactively to punish the fraudsters and continued its nature of eliminating LSR from every promotion selection list, at last CSO LSR approached the honorable High Court by filing writ petition during August in the year 2021 by mentioning all the facts. In response to the same, after one year Bank has filed its counter where in it has simply denied all the statements submitted by LSR without any supporting evidences. In view of Bank's counter, LSR through his advocate filed the rejoinder during October 2022, the brief content of the same is reproduced below:

REJOINDER FILED BY THE PETITIONER IN REPLY TO THE COUNTER FILED BY THE RESPONDENT BANK

The petitioner herein humbly submits this rejoinder to the counter affidavit filed by respondent Bank. That respondent Bank filed the counter affidavit full of blatant lies and false allegations against the petitioner. The petitioner herein denies all the averments of the counter filed by respondent bank except the facts specifically admitted herein in this rejoinder.

It is submitted that on the maintainability of the Writ Petition, the respondent Bank has mentioned that it is not maintainable at this high court as the respondent bank is not a government functionary and quoted 4 judgements of high courts which are not applicable to the facts of the present case.

Article 226 confers wide powers on the High Courts to issue writs in the nature of prerogative writs. Under Article 226, writs can be issued to "any person or authority". The term "authority" used in the context must receive a liberal meaning, unlike the term in Article12, which is relevant only for the purpose of enforcement of fundamental rights under Article 32.

Article 226 confers powers on the High Courts to issue writs for enforcement of fundamental rights as well as non-fundamental rights. The form of the body concerned is not very much relevant; rather, relevant is the nature of the duty imposed on the body. The duty is to judge the issue in light of the positive obligation owned by the person or authority to the affected party, no matter by what means the duty is imposed. If a positive obligation exists, the mandamus cannot be denied. "Considering its shareholding pattern, this Bank may be considered as a government-owned bank. In view of the assurance to the Parliament given on 8th December 2004 by the finance minister during the discussion on the Repeal Bill, 2003 that the Government holding in this Bank would always be above 51%, Bank is categorized under a new sub-group "Other Public Sector Banks". Therefore, the claim of the respondent that the writ petition is not maintainable is untenable and rejected summarily.

1. I submit that, if the Bank is privatised, modification to employees' service conditions is to be issued. But none of the employee's service conditions, including the petitioner's, have been modified as of date. Hence it cannot be treated as a private bank.

2. I submit that all that illegitimate acts of the Bank were committed on the petitioner prior to the declaration as a private bank. Hence the WP is maintainable

3. I submit that the SC ST reservation policy is still implemented in all recruitments conducted by the Bank post declaration of private bank

4(a). Like any public sector banks, the Annual Statement of Assets and Liabilities has been still as on the year 2022-23 obtained from all the employees of this Bank. Whereas there is no such practice in Private Banks.

4(b). The petitioner has been deputed for government election duty several times as Micro Observer/Presiding officer including in the year 2019. Private Bank employees will not be deputed for election duty. Hence this Bank shall not be treated as Private Bank.

4(c). The illegitimate penalty order was issued to the petitioner on the bank's letter head where in it is printed on the bank's letter head that it is a fully owned Government of India Bank.

5. In view of the above, the privatization declared in the year 2019 is actually not privatization at all, it is only for the purpose of submitting some returns by the Bank to RBI, it is treated on par with private banks

6. In reply to the averments of the counter affidavit of the respondent bank regarding the delay in filing the Writ Petition, it is submitted that the petitioner is pursuing the case with the Ministry of Finance Govt of India and the President of India. The petitioner not delayed the matter as alleged in the counter affidavit. Before both the authorities, the respondent bank submitted the same lies and did not conclude the case according to the orders of the ministry of finance dated 15/11/2019. The petitioner was forced to approach this Hon'ble court. Therefore, there is no delay in filing this writ petition.

7. In reply to Para C and D of the counter affidavit page No. 8, it is submitted that the contractual rights, even though they are not fundamental rights, can be enforced under Writ Jurisdiction according to the supreme court judgement in the case of M/s Zee Tele Films Ltd. and another v. Union of India and others: AIR 2005 SC 2677=2005 (4) SCC649. A Constitution Bench of the Hon'ble Supreme Court referring to the development of law by judicial interpretation culminated in the judgment of the 7 - Judge Bench in the case of Pradeep Kumar Biswas: 2002 (5) SCC 111, which did take note of the fact that earlier opinion in the case of Andi Mukta Sadguru Shree Muktajee Pandas Swami Suvarna Jayanti Mahotsav Smarak Trust and Ors. v. V.R. Rudani and Ors., 1989 (2) SCC 691, and observed that Article 226 confers wide powers on the High Courts to issue writs in the nature of prerogative writs

8. It is submitted that as per the visit report dt.26-02-2008 of Smt.V.K.N, the dealing Credmin officer of the subject SBEMPL loan case, said there were no operations at the work site of SBEMPL. Whereas, in contradiction to her own negative observations, Smt.V.K.N and Sri. N.R. C, the then dealing Manager and DGM,

irregularly disbursed loans to SBEMPL on 08-03-2008. Thus both Smt.V.K.N. and Sri.N.R.C (Bank dealing officers) have already colluded with the fraudsters and irregularly disbursed loans to SBEMPL despite there being no activity at the work site and despite there being no drawing power as per the stock statement submitted by SBEMPL. Thus both Smt.V.K.N and Sri.N.R.C have bye-passed Bank's internal guidelines. It is evident from documents No: P2 & P4 that the petitioner, Sri.LSR was not part of the irregular disbursement of the loan to SBEMPL on 08-03-2008.

9. It is submitted that, Prior to disbursing the Working Capital loan on 08-03-2008, Smt.V.K.N and Sri.N.R.C have irregularly allowed for a mortgage of the fake non-existing collateral property as security to this SBEMPL loan/s thus extended their cooperation to the fraudster borrower and mortgagors by not conducting pre-sanction/pre-disbursement visit to the collateral security and by not complying to the conditions stipulated in the Title investigation reports of this fake property which is the only reason for this account becoming NPA.

10. In response to the counter filed by the respondent bank vide Para No: ii, iii and iv on pages 11 and 12, it is submitted as follows:

Staff Accountability Committee (SAC) of the Respondent Bank was completely misguided by the then interested parties at Bank's Head Office so as to protect the internal fraudsters, which resulted in wrongly fixing staff accountability upon the petitioner as it was wrongly projected in its internal office notes submitted to SAC that the petitioner was the Credmin officer for this SBEMPL loan case during the year 2008.

Based on the fraudulently purported fabricated cyber-crime email dt.22-06-2008 (B-9), this misguiding information was captured in the office notes submitted to Bank's SAC by falsely projecting the petitioner as the dealing Credmin Officer of the subject loan case.

Bank, vide its response to the petitioner (during the inquiry proceeding) provided a copy of the P-10 (B-9) document to the petitioner; based on the same, it is evident that the respondent bank has falsely projected the petitioner as the dealing Credmin officer to SAC assuming the fabricated/false date 22-06-2008 as the date of work allotment order. They have underlined the above date and provided the P-10 document to the petitioner. In fact, the original work allotment order was issued vide email dt.23-01-2009. Even Bank's interested parties at its HO, without properly examining the B-9 (P-10) document, just underlined the fake date 22-06-2008 with pencil and provided this B-9 document to the petitioner during the internal inquiry proceedings as a response to certain documents sought for by the petitioner in writing. The interested parties in Bank's Head office were so eager to fix accountability upon the petitioner; as a result, they falsely recorded the petitioner's date of joining Bank's SME center at Hyderabad while submitting office notes to SAC; thus they created false record to make it believe that the petitioner is a longstanding officer in Bank's SME center Hyderabad. Subsequently, during the inquiry proceedings, all these records were proved as false information by the petitioner.

Further, in DE-6 SAC Minutes (P-12), it is mentioned that ME-3 (Visit report dt.26-02-2008) is satisfactory. In fact, in ME-3, it is mentioned that the activity at the borrower's unit was stopped many months back. Hence any mention in the note put up to SAC about ME-3 stating that ME-3 is satisfactory is nothing but again misguiding the Staff Accountability Committee. Due to the vested interests of a few officials at Bank's HO, SAC was misguided with such false information so as to protect the internal fraudsters and make the petitioner the scapegoat.

The margin brought in by the borrower was already confirmed by Sri.N.R.C in DE-11 (Draft TL disbursement note), which was brought by Smt.V.K.N into ME-7 (TL Disbursement note). The DE-11 was never routed through the petitioner, and it was confirmed and proved during the internal inquiry proceedings. Based on DE-11 finalized by DGM Sri.N.R.C, it was Smt.V.K.N who has proposed ME-7 and Sri.N.R.C approved the same. Still, in DE-6 [SAC minutes], accountability was irregularly fixed upon the petitioner for not ensuring borrower margin to be brought in. It is a grave irregularity on the part of Bank's HRD officials who have put up internal office notes to the Bank's Staff Accountability Committee, as the margin brought in was already confirmed by Sri.N.R.C himself in DE-11, which was prior to ME-7. All this false information submitted to Bank's SAC was only to make the petitioner a scapegoat as he belongs to SC Category and to protect the internal fraudsters. The accountability, in fact, needs to be fixed up on Smt.V.K.N as she had colluded with internal and external fraudsters and caused huge financial loss to the Bank.

In view of the above false information submitted to SAC, accountability was irregularly fixed upon the petitioner. Thus, the decision taken by Bank's SAC against the petitioner is another gross irregularity.

The internal inquiry proceeding happened in a transparent way except for the following flaws observed and noted hereunder:

a. The audio recording evidence offered by the petitioner (to prove his innocence and to identify the real internal fraudsters) was never accepted by the Inquiring authority for examination

b. Based on P-10 (fabricated cybercrime email of Smt.V.K.N), despite realizing that the petitioner was not the dealing Credmin officer for the subject loan case during the year 2008, the inquiring authority did not recommend for the re-examination of Staff Accountability so as to fix the staff accountability up on Smt.V.K.N.

c. During the inquiry proceedings, the evidence given by Shri. EKL, GM (the then AGM and SC category officer) was also not given weight-age where in Shri.EKL had very specifically confirmed that prior to obtaining the signature of the petitioner in TL disbursement note, Smt.V.K.N approached Shri.EKL for his signature too in the same. He has further confirmed that even if the petitioner would not have signed the TL disbursement note, the Term Loan would have been disbursed on 31-03-2008 by both Smt.V K N and Sri.NRC as how they have already disbursed Working capital loan to the same borrower on 08-03-2008 considering the same fraudulent immovable property as security.

d. The Respondent Bank did not follow the Principles of Natural Justice at all during the Disciplinary Proceedings. The interested parties at Bank's Head Office were more interested and rather eager to fix accountability somehow on some scapegoat. Accordingly, they have identified the petitioner as a scapegoat since he belongs to Scheduled Category and is a newly joined officer in the bank; they thought that he would keep quite due to the fear of higher authorities and illegitimate disciplinary action.

e. The comment of the Inquiry Authority in the concluding part of his report (P-15) that the charge numbers i, iv, v and vi are not proved against the petitioner is correct, but at the same time, due to the pressure from Bank's HRD, the Inquiring Authority has, in contradiction to his own findings during the inquiry process, made a false concluding comment that charge number ii and iii are partly proved against the petitioner. The entire episode of disciplinary action against the petitioner has been based on the false presumption that the petitioner was the dealing Credmin officer for the subject loan case during the year 2008, wherein the fraud took place. Whereas during the inquiry proceedings, the Inquiring authority himself has found that the petitioner was not the dealing Credmin officer during the relevant period and Smt.V.K.N was the dealing Credmin officer for the subject loan case during the relevant period in the year 2008. The Inquiring Authority has very specifically mentioned this fact in his report dt.24-12-2013 (P-15). However, in contradiction to his own findings, he had not recommended for the re-examination of staff accountability against Smt.V.K.N and due to the pressure from the interested parties in the Bank, he has falsely concluded that charge number ii and iii are partly proved. The reason stated by him for such a conclusion is that the petitioner, Sri.LSR, should have exercised proper due diligence before signing the TL disbursement note and its voucher both dt.31-3-2008.

f. Any inquiry report shall be based on documentary evidence and objective facts. Hence the conclusion of the two charges mentioned as partly proved is only the feeling of the Inquiry Authority. All that documentary evidence and objective facts contradict his feeling about the two charges as partly proved. Hence it is illogical and irrational to conclude that the two charges are partly proved against the petitioner. Please find the justifications for the same noted below:

- Bank has not provided Finacle (core banking) user ID and password to the petitioner from the date of his joining to till 05-05-2008, and he was not imparted with finacle training during the year 2008. Hence the petitioner cannot check the funds of the Working Capital Cash Credit loan already diverted/siphoned before 31-3-2008. Hence in the opinion of Inquiring authority, what kind of due diligence can the petitioner exercise in this context before signing TL disbursement note?
- The immediate supervisors of the petitioner in his previous Banks were honest and were having integrity. Being a newly joined officer in Bank's SME Center at Hyderabad with hardly one month of experience, how can the petitioner doubt that all three of them (i.e., his supervisor Sri.N.R.C, the previous Head, SME, Hyderabad Sri. VSV and his colleague Smt.V.K.N) have colluded with the fraudulent borrower? What kind of due diligence he can exercise in such circumstances as a newly joined officer?
- When there are no adverse comments in the TL disbursement note and when all the senior officers have assured the petitioner that they will ensure end use by issuing DDs and Pay Orders to the suppliers, as a newly joined officer, whether the petitioner can think and suspect on 31-3-2008 that those officers were telling lies and giving false assurances/false promises?
- Is there any possibility to exercise any due diligence by a newly joined officer when the assurances were already given by his superior officers and senior colleague regarding end utilization?
- As told by them, the WC CC loan was already disbursed many days back (on 08-03-2008) itself, hence being a newly joined officer, should the petitioner doubt that they have disbursed the WC loan by resorting to so many irregularities and by colluding with the external fraudsters?

- Whether the petitioner is a yogi to see the past irregular things that happened during his physical absence. Hence the conclusion of the inquiry officer about the two charges as partly proved is absolutely senseless.
- In fact, by the time the petitioner has got his Finacle user ID and password, even the TL funds were also diverted /siphoned.
- When files are not in the petitioner's custody (they were in lock and key custody of Smt. VKN in the year 2008), when the loan case was not allotted to the petitioner, when Finacle ID was not provided to him and when the petitioner's boss and ex-SME head, as well as one senior officer, are giving so many oral assurances about adhering to procedural guidelines by them, what kind of due diligence the petitioner was expected to exercise, not being the dealing office for this loan case?
- Where is the necessity for the petitioner to exercise any due diligence when funds are parked only in the current account but not outgoing from Bank?
- The Internal Inquiry officer of Bank Shri.PKK, instead of simply saying a vague statement that LSR should have exercised proper due diligence, should have clearly mentioned the points in detail in his report that attract exercising proper due diligence by the petitioner. Without mentioning any such point about due diligence to be exercised, simply concluding two charges as partly proved against the petitioner is illogical, illegitimate and irrational.
- When the IA was confirming in his report that Smt.V.K.N was the loan case dealing Credmin officer during the relevant period, i.e., the year 2008, he cannot give a false conclusion as the two charges are partly proved against the petitioner, which is in contradiction to his own findings of inquiry proceedings.
- The inquiry officer is fully aware that the two charges mentioned as partly proved are pertaining to the duties and responsibilities of loan case dealing Credmin officer, Hence

one side he found and declared in his report that Smt.V.K.N as the Credmin officer for this loan case and on the other side illogically he is saying that the petitioner should have exercised proper due diligence. This conclusion gives scope to doubt whether he was also influenced by the interested parties/ internal fraudsters to draw such an illogical conclusion.

- In fact, as an honest inquiry officer Shri.P.K.K should have ideally recommended for re-fixation of staff accountability upon Smt.V.K.N and should have concluded his report by mentioning that all the charges framed against the petitioner are NOT PROVED, but he did not do so.
- By looking at this entire episode of punishing the petitioner with a major penalty, it can be understood that the then disciplinary authority and appellate authority, in this case, have either not read the inquiry report of Sri.P.K.K or must have colluded with the internal fraudsters. Otherwise, they would not have taken such an illegitimate and illogical decision to order for imposing a major penalty upon the petitioner.
- The most pathetic point in this entire fraud story is a lady fraudster who has internally committed a financial crime and ultimately was appointed/made as a Management Witness for the false allegations made upon a scapegoat (the petitioner), in the fraud committed by herself. It is very important here to realize how Smt.VKN was appointed as Management Witness by the Bank in the internal inquiry proceedings initiated against the petitioner. Appointing Smt.VKN as Management witness is nothing but a thief giving witness against an innocent person in the crime/theft committed by the thief herself.
- All those officers, i.e., the Disciplinary Authority and the Appellate Authority who are supposed to find the facts and punish to internal fraudsters became supporters of internal fraudsters even after the truth and facts came to light.
- In view of the petitioner's signature appearing in ME-7 (as it was affixed in good faith and based on the assurance given

by his senior officers) and as it happened within one month of his joining the Bank SME Center, after completing the inquiry proceeding, ideally, Bank should have dropped all the charges framed against him rather than imposing a major penalty illegitimately. Thus, the Respondent Bank did not follow the Principle of Natural Justice during the Disciplinary Proceedings.

In response to counter in para no (v) page 13 of the respondent Bank, it is to submit that, in view of the illegitimate Major penalty imposed, the petitioner appealed against the said penalty order. Still, unfortunately, the Appellate Authority in the Bank ***(the then ED who was subsequently arrested by CBI in another case)*** also colluded and wanted to protect the internal fraudsters. Hence, he has confirmed the penalty imposed upon the petitioner by grossly neglecting to look at the factual information and it's supporting documentary evidence.

As a result, due to this illegitimate penalty order, the petitioner initiated many proactive steps in the form of various petitions and emails sent to various statutory and other competent authorities, including the Honorable President of India. However Bank's HRD started telling lies to the Ministry of Finance and to the honorable President of India by way of submitting its written reply letters containing mostly incorrect, irrelevant and misguiding information, which is very much unwanted. The representations of the petitioner, letters sent by the Ministry of Finance and honorable President's Secretariat and the incorrect, irrelevant and misguiding replies submitted by bank will be submitted to the honorable court if called for.

It is to submit that the respondent bank vide its para-wise replies vide item number (iii) in pages 13 and 14 of its counter submitted false statements to misguide this honorable court. It is not true, and Bank did not initiate appropriate criminal proceedings against the borrower and the mortgagors. In fact, this fraud was committed by the borrower and mortgagors in collusion with the then internal Bank Officers. As per RBI Circular dt. 01-07-2010 all that fraud cases wherein the amount involved is rupees one crore, and above, the criminal complaint shall be filed with CBI in such cases. Further, if staff involvement is there in such cases, the same shall be filed with CBI (Anti-Corruption Bureau). In this instant case, as has been found out by the petitioner, there is a deliberate bypass of the bank's guidelines by certain internal officers as they have colluded with the fraudulent borrower and mortgager. Secondly, some interested officers in the Bank who are directly and indirectly involved in this fraud have deliberately bypassed RBI guidelines and did not file compliant with CBI despite the approval was already obtained for the same by the petitioner on 13-11-2010 itself. It is only to protect the internal fraudsters, Bank did not take any steps against those who have bypassed RBI guidelines in the year 2010 and 2011, and to protect one of such internal fraudsters Smt.V.K.N, bank, instead of framing charges against her, made her Management Witness in the illegitimate inquiry proceedings initiated against the petitioner.

The colluding of internal fraudsters can be confirmed upon examination of the documentary evidence viz ME-3 [pre-disbursement visit report], ME-5 [WC disbursement note], DP fixation [excel sheet] in Cash Credit, Note for identifying officer to conduct PDVC, DE-2 [Re-fixation of repayment schedule in TL], ME-2 [Loan Sanction Letter], a Draft note of TL disbursement [DE-11] and DE-10 [Transaction sheet for conducting Loan Documentation] and all that representations made by the petitioner to the MD & CEO of the Bank, to the CVO of the Bank and other statutory authorities of Government of India including Honorable President of India where in the petitioner has been repeatedly reminding about the non-filing of complaint with CBI and demanding for the same for the past several years. Further, it is not due to oversight but deliberate bypass of RBI guidelines by the officer/s in the years 2010 and 2011 in SME Center, Hyderabad, as they were involved and interested parties in this fraud loan case.

Further, it is objected to Banks counter wherein it is argued that this WP is not maintainable. While objecting to such escapist counter filed by the Bank to see somehow this petition is to be dismissed, it is really important and relevant here to bring to the notice of the honorable court that the ***bank is still monitored by the Chief Vigilance Commissioner of India through its representative, i.e., CVO of the bank. The current CVO in the bank was appointed as per the notification issued by***

the Ministry of Finance in the year 2022. There is no such practice of appointing CVOs in private sector Banks. Over and above all, the combined share capital of the government of India and ZIC (being the government of India undertaking) together forms 94.72% of the entire share capital of the Bank. It is evident to the public that the government of India has off-loaded its share to ZIC recently during the year 2019, which is post imposition of illegitimate penalty order upon the petitioner.

Again, it is very sad to see the Bank's false denial regarding the Petitioner's confirmation about detecting and reporting of this fraud by him to Respondent Bank's Head Office on 13.11.2010. The bank should not falsely deny this because, as per Document No: P-11 already submitted to this honorable court, it is very much evident that the petitioner was instrumental in detecting and reporting this fraud. Further, all that the then officers present in SME Center, Hyderabad can also be inquired about if required to realize this truth.

The respondent bank is again trying to mislead this honorable court with the following statement reproduced below from its counter " It is noticeable that the account was marked as NPA on 13.12.2009 and was reported to ACB on 30.04.2010, i.e. much before the reporting done by the Petitioner, if any, as alleged by the Petitioner".

It is to submit that the account becomes NPA if the dues are not repaid for more than 90 days, and every NPA will be reported to the ACB (Audit Committee Board) of the Bank. Whereas reporting any loan account as fraud happens only if the fraud elements are observed, investigated and confirmed. In this instant loan case, the incident of fraud came to light during the visit undertaken by the petitioner to the collateral security as the preliminary step/preliminary due diligence before going ahead with actions as per SARFAESI Act. In this context, the petitioner observed that the physical structure as per the documents is not there and the boundaries of the immovable properties are not matching with what is reflected in the title deeds. Hence, he has detected and reported this fraud, but the respondent bank is trying to mislead this honorable court.

In response to counter in para no (iv) pages 14, 15 and 16 of the respondent Bank, it is to submit that the respondent bank is again trying to misguide the honorable court as if it is due to the petitioners negligence, Bank was exposed to hug financial loss. It is strongly objected.

The details about how the internal Bank's fraudsters have extended cooperation to the external fraudsters, the modus operandi followed by them, and how they have further tried to postpone the inquiry proceedings by remitting Rs.50.00 lakh into this loan account by committing frauds in some other loan accounts and how these internal fraudsters have bypassed even RBI guideline by not filing compliant with CBI ACB are explained in detail in this document.

The respondent bank trying to defend its illegitimate actions by showing the petitioner's work experience prior to joining this Bank as the basis for imposing a penalty upon him. In fact, it is a false justification made by the respondent Bank. The Disciplinary Authority and the Appellate Authority of the Bank did not take a holistic view but acted in a biased and suppressive manner to protect the internal fraudsters.

The respondent Bank needs to answer the following questions:

1. What is the reason for these loan accounts becoming NPA? Is it because of fraud in Collateral security or not?
2. Whether Smt. V.K.N or Sri. N.R.C has/have ever visited the collateral security prior to Sanction and disbursement of loan to this borrower?
3. Is it not bypassing Bank's guidelines by Smt. V.K.N and Sri.N.R.C to conduct loan security Documentation without obtaining approvals for the deviations viz not obtaining property tax receipt, and not visiting collateral security?
4. How the working capital loan was disbursed to the fraudulent borrower on 08-03-2008 by Smt.V.K.N and Sri.N.R.C despite the presence of fake high-value debtors in the stock statement?
5. Whether the PDVC certifying officer Smt.RE was misguided by providing irrelevant documents by Smt.V.K.N and Sri.N.R.C for vetting by her.

6. Why Smt.V.K.N has not brought the adverse observations of unit visit report dt.26-02-2008 into the working capital disbursement note dt.08-03-2008?

7. Whether the fraudsters (both internal and external) have already successfully cheated the Bank on 05-03-2008, 08-03-2008 and 17-03-2008, which are/is prior to obtaining the petitioner's signature in ME-7 on 31-03-2008?

8. How and under whose influence Smt.V.K.N was appointed as a Management witness in the disciplinary proceedings initiated against the petitioner, instead of making her the accused?

9. By hiding all the above and by illegitimately punishing the petitioner without examining and without considering the context under which the petitioner's signature was obtained in the ME-7, is it right on the part of the respondent Bank to impose a penalty upon the petitioner by making Smt.V.K.N as Management Witness?

10. ***Whether ignoring all the above irregularities by the respondent Bank is called a holistic approach as falsely claimed by it in its counter?***

In view of the above, all the actions done by the respondent bank against the petitioner are illegitimate and the false reasons given in the counter filed by the Bank are baseless, escapist and misguiding.

In response to the counter in para no (v) page 16 of the respondent Bank, it is to submit that this counterpoint is another escapist argument the respondent Bank has put forth so as to further suppress the petitioner's career growth.

This petition is very much maintainable in view of the following reasons:

a. Either directly or indirectly still, the respondent Bank is a fully owned government of India Bank as the shareholding of the Government of India and ZIC jointly is 94.7% as of date.

b. Bank is still supposed to follow RBI guidelines on frauds w.r.t, filing compliant with CBI etc. as applicable to public sector

Banks. Whereas the same is not applicable to private sector banks.

c. Bank is still watched and monitored by Central Vigilance Commissioner through the CVO appointed by the Ministry of Finance in the Bank. There is no such practice in Private Banks.

d. This entire fraud case happened prior to offloading of part of share capital in this bank by the government to ZIC.

e. Illegitimate Penalty imposed upon the petitioner was prior to offloading of part of share capital by the government to ZIC.

f. Bypassing RBI guideline on frauds by not filing compliant with CBI in this case happened in this bank prior to offloading part of share capital in this bank by the government to ZIC.

g. If Bank is privatized, modification to employees' service conditions is to be issued, but none of the employee's service conditions, including the petitioner's have not been modified as of date. Hence it cannot be treated as a private bank.

h. The SC ST reservation policy is still being implemented in all recruitments conducted by the Bank as on today.

i. By filing this kind of baseless, false and misguiding counter by the respondent Bank, it is not only protecting the internal fraudsters but also leaving the external fraudsters scot-free even after 14 years of happening of this fraud in the respondent bank.

This Bank already tried to misguide the honorable President of India, the Ministry of Finance, and now it is trying to misguide this honorable court with its illogical and misguiding arguments.

In response to counter in Para no (vi), pages 16 and 17 of the respondent Bank, it is to submit that the petitioner is governed by its Officers service rules. In fact, all the time during his service in this bank, the petitioner is strictly acting as per the service rules only both in detecting and reporting about this fraud, in openly putting it in writing in his replies

dt.13-03-2013, in his overall presentation dt. 30-11-2013 and in his other petitions /representations submitted to other statutory authorities as to how this fraud happened and how the fraudsters have been protected. In fact, the petitioner's signing of Management Exhibit-7 was rather the right action as the petitioner being the then officer on probation had acted under the direction of his supervisor, which is as per Rule 5 (3) of the Officer's Conduct Rules.

It is also important to mention here that Bank's Officers' (Discipline & Appeal) Rules 2006 do not encourage protection to internal fraudsters, do not accept caste-based discrimination and do not agree with bypassing regulatory and internal guidelines on frauds as how some officers in the respondent bank have been bypassing them due to the pressure from the interested parties in the Bank.

In fact, as per current circular guidelines of the Bank, the petitioner can continue up to 10 years in Hyderabad/ Secundrabad Metro city, whereas so far, he has completed only four years as on June 2022, and for another six years, he can be continued if the bank does not want to cause further harassment to the petitioner by way of transfers as he has filed this Writ Petition challenging respondent bank's actions against him.

In response to counter in Para no (vii), pages 17 and 18 of the respondent Bank, it is to submit that the internal interested parties in the respondent Bank have not initiated steps for appropriate criminal action until the year 2012 against the fraudulent borrower/mortgagor despite the petitioner obtained the approval for the same in the year 2010 itself. It is only to protect both internal and external fraudsters, the then DGM Sri. VSV intentionally caused delay in this connection and he bypassed RBI and Bank's guidelines in this regard. In fact, as seen from the documentary evidence, it was Sri. VSV who was instrumental in sourcing this fraud loan account to this bank in the year 2007 and it is he who ensured its irregular disbursement. Upon examining the audio record evidence that the petitioner has requested the respondent bank to accept as additional evidence, all the truths would come to light, including how Sri. VSV bypassed RBI guidelines by not filing the complaint with CBI. It was in the year 2012, under the leadership of another GM, Sri. VDS, these irregularities/non-compliance done by Sri. VSV were observed and suitable steps were initiated by Sri.VDS, however his efforts were not fruitful in filing the complaint with CBI. As a result, ultimately still, as of date, this case is not filed with CBI for investigation. Even the local police complaint filed in this regard was also managed for the disappearance. This is how things have been moving irregularly in the respondent bank with regard to compliance to RBI guidelines on frauds and this Bank so far did not take any action against Sri. VSV for not filing compliant with CBI during his second tenure at Bank's SME center, Hyderabad during the year 2010 and 2011. One of the interested parties in the respondent bank is Sri. VSV, the then DGM now CGM, who is the root cause for happening of this fraud in this Bank and who intentionally bypassed RBI guidelines on frauds.

It is to submit that all the points mentioned in para number 9 of the WP are true and correct. The petitioner has already produced relevant documentary evidence for all that points from 'a' to 'j'. The respondent bank vaguely submitted its counter vide para number viii, pages 18 & 19 despite knowing that every point mentioned by the petitioner is true and correct. In this connection, it is to submit that the respondent Bank is trying to defend its suppressive action of non-promoting the petitioner for unjustified reasons. The facts are as follows:

a. Upon this fraud is detected and reported by the petitioner in the year 2010 end, certain internal interested parties who are directly/indirectly involved in this fraud have managed for non-promotion to the petitioner in the year 2011. It was due to the fear that those internal officers' irregular activities would be brought to light by the petitioner in case he is promoted.

b. During the years 2012 and 2013, the promotion process was not conducted to petitioners' batch of leftover un-promoted AGMs

c. Again, in the year 2014, despite the best performance of the petitioner in the promotion interview process, his selection results were ***kept in sealed cover*** as the disciplinary action orders were not issued yet and as they had already decided to impose an illegitimate penalty upon the petitioner, that sealed cover has not been opened.

d. In the year 2015, in view of the illegitimate penalty order imposed upon the petitioner, he was not called for the promotion process.

e. There has been an unwritten practice in this bank that the interview committee members, while conducting the interviews, are given access to view the disciplinary actions initiated, under process/orders passed, if any, against the promotion aspirants. It is a general practice that such individual officers against whom major penalty were imposed will be generally excluded from the promotion selection list. Thus, from the year 2016 to the year 2021, the petitioner's name was excluded from the promoted officers list. In the year 2022, though such provision of viewing the disciplinary action details is disabled to the interview committee, since this WP is filed in the year 2021, highlighting how irregularly the petitioner is put to harassment and suppression by the respondent bank, obviously his name was eliminated from the promoted officers list. Thus with the promotion year 2022 all the promotion attempts of the petitioner exhausted as per Bank's promotion policy and he will not be called for promotion at all from the year 2023.

Thus, some of the then AGMs of the year 2008 are now CGMs, and some of the then DGMs are now Executive Directors of the Bank, whereas the petitioner joined as AGM in the year 2007 and still remained as AGM due to suppression with an illegitimate penalty order.

In reply to para number 'ix' on pages 19 and 20 of the respondent bank's counter is a false submission. It is already submitted under various points in this document as well as in the WP filed by the petitioner as to how the principles of natural justice have been violated and how the petitioner was made a scapegoat by the respondent bank. Right from submitting internal office notes to SAC of the Bank till today in giving false justifications by the respondent bank to this WP while filing its counter, all the methods resorted to by the respondent Bank are against the principles of natural justice.

11. It is humbly submitted and reiterated that the respondent bank blindly, without considering the facts and documentary evidence, framed charges against the Petitioner in the year 2013 and illegitimately punished the Petitioner with a major penalty in the year 2015 vide its penalty order dated 09.03.2015. further, it is still trying to defend its actions with misguiding statements as mentioned in its counter vide para number X on pages 20 and 21. In strong objection to the same, please find the following documentary evidence in defense of the petitioner's above statement:

    a. Management Exhibit -5 [Cash Credit disbursement note] dt.8-3-2008 is the root cause for financial loss to the respondent Bank and the petitioner has not recommended the same,

    b. Management Exhibit -3 [pre-disbursement visit report] dt.26-2-2008 observations were intentionally not brought into disbursement notes by Smt. V.K.N and the petitioner is not part of the same

    c. DP fixation [excel sheet printed signed copy] in Cash Credit irregularly fixed by Smt.V.K.N on 8-03-2022, and petitioner is not part of the same

    d. Note for identifying the officer to conduct PDVC is moved by Smt.V.K.N on 8-03-2022, and the petitioner is not part of the same. As per the PDVC (Pre-disbursement verification) report, it is found that Smt.V.K.N has misguided the PDVC officer

    e. DE-2 [Re-fixation of repayment schedule in TL],

f. Draft note of TL disbursement [DE-11] is moved by Smt.V.K.N and the petitioner is not part of the same.

g. DE-10 [Transaction sheet for conducting Loan Documentation] dt.05-03-2008 conducted by Smt.V.K.N is the root cause for this fraud happening in the respondent bank and the petitioner is not part of the same.

h. P-12 Copy of Bank's SAC (Staff Accountability Committee) Minutes confirming that the Bank has falsely believed that the petitioner was a Credmin Officer during the year 2008 to this SBEMPL borrower loan case

i. P-10 Copy of Fabricated cybercrime email of Smt.V.K.N submitted to the bank to misguide as if the petitioner was the Credmin officer for the SBEMPL in the year. The documentary response given by the inquiry team evidences the same.

j. P-9 Copy of Email Confirmation given by ZINTEC on providing FINACLE User ID to the Petitioner, which proves that the petitioner was not having FINACLE user ID up to 5-5-2008 at least to view at the loan accounts transactions.

k. P-15 Copy of Bank's Internal Inquiry Officer Shri. P.K. K's Report – on the charges levelled against the petitioner reveals that the petitioner was not the Credmin officer during the year 2008 and confirms that all charges framed against the petitioner are broadly not proved as per the documentary evidence.

l. ***The false and misguiding replies submitted by the respondent Bank to the Ministry of Finance and to the honorable President of India are also additional evidence for the suppressive action of the respondent bank against the petitioner.***

Upon perusing all the above documentary evidence, it is evident that certain interested parties in the Bank have been protecting internal and external fraudsters in this loan case and harassing the petitioner by depriving him of promotion for the past 12 years (since 2011). It is V.K.N, VSV and other interested parties who had been not adhering to the Bank's established procedures, systems and processes and guidelines of RBI. Hence all the contentions made by the petitioner are valid and justified.

12. In reply to para number 'xi' on page 22 of the respondent bank's counter, it is to submit that the respondent Bank is more interested in protecting the internal and external fraudsters. That is why it has still not filed compliant with CBI and still continuing career suppression of the petitioner as he belongs to the S.C category and trying to misguide this honourable court with its false averments in its counter.

    What is neglected in the internal inquiry proceedings and in the report submitted by the Inquiry Offers are brought to light in detail in these documents and in the WP filed by the petitioner and how the respondent bank's appellate authority has paid a deaf ear to look at the factual documentary evidence is also mentioned in detail in all the representations and appeals made by the petitioner including in this document.

13. In reply to para number 'xii' on pages 22 and 23 of the counter filed by the respondent bank, it is submitted that if Smt VKN is not an internal fraudster, then what about all that documentary evidence viz ME-5 [Cash Credit disbursement note], ME-3 [pre-disbursement visit report], DP fixation [excel sheet printed signed copy] in Cash Credit Note for identifying the officer to conduct PDVC, DE-2 [Re-fixation of repayment schedule in TL], Draft note of TL disbursement [DE-11], DE-10 [Transaction sheet for conducting Loan Documentation] which are confirming that she was knowingly and intentionally bypassed bank guidelines? Petitioner's role or involvement is nowhere in the above documents and these are the documents which confirm that Smt.V.K.N is one of the internal fraudsters who has colluded with fraudulent borrowers by not adhering to banks' guidelines.

14. The Disciplinary Authority and the Appellate authority of the respondent bank did not take a lenient view as claimed. Still,

rather biased, suppressive and anti-SCST action they have resorted to against the petitioner, which is against the principles of natural justice. This unlawful act was committed by the respondent bank only to protect the internal and external fraudsters and to make the petitioner the scapegoat.

15. In reply to para number 'xiii' on page 23 of the counter filed by the respondent bank, it is submitted that the respondent Bank is repeatedly trying to misguide with baseless points in its counter. Petitioner has produced number of documentary evidence in support of his claim that the inquiry officer Shri. P.K.K, in contradiction to his own findings, documentary evidence and against his own conscience, made an illogical and irrational conclusion about the two charges as partly proved. All those documentary evidence, along with justification proving that the Inquiry officer's conclusion is illogical, is once again in detail mentioned in this document. Hence everything submitted by the petitioner is true and valid.

16. ***In reply to para number 'xiv' on pages 23 and 24 of the counter filed by the respondent bank, it is to submit that the Appellate Authority Sri. S.KV (who was subsequently arrested by CBI in another case), Sri.*** VSV ***the then DGM now CGM who is instrumental in bringing this fraud loan to this Bank and ensured its irregular disbursement and bypassed RBI guidelines by not filing compliant with CBI and Smt.V.K.N who has resorted to all that irregularities in this fraud loan case by not adhering to banks guidelines, all the above three individuals belong to the same so-called upper caste/upper community. Hence the appellate Authority has obviously reflected a vested interest in protecting the remaining two individuals at the cost of the petitioner's professional career, as the petitioner belongs to the SC category.***

17. In reply to para number 'xv' on page 24 of the counter filed by the respondent bank, it is humbly submitted that the respondent Bank is completely bypassing the conspiracy and fraud angle in this fraud loan and not at all considering how the petitioner's signature

was obtained in ME-7 fraudulently by Sri. N.R.C, Sri. VSV and Smt.V.K.N. The same was in detail explained by the petitioner in his replies to the charges vide his letter dt.13-03-2013 and in his overall presentation, dt.30-11-2013 and the gist of the same is also mentioned in this document. Based on the counter filed by the Bank against this specific point, it is again proved that neither the DA nor the AA in the Bank has read the petitioner's above-mentioned two documents. Hence the respondent bank cannot deny the petitioner's point as baseless. Further, the respondent bank should also give in detail what made it simply act blind to all that documentary evidence against Smt.V.K.N and how she was excluded from the disciplinary proceedings against her. It is a very clear case of punishing the petitioner as a scapegoat instead of punishing the real internal fraudster Smt.V.K.N.

18. In reply to para number 'xvi' on pages 24 and 25 of the counter filed by the respondent bank, it is respectfully submitted that all the statements made by the petitioner are true and factual and supported with documentary evidence. The respondent bank's counter is baseless. As has been already reiterated that this is a planned conspiracy with the involvement of internal fraudsters and by giving false assurance, the internal fraudsters have obtained the petitioner's signature in ME-7 so as to dilute the negative impact upon them if the fraud comes to light in future.

19. The supervisors of the petitioner in the previous banks where he had worked were not the fraudsters as how he is made a scapegoat in this loan case with false assurances by NRC. In fact, the petitioner has unblemished banking career history for the past 25 years of his career.

20. In reply to para number 'xvii' on pages 25, 26 and 27 of the counters filed by the respondent bank, it is respectfully submitted with a strong objection to the counter filed by the respondent Bank that, as claimed by the respondent Bank, the Disciplinary Authority and Appellate Authority of the Bank have not taken a holistic view. Still, their view was more biased, fraudsters protective and suppressive in nature against SC/ST Officers.

It seems these two authorities did not bother even to read the Inquiry officer's report thoroughly. over and above this, even the petitioner's overall presentation dt.30-11-2013 and his replies dt.13-03-2008 were not at all looked into by these two authorities, it seems. If at all these documents would have been examined properly, the following very simple commonsensical points would have been observed by them and they would not have imposed any penalty at all and they would have withdrawn all the charges framed against the petitioner:

1. Fraud happened in the Bank by disbursing a WC loan to the borrower. The petitioner was not part of the WC loan disbursement.
2. Fraud allowed to happen by conducting documentation by Smt.V.K.N irregularly bypassing all internal guidelines of the Bank. The petitioner was not part of the officers who conducted documentation
3. Bank's Inquiry Authority very specifically mentioned that Smt.V.K.N was the Credmin officer for this SBEMPL loan case during the year 2008, and the petitioner Sri.LSR was not entrusted with any responsibilities of this loan case.
4. All the charges frame against the petitioner were pertaining to the duties and responsibilities of the loan case dealing Credmin officer

21. ***It is generally appreciable if any individual or institution realizes its mistakes and initiates corrective steps in a positive direction. Whereas this instant case, the respondent bank has been repeatedly giving false and baseless justification to defend its illegitimate action initiated against the petitioner.***

22. In addition to the above, in this SBEMPL loan case, the respondent Bank was never bothered to protect public money being the custodian of public money that is why it still has not filed the case with CBI as on date and it has not taken any disciplinary action against the officer Sri. VSV who intentionally

avoided filing the complaint with CBI during the year 2010 and 2011.

23. One of the very important reasons as to why Smt.V.K.N was not punished in this case is because of the influence of Sri. VSV who in turn managed everybody at Bank's Head office for excluding Smt.V.K.N from punishment. His fear and vested interest were that if she was going to be charge-sheeted, she would definitely give all oral and documentary evidence confirming that she had done all that irregularities due to the pressure she faced from Sri. VSV. Further, if the CBI case is filed, again, ultimately, it would come to light in the investigation that Sri. VSV was the prime person who knowingly brought this fraud case to the Bank and ensured its irregular disbursement by misusing his power and position. In view of the above, as well as to make somebody a scapegoat, the respondent Bank's Appellate Authority taking a biased view, did utmost favour to Smt.V.K.N by imposing an illegitimate penalty upon the petitioner.

24. This illegitimate and illogical actions of the Bank and its non-filing of the case with CBI is nothing but directly protecting the fraudulent Borrower and fraudulent mortgagors too. Every point mentioned by the petitioner in the WP has supporting evidence. Hence the counter filed by the bank is just an attempt to misguide this honourable court.

25. In reply to para number 'xviii' on pages 27 and 28 of the counter filed by the respondent bank, it is to submit that the respondent Banks counter is strongly objected as all its actions in this particular loan case are nothing but encouraging fraudsters, protecting internal Bank's fraudsters and disobedience towards RBI guidelines and misguiding the honourable President of India including Ministry of Finance. ***Thus the error of law is very much apparent on the face of the record that the internal fraudster Smt. V.K.N has been protected by the respondent bank, duly ignoring all the documentary evidences confirming her non-compliance to bank guidelines.***

26. Further, it is blindly overlooked and completely paid a deaf ear to the inquiry report submitted by the Inquiry Officer. At least before issuing the penalty order in the year 2015, they never bothered to ensure whether CBI Complaint was filed or not.

27. Hence the action of Appellate Authority Sri.S.K.V (who in turn arrested by CBI in another case) was completely caste biased, SC/ST suppressive, fraudsters protective and he did not bother whether the Bank's interest was protected or not. Thus, the error of law is very much apparent on the face of the record.

28. The respondent bank just wants to show on record that somebody (some officer) is punished since this is a fraudulent loan case. For the sake of showing to the Vigilance department, they have chosen the petitioner's name for making a scapegoat.

29. In reply to para number 'xix' on page 27 of the counter filed by the respondent bank, it is respectfully submitted and reiterated that the respondent bank has no justified grounds for its irregular and illegitimate actions committed upon the petitioner. In a very irresponsible manner, they have imposed a penalty upon the petitioner. The vague excuse given by the respondent bank for not even listening to the audio evidence offered by the petitioner is completely irresponsible in nature and it was gross injustice committed by the respondent bank. It looks like the concerned authorities of the respondent bank have been more enthusiastic about illegitimately punishing a scapegoat rather than protecting Bank's interest.

30. In reply to para number 'xx' on page 28 of the counter filed by the respondent bank, it is submitted that para 31 of the Writ Petition is very much relevant because it shows how diligently the petitioner have been active in protecting Bank's interest in the past. In fact, this para further confirms that the petitioner's supervisors in this Bank repeatedly forced him to recommend for irregular disbursement of an Rs.6.50 Cr loan to another borrower. Still, the petitioner did not agree to the irregular instructions of his supervisors. This incident happened in the year 2014 which

was prior to imposing an illegitimate penalty upon the petitioner. Despite the petitioner's objection, this loan was irregularly disbursed to JSL without obtaining the petitioner's signature on the disbursement note. Subsequently, for a year, he had been harassed by his supervisors to sign the backdated disbursement note of JSL SEFAESU loan of Rs.6.50 Cr. In fact, that loan also has become NPA subsequently. Still, no action was initiated against the officers concerned who have irregularly disbursed that loan despite the petitioner's strong objection to its disbursement. It was just not a non-adherence to the bank's sanction terms but gross negligence on the part of the officers who disbursed it and a clear case of evidence for their vested interests.

31. It is submitted that it is again a very blind approach by the respondent bank in mentioning that Rs.50.00 lakh was remitted by Sri. N.R C at Rajahmundry branch in this SBEMPL loan case is not relevant. In fact, it is very much relevant as the same was nothing but some other fraudulent loan proceeds committed by Sri. N.RC at Rajahmundry. He had remitted that amount into this SBEMPL loan case only to show apparently as if recovery is coming into the loan account so that he anticipated that initiation of inquiry proceedings could be postponed. This is another example of the involvement of internal fraudsters and their conspiracy in this loan case where the petitioner is made as a scapegoat.

32. Further, it is submitted that TSL fraud is another big loss to the respondent Bank and to many public sector Banks. It is because of the petitioner's proactive steps he saved an additional loss of Rs.80.00 Cr to this Bank in this loan case. It is a fact, worth mentioning examples to show the diligent nature of the petitioner in protecting the Bank's interest.

33. It is more important to bring to this honourable court's notice that the petitioner, despite being so proactive in protecting the Bank's interest and despite being a positive performer for the benefit of the respondent bank, his professional career progression has been completely halted due to the illegitimate penalty imposed upon him.

34. In reply to para number 'xxi' on page 28 of the counter filed by the respondent bank, it is to submit that the respondent bank in its counter in a very casual way trying to defend its anti-governmental and anti-SC/ST tendencies. It is a unique case where this Bank is the custodian of public money and still has been encouraging internal and external fraudsters. For example, even today complaint with CBI is not filed against the external fraudster despite the case already reported as fraud to RBI. Further the respondent Bank has been, since the year 2011, promoting those officers who have extended full support to the external fraudsters and till today did not take any action against them both for bypassing RBI guidelines on frauds as well as for extending cooperation to the external fraudsters. The petitioner, despite being declared by the Inquiry officer that he was neither a Credmin officer for this SBEMPL loan case during the year 2008 nor having Finacle User ID (Soft wear) up to 05-05-2008 (being a newly joined officer- He has joined the this Bank SME Center at Hyderabad on 25-2-2008 as per Office Order No: 1862 Dt.15-02-2008), ***Bank is still not ready to accept the irregularities happened while fixing staff accountability upon the petitioner***. Since he was a newly joined officer with hardly one month of experience and was not having any Knowledge about Bank's Core Banking software, i.e., 'FINACLE' (Bank has not provided him FINACLE User ID up to 05-05-2008) up to July 2008, it should not have framed any charges against him at all because the entire fraud and diversion of funds happened during March and April 2008 itself. Smt.V.K.N and Sri.N.R.C (the then DGM) have already cooperated for diversion/siphoning of all that loan funds from 'FINACLE' core banking software loan accounts before 31-03-2008 (from CC) & before 22-04-2008 (from TL) itself and by suppressing this diversion of funds aspect, on 22-4-2008 both of them have recommended for re-fixation of repayment schedule in Term Loan account of SBEMPL so as to postpone this fraud coming to light in case detected in future. The petitioner was made Credmin head on 23-1-2009 and so far, he has never dealt as a direct dealing Credmin officer for this loan case. Even upon

the issue of loan cases distribution office order vide email dt.23-1-2009, this SBEMPL loan case was allotted to some other officer in the Bank at Hyderabad SME Center.

35. Despite having so many points and evidence, as explained above, without accepting the mistake took place at the stage of fixing staff accountability upon the petitioner, the respondent bank, in a casual way trying to defend its illegitimate acts at the cost of huge financial loss to Bank; thus it has violated principles of natural justice and caused professional career loss to the petitioner

36. It is to submit that the respondent Bank being a fully owned government Bank till today, has to obviously follow the guidelines on SC/ST reservations. There is nothing special in repeating such a point in its counter in para number 'XXII' (pages 28 and 29). In fact, what is special here is to protect a so-called upper caste internal fraudster Smt.V.K.N; the interested parties in the Bank who belong to the same upper caste category made the petitioner as a scapegoat as he belongs to SC Category. All that documentary evidence referred to in this case is more than a hundred per cent confirming that intentionally and by indulging, Smt.V.K.N had committed this fraud with the support of other fraudster officers in the Bank. ***In fact, the primary attempt was made by these internal fraudsters to obtain the signature of another SC category officer Shri.EKL the then AGM. However, considering the then-existing time and context at SME Center Hyderabad on 31-3-2008, these internal fraudsters chosen to obtain the petitioner's signature in ME-7 and skipped approaching again to Mr EKL. It is a planned conspiracy done by internal fraudsters. The respondent bank cannot try to escape by simply saying this point is baseless; It needs to submit all the internal office notes to this honourable court showing how Smt.V.K.N was excluded from getting staff accountability and other internal notes that made Smt. VKN as Management witness in the inquiry proceedings initiated against the petitioner. The context under which the P-10 documents were received by Bank's Head office and how it was projected in the internal***

office notes while excluding Smt. V.K.N from staff accountability also need to be seen. In fact, the petitioner has already requested the respondent bank in writing to provide him with the copies of internal office notes moved while fixing staff accountability against all the officers in this SBEMPL loan case and the preliminary replies/ comments obtained from Smt. V.K.N in this case prior to issuing charge sheet to the petitioner. Suppressing all those documentary evidence, simply saying the petitioner's point is baseless is nothing but a fraudster protective policy adopted by the respondent bank.

37. In reply to para number 'xxiii' on page 29 of the counter filed by the respondent bank, it is to submit that the respondent Bank did not take into account the documents evidencing the reasons for this SBEMPL loan account becoming NPA. For example:

- By disbursing WC Cash Credit loan to the borrowers on 08-03-2008 by Smt.V.K.N and Sri.N.R.C, the fraud already happened (P-4),
- By irregularly conducting security documentation for a non-existing property on 05-03-2008 by Smt.V.K.N and Sri.N.R.C duly colluding with the fraudulent borrowers/mortgagors, the respondent bank was already cheated (P-3).
- By allowing siphoning/diversion of funds by Smt.V.K.N and Sri.N.R.C between 08-03-2008 to 22-04-2008, they completed the fraud to happen in the Bank (P-5).
- By initiating the internal office note for the re-fixation of repayment schedule in the Term Loan of SBEMPL, Smt.V.K.N and Sri.N.R.C have further tried to postpone the fraud coming to light (P-8).

Thus, by blindly ignoring the above documentary evidences, the authorities in the respondent Bank have taken a biased view and illegitimately imposed a penalty upon the petitioner, thus ruined the petitioner's professional career growth.

38. Further it is true that the petitioner was not having any assigned role in the subject loan case during the year 2008. The audio record evidence and the P-10 document confirm the same. Hence the respondent Bank saying the petitioner's affidavit as baseless, is nothing but its refusal to look at the available evidences due to its pro-fraudster tendency.

39. In fact bank's counter is incorrect and misleading the honourable court as it is a hundred per cent a planned conspiracy and caste based discrimination against the petitioner as all the three, i.e., Smt.V.K.N, Sri. VSV and Sri.S.K.V who belong to the so called upper caste have suppressed the petitioner as they have colluded to protect the fraudsters.

40. It is to submit that the rule position mentioned by the respondent bank at counterpoint 'xxiv' on pages numbers 29, 30 and 31 is correct as far as the set-out rule positions are concerned. Whereas with regard to the experience, meritorious performance and honest nature of the petitioner is concerned, he deserves promotion right from his first interview held in the year 2011 itself, because he had detected fraud in this SBEMPL loan case, certain interested parties at Bank's HO did not like it. Hence, they have ensured that he is not promoted. The above point is true but unwritten. The bank is only taking shelter under the set-out rules as a false excuse for not giving promotion at all to the petitioner. The real hidden reason for the petitioner's non-promotion is due to fear that he will unearth all the fraudulent activities committed by these interested parties, which in turn may pose a threat to these internal fraudsters' professional careers in the Bank.

41. The petitioner has very high academic and professional qualifications with a proven meritorious performance track record. In addition to the above, he has experience as faculty and handled more than 1000 training sessions of one and half hours duration each and the majority of the training sessions handled by him were rated excellent by the participants.

42. In fact, it is shameful on the part of the respondent Bank for its false defence counter-taking shelter under the rule position and justifying its illegitimate actions against the petitioner. It is true that the petitioner hundred per cent deserves promotion, but he has been denied only to protect the internal fraudster and to make the petitioner the scapegoat.

43. It is to submit that all that mentioned by the petitioner at para number 36 in this WP is true and factual. The respondent bank does not have any basis nor any documentary support to disagree with the same at its point Number 'xxv' page 31 of its counter. To confirm the same, the petitioner's points are once again reproduced below:

"I submit the following justification in support of my prayers for the three promotions as noted below: First time I appeared for the DGM Promotion interview in the year 2011, my performance in the interview was outstanding, but my career progression was suppressed as I have detected and reported SBEMPL Loan fraud during November 2010 which was not liked by certain higher authorities in the Bank HO. Secondly, some of my batch AGMs who became DGMs (Deputy General Manager) in the year 2011 were promoted as GMs (General Manager) in the year 2016 and again, some of the GMs of the year 2016 promotion batch have become CGMs (Chief General Manager) in the year 2021. If they would not make me a scapegoat in this SBEMPL fraud loan case, obviously, I would have become CGM in the year 2021. I have been proving meritorious since my childhood, and I am a Double Postgraduate from Central University, Hyderabad and Osmania University. I was qualified for UGCs JRF in the year 1993 in the first attempt itself and subsequently got UGCs Senior Research Fellowship also in the year 1996. I have cleared Banking related JAIIB and CAIIB Exams in the first attempt itself. Joined Bank at Kakinada on 29-12-2007 in AGM grade as this Bank is a fully owned Government of India Enterprise and Recovered crores of rupees from many NPA borrowers

and fraud declared loan cases. Started my Banking career in the year 1997 and so far gained 25 years of experience in banking by working in various capacities viz., Branch Head (at Adoni, Nandyala, Kurnool and Vijayawada), Vigilance and Audit Officer (in Chennai), Credmin Head in MSME (in Hyderabad), Credmin Head in Large Corporate Loans department (in Chennai), Regional Coordinator (in Chennai), AGM of Central Loans Processing Center (in Chennai), Recovery Officer (In Hyderabad) and as Faculty in Training department in the Bank from December 2010 to June 2014. Over and above all, I had been given an excellent rating by the majority of the trainee participants for more than 1000 training sessions handled by me at Bank's Apex Staff Training College, Hyderabad and at Zonal Staff Training College at Chennai for imparting quality inputs. Despite so many positive contributions from my side and an unblemished banking career, this Bank authorities have been causing a lot of mental agony to me since the year 2011 for working honestly and for protecting Bank's interest."

44. In reply to the Para number 'xxvi' on pages 31 and 32 of the respondent bank's counter, it is a false statement. It contradicts various documentary evidence quoted both in the WP and in this document filed by the petitioner. As the respondent Bank has no documentary evidence to defend its stand, it is simply stating that the petitioner's statements in his affidavit in WP are baseless. All the statements made by the petitioner at para no: 37 and 38 in WP are based on strong documentary and audio evidence. The statements of the petitioner are reproduced below:

    I submit that both the disciplinary authority (CGM), as well as the appellate authority (ED) of the Bank, have imposed and confirmed a penalty upon me by mentioning some false defense statements in their respective orders. Upon studying the same with reference to my overall presentation as well as the inquiry officer's report, it can be easily understood that the penalty imposed upon me is the most illogical and illegitimate. It is a preconceived decision to make me a scapegoat so as to protect Bank's internal fraudsters.

45. I humbly submit that as per the SAC policy of the bank and as per the Officers Conduct Rules, normally, any officer deserves punishment if they reflect any mala fide intentions or gross negligence of duty. In the instant case, there are no allegations against me about any mala fide intentions and the two charges mentioned as partly proved against me are not pertaining to gross negligence of duty as it was confirmed by the Inquiring Authority that I was not the Credmin Officer for this SBEMPL loan case in the year 2008. I have obeyed my supervisor's instructions based on the assurance and confirmation given by him on 31-3-2008 and signed the TL disbursement note and its voucher. Further, I was a newly joined Officer with hardly one month of experience in SME Center, Hyderabad as of 31-3-2008 without having Finacle user ID.

46. It is to submit that upon perusal of the above statements made by the petitioner in his affidavit in WP, he is referring to all the documentary evidence produced in the internal inquiry process both by the Bank's Management as MEs and by himself as DEs. Despite having so much documentary evidence (in addition to audio files) respondent bank wants to be blind to look at them as it was a preconceived decision on the part of the respondent bank to make the petitioners a scapegoat so as to protect the internal fraudsters.

    In view of the above, it is needed to seek Bank's specific response to the following points:

    a. Whether the petitioner disbursed a Cash Credit loan in this SBEMPL loan? (Answer: No)

    b. Who allowed the external fraudster to cheat the bank? And on which date/s? (It was Smt.V.K.N and Sri.N.R.C on 05-03-2008, 08-03-2008 and 31-03-2008)

    c. Who misguided the PDVC officer prior to disbursing TL in the SBEMPL loan case? (it was Smt.V.K.N and Sri.N.RC)

d. Who was supposed to conduct a collateral security visit prior to disbursement/sanction? (it was Smt.V.K.N and Sri.N.R.C)

e. Whether the DE-11 was routed through the petitioner. (The answer is 'No').

f. Who allowed and encouraged diversion and siphoning of Bank funds by the SBEMPL borrower from their loan accounts. (It was Smt.V.K.N and Sri.N.R.C).

g. Who disbursed WC loan to SBEMPL on 08-03-2008 in contradiction to their own observations during works site visit dt.26-2-2008? (It was Smt.V.K.N and Sri.N.R.C)

h. What is the only reason for this SBEMPL loan to become NPA? (It was Collateral Security fraud)

i. Who encouraged and ensured this collateral security fraud, and on which dates? (It was Smt.V.K.N and Sri.N.R.C encouraged and ensured this collateral security fraud to happen in the Bank on 05-03-2008 and on 08-03-2008 by conducting illegal security documentation and by disbursing WC cash credit loan irregularly.

All the above noted are primary questions, and the answers confirm that Smt.V.K.N and Sri.N.R.C are internal fraudsters, and because of them, Bank has incurred huge financial losses.

Then why is the bank still making the petitioner a scapegoat and continuing its suppressive measures upon the petitioner by trying to misguide this honorable court as how it already tried to misguide the Ministry of Finance and Honorable President of India's office? The only answer to the above question is because the interested parties in the respondent Bank want to protect the internal and external fraudsters even today.

As falsely alleged by the respondent Bank, signing ME-7 was not misconduct on the part of the petitioner. Still, it is rather a right action as the petitioner being an officer on probationary period, had acted under the direction of his supervisor, which is as per Rule 5 (3) of the Bank's Officer's Conduct Rules.

47. I further submit that it is appropriate to refer the SBEMPL NPA loan case to CBI for investigation as the respondent bank is not filing a complaint for more than a decade, therefore, preventing an investigation in the fraud of public money.

Therefore, in view of the facts and circumstances explained above, I pray this Hon'ble court to reject the counter affidavit filed by the respondent bank in the interest of justice and render justice.

Chapter-8

The Judgment Predicted

The respondent Bank in its counter mentioned that this WP is not maintainable as the Bank is recently declared by RBI as a private Bank and informed this court to advise the petitioner to approach a lower court. They have further mentioned in its counter that the petitioner's appeal is time barred.

In this connection, before going in to thorough examination of the case details, it is of equally and more important to decide upon whether the WP filed by the petitioner is maintainable at this high court. Hence, the above objections raised by the Bank are examined in detail and it is pronounced as follows:

a. Penalty order dt.09-03-2015 was issued to the petitioner on Bank's letter head wherein, on the letter head itself it is printed that Bank is 'A Government of India Owned Bank.

b. Still as on today (9-01-2023) the combined share capital of government of India and ZIC (being government of India enterprise) together forms 94.72% of entire share capital of the Bank. It is evident that the government of India has offloaded its share partially to ZIC recently during the year 2019 which is post imposition of illegitimate penalty order upon the petitioner.

c. Still for all the purposes, the Bank is considered as Government of India owned Bank because the Chief Vigilance Officer (CVO) in the Bank is appointed by the Chief Vigilance Commissioner of India (CVC). There is no such practice of appointing CVO by CVC in private sector Banks.

d. The Bank has been in receipt of its CVO's appointment orders issued as per Government of India, Ministry of Finance instructions including the one recently issued by Ministry of Finance on 25th April 2022 appointing Ms.AR as CVO of the Bank. Based on the same, the Bank in turn issued office order no: 212 dt.May 11th 2022 appointing Ms.AR as CVO of the Bank.

e. In view of appointment and continuation of CVOs in the Bank even after offloading its share capital by Government of India to ZIC of India and even as on date either directly or indirectly the Government of India is still holding 94.72% of entire share capital of the Bank as ZIC of India is also a government of India enterprise, the Bank shall be treated as public sector Bank by this court for the purpose of pronouncing judgement in this WP unlike RBI considering it as private Bank for the purpose of submitting some MIS returns. Hence this WP is very much maintainable by this court.

f. It is also observed and understood that except for the purpose of submitting certain MIS data to RBI, for all the remaining statutory compliances to be submitted to government of India/ RBI/ Ministry of Finance, the respondent Bank is bound to comply with all the norms on par with other Nationalized Bank in India.

g. Petitioner's appointment in the Bank, the disciplinary proceedings initiated against the petitioner, all his appeals, representations and further appeals to various statutory authorities including filing of this writ petition before this High Court have been taking place before the sale of of the Bank to private buyers is concluded. In fact as on today the sale to private players is not concluded. Hence till today (9th January 2023) the Bank shall be treated as fully owned Government of India Bank both directly and indirectly.

h. The share capital of Government India in the Bank (Including ZIC's share) is never reduced to below 50% as on date. Hence the respondent Bank being fully owned government of India Bank, it ought to protect public interest as well as government of India and other shareholders interest and their reputation.

i. As per RBI Circular dt.01-07-2010, Bank was supposed to file compliant with CBI soon after the petitioner detected and reported the fraud on 13-11-2010 in this fraud loan case collateral security, but Bank has not adhered to RBI norms during the year 2010-11. This act of noncompliance to statutory and RBI norms committed by the Bank even before transfer of its partial shareholding to ZIC of India. Bank is answerable to this court and to government of India in what capacity it had not adhered to RBI guidelines on frauds and shall submit its detailed explanation on the action taken by the bank on the individual officers who have bypassed RBI guidelines without filing compliant with CBI during the year 2011. Any slackness by Bank in this regard would be presumed as there are interested parties at its Head Office protecting internal and external fraudsters.

j. If Bank is privatised, modification to employees' service conditions is to be issued, but none of the employee's service conditions, including the petitioner's, have been modified as of date. Hence it cannot be treated as a private bank.

k. The SC/ST reservation policy is still implemented in all recruitments conducted by the Bank as on today. Hence bank's request for not to entertain this WP is baseless and appears as biased.

l. Like any public sector banks, the Annual Statement of Assets and Liabilities has been still as on the year 2022-23 obtained from all the employees of this Bank. Whereas there is no such practice in Private Banks.

m. It is argued in the counter filed by the respondent Bank sating that the petitioner's appeal is time barred, but on perusal of the available documentary records, it is observed that the petitioner never stopped appealing in this case soon after imposition of Major Penalty upon him by the Bank. He has been making representations and appeals to various authorities in Bank as well as various statutory authorities including Ministry of Finance, Government of India and honourable President of India. Few examples of appeals made by the petitioner as well as replies received are as follows:

1. Petitioner's appeal dt. 10-04-2015 to the Executive Director of the Bank,
2. Petitioner's appeal dt.01-02-2017 to the MD and CEO of the Bank,
3. Email dt. 19-05-2018, 31-05-2019 and some more mails and letters submitted to MD & CEO as well as to the CVO of the Bank and other statutory authorities
4. President's Sectt Letter No.P1/E/2407190169 dt.24-07-2019,
5. Lr.No:20/25/2019-Welfare dt.20-08-2019 of Under Secretary to the Government of India, Ministry of Finance, Department of Financial Services.
6. Petitioner's representation dt.08-7-2019 submitted to the Honourable President of India.
7. NCSC Delhi's Compliant reference Dairy No: 30586/CR/2019,
8. Director, NCSC, Hyderabad's letter F No: 1/59/19/TS-SER dt.26-7-2019 sent to CGM of the Bank at Mumbai,
9. CVC Compliant reference no: 132552/2019/vigilance-3,
10. Bank's Lr HRD NO.2919/Representation dt.04-10-2019 addressed to Ministry of Finance,
11. Petitioner's representation dt.14-10-2019,
12. Lr.No:20/25/2019-Welfare dt.15-11-2019 of MOF-GOI-DFS,
13. Bank's letter ref no: HRD/ERS/2019-20/7726 dt.11-03-2020 addressed to the Under Secretary to GOI, DFS, Ministry of Finance and some more emails of the petitioner.
14. Bank's letter ref no: HRD/ERS/2019-20/7726 dt.11-03-2020 addressed to the Under Secretary to GOI, DFS, Ministry of Finance and

15. Petitioner's letter dt.30-07-2020 addressed to the honourable President of India under copy to Bank's MD & CEO

    Thus it is observed that the appeal matter has been continuously represented by the petitioner to various statutory authorities including Bank's authorities. Hence as argued by the respondent Bank, the issue of filing Time barred WP by the petitioner does not arise.

In view of the above it is confirmed that this WP filed by the petitioner LSR is very much maintainable at this High Court.

Over and above the same, it has come to the notice of this court that vide its letter dt.August 05th 2022 the vigilance department of the respondent Bank have advised CBI, ACB, Hyderabad that the matter about permitting prosecution of some of its employees by CBI is presently under consideration of CVC of India and as advised by Vigilance department it has sought for the permission of Department of Personnel and Training (DPT) of Government of India through the Ministry of Finance whether to allow some of its employees to be prosecuted by CBI, ACB, Hyderabad in some other compliant filed by the respondent Bank with CBI ACB, Hyderabad and registered vide FIR dt.22-03-2018 based on Bank's compliant. Though this case is not relevant to the petitioner LSR's case, to properly examine and understand whether to treat the respondent Bank as Pubic Sector Bank or Private Sector Bank, it has much relevance to take in to account the above referred FIR dt.22-03-2018 registered by CBI.

Those fraud pisciculture loans on which FIR was registered by CBI are pertaining to the year 2010 and 2011 and Bank vide its letter dt.05-08-2022 sought for permission of Department of Personnel and Training of Government of India through the Finance ministry whether to allow CBI to prosecute some of its officers involved in Pisciculture fraud loans. If the respondent bank is following the logic and concept of private bank in total for all purposes, then the need to refer the matter to DPT through finance ministry does not arise for allowing/not allowing to prosecute its employees. In this connection, as claimed and argued by the respondent Bank that it is a private Bank and petitioner cannot file this

WP in this high court, how come the respondent bank being a private bank sought for DPT permission? Here it is evident that the respondent bank is not a private bank as evidenced by its letter dt.05-8-2022 and it cannot change its stand from case to case and person to person.

The petitioner's appointment happened in the Bank on 29-12-2007 at its Kakinada branch. The fraud pisciculture loans incidence happened in the Bank during the year 2010 and 2011. Comparing these two different aspects, when bank has proceeded as a public sector bank and sought for DPT permission on prosecuting its employees, referring the matter to CVC as how other public sector banks do, it cannot object for entertaining the WP filed by the petitioner as not maintainable claiming itself as a Private Bank? These two stands of this respondent Bank in two different matters are contradicting to each other.

Rules and standards of the respondent Bank cannot be changed from person to person and from case to case. Secondly in a broader perspective, as claimed by the petitioner, the disciplinary proceedings initiated upon the petitioner by issuing charge sheet dt.28-2-2013, internal departmental inquiry proceedings conducted in the year 2013 and major penalty order imposed upon him during March 2015. During this entire period, Bank completely remained both directly and indirectly as a fully owned Government of India Bank as claimed and printed by the respondent Bank on its letter head containing the major penalty order issued to the petitioner.

The primary pray in the WP is to declare the major penalty imposed upon the petitioner by the respondent Bank as illegitimate. If this court agrees that the major penalty imposed upon the petitioner during the year 2015 is irregular and illegitimate, obviously he would be entitled to all internal promotions in Bank's career ladder. It is because the Bank has given access to the interview committee members all these years up to the year 2022 to view the disciplinary action proceedings initiated/ imposed upon every candidate appearing internal promotion process, obviously the respective interview committees must have developed a kind of negative opinion upon those candidates (having some disciplinary proceedings pending/completed) appearing for promotion and must have excluded them from the selection list.

In addition to the above, it is observed that the same respondent Bank has selected the petitioner for the Faculty position in its apex training college based on a separate selection process conducted by the bank in the year 2010 (prior to detection of this fraud) itself. Among those officers who appeared for faculty selection process along with the petitioner in the year 2010 are now in the position of Chief General Manager, and Senior General Manager. In fact one of the then Faculty position aspirant, appeared for the selection process along with the petitioner in the capacity of the then AGM, but not selected as Faculty is now working CGM and got three promotions since the year 2011.

Hence if the Major Penalty order imposed upon the petitioner is found as illegitimate by this court, obviously he has to be allowed with thribble promotion directly up to CGM cadre as prayed by the petitioner LSR in his WP.

Further the respondent Bank in its counter stated that neither the Central Government nor any of the State Governments exercise deep and pervasive control over the Respondent Bank. Also the Respondent Bank does not perform any public, statutory or sovereign function.

This court is denying with the above statement of the respondent Bank and considering it as fully owned government Bank directly as well as indirectly as on date, hence, it cannot make such statement and being the custodian of public money it is illegitimate to make such statement and it is a damage to the authority of Government of India being the majority stakeholder (directly and indirectly) in this Bank. It is observed that, for all the purposes, this Bank is still being monitored by Government of India through CVC, RBI, Ministry of Finance, CVO and other statutory agencies/authorities.

Upon examination of the charges framed by the Bank against the petitioner LSR, his replies denying the same, internal departmental inquiry proceedings conducted by Bank officials, the overall presentation made by the petitioner LSR, the Bank's departmental inquiry officer's report, the major penalty imposed upon the petitioner LSR, his various appeals made to both Bank's Management as well as to various statutory authorities, the writ petition filed by the petitioner LSR, the counter filed by the Bank, the rejoinder filed by the petitioner LSR and subsequent arguments together with various documentary as well as audio evidences produced to this court, it is observed as follows:

In any organization, recruitment and maintenance of its employees and putting the efforts to improve their skills from time to time are important tasks of the management. The quality of trainings and other inputs provided by the organization to its employees play crucial role in maintaining the integrity levels of the employees, their respective job knowledge as well as ability for protecting the interest of the organization as a whole.

Especially with regard to Banks, since they deal with public money, Bank's management needs to be more alert and cautious in protecting public interest at large without compromising on any aspects. It is the primary responsibility of Bank's management to prescribe clear guidelines in writing in the form of circulars, policies etc. as to the systems and procedures to be followed without any slackness on the part of any employees are concerned and there should be a mechanism to frequently monitor whether there is any bypass attempted by any employee to the established procedural guidelines.

Since Banks survive on the interest difference margin and other miscellaneous income, any slackness on the part of either its management or its employees in adhering to the guidelines to be viewed seriously and it equally applies to all the individuals from top to bottom in the Banking organization.

In this instant NPA loan case of SBEMPL the biggest debate happened so far is on the discernibility of accountability on the employees. This entire disciplinary action episode though looks like a small issue which is mostly routine type in many Banks, the non-compromising nature of the petitioner and his continuous efforts have taken this case to an entirely different angle to be viewed at. In this connection the following two basic questions need to be addressed before promulgating judgment.

1. What are the rules and guidelines prescribed by Bank for sanction, disbursement and monitoring of Loans?

2. What are the systems and procedures to be adhered to while fixing staff accountability upon any employee?

With regard to rules and guidelines prescribed by Bank for sanction and disbursement and monitoring of Loans is concerned, even a layman can say that the purpose of the loan is important to take a decision to lend for a business entity. If the purpose is legitimate, obviously its legal compliance part becomes the first and foremost aspect to be taken care; for example in this instant loan case since it is Mining activity, the need for working capital arises only when the activity is continuously happening. In the absence of pre-sanction visit reports to confirm whether activity was going on or not, the pre-disbursement visit automatically occupies importance to decide whether to disburse the loan or not, provided it is assumed that this business has all that statutory approvals, permissions licenses etc.,

ME-3 (visit report) says that there has been no activity since April 2007, hence the disbursement of Working capital in the month of March 2008 does not arise at all. The officer concerned i.e. VKN despite conducting visit to the borrower's works site at the end of February 2008 and reporting that there was no activity since April 2007 and the head of the department DGM NRC having noted the content of the ME-3 unit visit observations, must have sought for explanation from the borrower insisting justification for its request for disbursement of WC loan on 08-03-2008.

Since no justification was sought for from the borrower for WC disbursement, the following two conclusions can be drawn in this regard:

a. The Banks dealing officers VKN and NRC must be either not having respective job knowledge and skills for the duties discharged by them or

b. They must have colluded with the borrower. This colluding aspect altogether takes this case to a different angle from which this is to be viewed.

For verification, audit, inspection and other justification purposes, it is understood that any loan disbursement office note must contain the full information about the compliance part so as to go ahead with disbursement. NRC and VKN not bringing the important observations of ME-3 in to WC disbursement note (ME-5) cannot be treated as lack of knowledge and it definitely amounts to suppression of facts. Thus both of them have caused financial loss to Bank by irregularly disbursing WC to the borrower SBEMPL despite there is no activity.

With regard to outgoing money from the Bank in the form of loan is concerned, like any common man while giving a hand loan to his friend or relative, the minimum care how he or she takes, similarly, the officers disbursing loans shall give a minimum thought at it as to whether this amount would be ultimately utilized for the purpose it is sanctioned and whether it results in enabling the borrower's capacity to repay the loan with interest to the Bank. When the primary activity itself is not happening, then what for the money disbursed will be utilized? To have this basic understanding, one does not require any professional qualifications or experience since it is a basic commonsensical point. Obviously the amount disbursed without the activity under operation would be siphoned off for other purposes.

Secondly whether the WC disbursing officers have mala fide intentions or not, what is the necessity to disburse the WC loan despite there is no activity. Hence there is a benefit of doubt whether the WC disbursing officers have colluded with the borrower and intentionally encouraged diversion/siphoning of Bank funds?

This hurried disbursement of WC without there being no activity and without ensuring end use draws attention to have a broad examination of this loan proposal, its sanction and security creation etc., Hence the Bank is advised to refer back to all the sanction memorandums submitted to respective sanctioning authorities for getting this loan sanctioned during the year 2007, prepare a detailed report on the lapses if any observed in contradiction to the Bank's guidelines prescribed, get it certified by both its credit department head and HRD head of the Bank and submit a copy of the same to Bank's board of directors for their notice and to initiate suitable action against those individuals involved in this case, provided any lapses are observed in the sanction process as pointed out by the petitioner in his overall presentation dt.30-11-2013.

With regard to security creation by way of loan and mortgage documentation, Bank should immediately order for internal inquiry by appointing its legal department head to find out the lapses if any on the part of the officers involved in conducting security documentation with reference to sanction stipulation, circular guidelines and other systems and procedures prescribed by Bank including misguiding the PDVC officer occurred if any. Upon receipt of that report from Bank's legal department head, Bank's board of directors shall examine the same and initiate appropriate action by issuing suitable guidelines to avoid such occurrence in future to protect public money. Simultaneously Bank should also initiate appropriate action upon the individuals concerned for committing the lapses in mortgage and other documentations procedures.

Coming to the incidence of security creation and loan documentation is concerned, this court has made the following observation:

1. The immovable property stipulated as collateral security to this SBEMPL loan case as per the sanction stipulation is different from that of the immovable property upon which the security was created prior to disbursement of WC facilities to SBEMPL.
2. The approvals for change in collateral security were not obtained from the competent authority as per Bank's guidelines/practice.
3. As a matter of precaution to safe guard bank's interest, PDVC was prescribed by Bank, but it is found that this PDVC concept was completely misused and PDVC officer was not provided with the correct documents which ultimately resulted in defeat to the purpose of PDVC prescription.
4. As prescribed in Bank's circular guidelines, the visit to the collateral security was not conducted by the WC disbursing officers during pre-sanction and pre-disbursement stages.
5. The title investigation report issued by the Bank's panel advocate and the valuation report issued by the Bank's empanelled valuer were either not perused or intentionally paid deaf year by the officers who have conducted documentation/security creation;

    a. by not obtaining approval for change in collateral security

b. by not observing that the valuation given was only for open plots

c. by not seeking clarification from the valuer for exempting/ excluding building valuation

d. by not obtaining Property tax receipts as prescribed by Bank's advocate and

e. by not obtaining mutation confirmation with regard to the ownership of collateral securities.

If at all the visit to the collateral security could have been conducted, the openly visible lapses could have come to light before conducting documentation and security creation itself. Thus by neglecting to conduct visit, VKN and NRC completed documentation and security creation execution process which resulted in mortgaging a fake property as security to loan availed by SBEMPL.

It amount to gross negligence of duty on the part of VKN and NRC, but whether both of them are already aware about this fake immovable security can be commented by this court only after receipt of investigation report from CBI.

With regard to the fixing drawing power in the CC (WC) loan account on 08-03-2008 by VKN and NRC and allowing diversion and siphoning of WC funds without monitoring the account operations are though technical aspects, still it is observed that there are some commonsensical points to be observed there in;

a. Where there is no activity, there cannot be book debts (receivable) falling due within ninety days period

b. Future book debts which are subsequent to the date of stock statement date cannot form part of stock statement (stock statement dt.29-02-2008 and book debt dt.04-03-2008)

c. The first stock statement shall never contain High value book debts which are neither forming part of the loan sanction appraisal memorandum not found at the time of unit visit conducted by the Bank officials. Here in this SBEMPL first stock statement submitted to the respondent Bank, two high value book debts are mentioned in the stock statement (Lakshmi Aruna minerals and Singan projects) to make it eligible for arriving at drawing power for the WC disbursement.

d. No clarification nor justifications was called for from the borrower by VKN and NRC after finding entirely new high value book debts in the stock statement and both of them simply fixed drawing power and allowed withdrawal of WC funds by borrower which ultimately diverted and siphoned off as observed from the internal investigation report submitted by DGM RSR.

Thus the fraudsters successfully committed fraud and bank was exposed to financial loss as on 08th March 2008 itself.

Despite the above mentioned basic points are very much visible in all the documentary records, Bank has grossly failed in fixing staff accountability upon VKN and instead it has appointed VKN as Management witness in the departmental inquiry proceedings initiated against the petitioner LSR. Further Bank has refused to provide majority of the copies of documents pertaining to internal office notes and other papers sought for by the petitioner. This act of Bank amounts to suppression of factual information by not allowing transparency thus depriving the petitioner to have access to the documents that made him as accused in the in the charge sheet issued by the Bank.

If bank would have provided the copies of documents containing internal office notes submitted to the staff accountability committee, the explanations received from VKN prior to fixing staff accountability up on the petitioner LSR, definitely some more important points must have come to light as to where and how the concerned officers in the Bank have done mistakes in misguiding the staff accountability. For example, the petitioner LSR asked for works allocation order if any issued in the year 2008, in response, bank provided him the works allocation order issued in the year 2009. The particular document is a printed copy of an email pertaining to the year 2009, but it was managed as if it was forwarded in the year 2008 by changing the computer system date. Bank has grossly failed to see what is very much visible on this email printout copy as to when this works allocation order was released and it has underlined the fake date of the year 2008 (by changing computer system date) and provided a copy of the same to the petitioner. This single cybercrime email document alone is the best example to understand that the internal office notes submitted to Bank's staff accountability committee must have been containing majority of false information about the petitioner's role as to dealing with this NPA borrower loan case while. This high court is of the opinion that the Bank's concerned HRD officers intentionally did not provide the documents as sought for by the petitioner vide his letter dt.04th May 2013.

If at least the internal office notes put up to the SAC and the replies submitted by VKN along with the attachments if any to the Bank were provide to LSR in response to his letter dt.4th May 2013 addressed to the IA PKK, it is believed that all those mistakes committed by the Bank's HO and HRD officials must have been identified and brought to light by LSR then and there during the internal departmental inquiry proceedings as submitted in his overall presentation. This act of lack of transparency shown by the bank is highly irregular and illegitimate.

However for clarity sake it is presumed as follows and bank has to prove whether the following presumptions are right or not;

1. VKN while replying to Bank during preliminary comments called for in the year 2012-13, must have replied to Bank saying that she was not the dealing officer for this SBEMPL loan case for its post sanction credit disbursement and monitoring process.
2. To support her point 1 noted above, she must have enclosed the cybercrime email (date changed as **22-6-2008**) works allocation order.
3. Since this cybercrime email is dt.22nd June 2008, the HRD officers at Bank's HO must have taken petitioners appointment and joining bio data from its HRD data base and incorporated in its internal office notes submitted to SAC stating that from the date of joining the Bank i.e. since 29th December 2007, the petitioner has been working in its SME department, Hyderabad branch and must have projected that, according to the works

allocation order dt.22-06-2008 (fake date), LSR was the dealing officer for this loan case in post sanction credit matters since the date of its sanction. It must also have intentionally supressed in its internal notes submitted to SAC, the facts about WC disbursement note dt.8-03-2008 and drawing power fixation excel sheet, TL repayment re-fixation note, Documentation conducting attendance sheet etc. as who have initiated and approved them and about LSR's no role in the same.

4. The HRD officials must not have mentioned at all in the internal notes put up to SAC, about LSR joining at Kakinada branch upon receiving appointment order. Also there must not be any mention about his transfer to Hyderabad from Kakinada and joining its Hyderabad branch on 25-02-2008 in the notes submitted to Bank's SAC.

5. There are hardly the following documents pertaining to post sanction credit matters in this subject loan

Sl no	Name of the exhibit	Date of Exhibit	Officers signed the same
1	Sanction Letter (ME-2)	02-11-2007	VKN & NRC
2	Pre-disbursement visit report	23-02-2008	VKN & NRC
3	Documentation Attendance sheet	05-03-2008	VKN & NRC
4	Working capital CC disbursement note	08-03-2008	VKN & NRC
5	WC Drawing power fixing sheet	08-03-2008	VKN & NRC
6	Pre-disbursement vetting office note	17-03-2008	VKN & NRC
7	Term Loan disbursement draft Note	31-03-2008	VKN & NRC
8	Term Loan disbursement Note and its voucher	31-03-2008	VKN & LSR & NRC
9	Finacle screen shot parking TL funds in CA account (voucher prepared by VKN)	31-03-2008	VKN & NRC
10	Term Loan repayment re-fixation note	22-04-2008	VKN & NRC

Sl no	Name of the exhibit	Date of Exhibit	Officers signed the same
11	Account Monitoring and its control	During the relevant period of diversion and siphoning of funds up to 30-04-2008	VKN & NRC

Out of the above eleven documents, the petitioners signature appeared only in one instance where as VKN's signature appeared on all the eleven documents/instances. Definitely the Bank's HRD officers must not have provided the correct information to its SAC as noted above.

If bank fails to prove that the five points as mentioned above are wrong, obviously suitable disciplinary action must be taken immediately against those officers who misguided Bank's SAC in fixing staff accountability upon the petitioner LSR.

With regard to fixing staff accountability upon the petitioner LSR, irrespective of all the documentary evidences and other exhibits, the following primary and foremost points need to be considered;

a. LSR was a newly joined officer in the Bank with hardly one month of experience in SME, Hyderabad branch as on 31-03-2008 (the date of incidence of signing TL disbursement note)

b. He was **on probation period for one year** from his date of joining as per the appointment order issued to him.

c. **Any probationary officer, unless proved having mala fide intentions, shall not be fixed with staff accountability in routine procedural matters.**

d. The probationary officer's supervisor and other senior colleagues in the department shall take the responsibility and provide proper training to him in addition to Bank's formal induction training if any planned for.

e. If the supervisor and or any senior officer signs a document/ office not where in the probationary officer also signed the same, that supervisor/senior colleague only shall he be held responsible in case of fault if any found in such documents/ office notes.

f. No individual works shall be allocated to a probationary officer to handle them independently during the probationary period.

g. The probationary officer must be imparted with proper training in his area of work and must be given access to acquaint with the systems, procedures and guidelines of the Bank during the probation period.

h. Especially while working in a computerized core banking software working environment, the probationary officer must be given separate technical training to learn and understand the core banking software operations.

It is understood from the overall presentation submitted by the petitioner and other exhibits that he was not provided with Finacle (core Banking software) training by the Bank up to May 2008. Hence it is illogical to seek clarification from the petitioner about loan account monitoring aspects in Finacle (core Banking software) as the loan funds were already siphoned off as on 22nd April 2008 itself. In fact as understood, the petitioner, prior to joining the respondent bank, worked in two banks where there was no computerization at all in the first bank and the second bank was functioning in MS DOS platform. Hence it is evident that the petitioner was completely unaware about Finacle (core Banking software) operational matters.

In view of the above, the following mistakes/faults/irregularities observed on the part of the respondent bank and it's all dealing officers who have directly and indirectly caused for imposition of major penalty upon the petitioner LSR;

1. **Bank and its officers have completely forgotten the concept of Petitioner's Probation Period before fixing staff accountability up on the petitioner LSR**

2. Bank has not made any allegations on LSR about any mala fide intentions and all the charges irregularly framed against him were pertaining to routine loan disbursement and monitoring procedural issues. Since the officer was on probation (being a new joinee) for one year as per Bank's appointment order, Bank shall not frame charges upon him on such routine procedural aspects like disbursement, monitoring etc. His supervisor and other senior colleagues/staff working in the same departments and have been dealing with those matters during the relevant period must be held responsible for the same.

3. Bank made false allegations on the petitioner about working capital disbursement without even looking at the respective internal office notes. It amounts to gross negligence of the work on the part of the officers who have drafted and approved those charges for reflecting in the charge sheet issued to the petitioner. Petitioner has not signed the WC disbursement note at all.

4. Bank and its officers completely misguided its Staff Accountability Committee both by not providing certain important information as well as by providing certain wrong information to it which resulted in falsely fixing staff accountability upon the petitioner LSR. It amounts to mis-conduct on the part of the officers who have prepared and submitted those office notes to Bank's SAC.

5. Bank failed to adhere to its own loan sanction guidelines stipulated, thus sanctioned WC loan for a non-existing activity. Bank shall take suitable action upon the responsible officers who caused such non adherence to established procedural guidelines of the Bank.

6. Bank failed by approving sanction of a Term Loan without knowing the vendors/suppliers for the proposed project/activity. Bank shall take suitable action upon the responsible officers who caused such non adherence to established procedural guidelines of the Bank.

7. Bank made false allegation against the petitioner in its charge sheet dt.27-02-2012 saying that because of his acts of negligence Bank

was exposed to huge financial loss. Thus Bank has grossly failed to identify the real reasons for financial loss and caused irreparable professional career loss to the petitioner and put him to lot of mental agony.

8. Bank has not accepted the audio evidences offered by the petitioner. Thus it did not provide equal opportunity to present his full version to defend his stand that he was not the dealing officer at all to this SBEMPL loan case. This amounts to Bank's action in contradiction to the principles of natural justice. Further such autocratic tendency of Bank resulted in protecting the internal fraudsters of the bank and punishing the innocent (the petitioner)

9. Bank has not conducted the departmental inquiry in a transparent manner by refusing to provide copies of certain important documents/office notes sought for by the petitioner LSR. Thus it did not provide equal opportunity to present his full version to defend his stand. Further such autocratic tendency of Bank resulted in protecting the internal fraudsters of the bank and punishing the innocent (the petitioner)

10. It appears that Bank and its HO officials have influenced/pressurized the internal departmental inquiry officer PKK. Though the IA PKK finally concluded that the petitioner LSR was not the credmin officer during the relevant period for SBEMPL loan case and having declared that the charges are not proved against him, still very illogically concluded that the two charges are partly proved out of six charges saying that petitioner did not appear to have exercised proper due diligence before signing TL disbursement note and its voucher dt.31-03-2008. In this context the IA PKK has:

    a. failed in mentioning elaborately the details of due diligence point wise that are expected to be exercised by a newly joined probationary officer

    b. failed in remembering that the petitioner was neither having finacle user ID nor finacle knowledge

c. failed to take in to account all that procedural lapses and irregularities committed by VKN

d. failed to recommend for re-examination of Staff Accountability of VKN

e. failed to remember under whose custody the keys of the file keeping almerah were in the year 2008

f. failed in realizing that the two charges which he mentioned as partly proved against the petitioner are actually the duties of respective Credmin officer of the loan case as per Bank's circular guidelines

Thus IA PKK has contradicted with his own findings of his inquiry report by mentioning that the two charges are partly proved. This illogical conclusion of IA PKK by not even accepting the audio evidences offered by petitioner is giving scope to suspect that the Bank and its HO officials have influenced and pressurized the internal departmental inquiry officer PKK to give a false conclusion in his report so as to protect VKN and other internal fraudsters by making the petitioner a scapegoat.

1. Bank and its officers did not properly studied the internal inquiry report submitted by PKK and if Bank and its officers would have studied the same, they must have recommended for re-fixation of staff accountability upon VKN duly exonerating the petitioner LSR from the Staff Accountability.

2. Bank and its officers neglected fraud angle in the collateral security of the SBEMPL loan case and it has not conducted investigation to identify the involvement of its internal officers if any in this collateral security fraud. Thus bank directly and indirectly protecting all the fraudsters.

3. Bank did not file compliant with CBI as per RBI guidelines dt.01-07-2010 nor taken any action against those individual officers who have caused such breach of RBI guidelines. It is reflecting that bank is acting in a biased manner to protect some individual officers despite they caused damaged to Bank's reputation.

4. Bank and its officers did not follow the basic guidelines ought to be followed before fixing staff accountability viz obtaining the details of chronology of events happened and the officer/s involved in each activity/incident as per the chronology.
5. Bank did not verify even the basic document like Credmin works allocation order date thus committed a grave mistake, it amounts to negligence on the part of the officers responsible for it. Thus the staff accountability was wrongly fixed upon the petitioner LSR.
6. Bank did not read the concluding part of the replies to charge sheet dt.13-03-2013 submitted by the petitioner LSR. If it would have read it, it must have brought the content of the same in to the office notes submitted to SAC about the role of VSV and internal officers' in fraud angle.
7. Despite the petitioner reminder several times, Bank and its officers did not pay any attention on how Rs.50.00 lakh remitted in cash into this SBEMPL Loan account at its Rajahmundry branch. Thus it has indirectly encouraged the frauds and fraudulent officer who have remitted the same by committing some other frauds at its Rajahmundry branch.
8. It was pre-decided by Bank and its HO officers to impose Major penalty upon the petitioner LSR irrespective of inquiry findings, that is why despite the IA PKK bringing to light in his report as to who was the Credmin officer for this loan case during the relevant period, Bank paid deaf ear to his findings and imposed Major penalty upon the Petitioner.
9. Bank and its officers have been providing wrong, misguiding, irrelevant and unsolicited information to various statutory authorities including honourable President of India, Ministry of Finance etc. This amounts to misconduct on the part of the officers who have prepared and who have approved such reply letters.
10. Bank and its officers are not ready to accept its mistakes committed in the routine procedural disciplinary matters pertaining to the petitioner LSR.

11. Bank and its officers trying to take false shelter under the concept of Private Bank though this WP matter is pertaining to the incidents happened during the years 2008 to 2015. It amounts to escapism and double standards on the part of the Bank.

12. All the responses displayed by the Bank and its officers in this case are conveying that it has adopted illegitimate suppressive actions against the petitioner LSR who belongs to downtrodden sections of the society (SC category) so as to protect the internal and external fraudsters.

Upon examining the case details in depth with reference to the original charge sheet issued to the petitioner LSR, the replies submitted by LSR denying all the charges, the inquiry officer PKK's reports dt.24-12-2013 and 18-01-2014 and subsequent appeals and representations made by LSR to the Bank officials as well as to various statutory and regulatory authorities, the following judgment is pronounced.

Order

Detection of the collateral security fraud by the petitioner LSR in this SBEMPL loan case is true and correct. Hence he deserves appreciation. This court believes that there is cooperation extended by its internal officers in allowing the external fraudsters to commit fraud successfully by mortgaging a fake and non-exiting property and by getting disbursement of WC and TL loan funds. This court believes that some of the influential officers at the HO of the respondent Bank did not like this fraud detected by the petitioner LSR, hence they must have influenced for elimination of petitioner's name from the DGM promotion list of the year 2011 promotion process. Subsequently the petitioner did not get promotion as the promotion interview committees were given access to view all the disciplinary actions proceedings initiated and completed upon the promotion aspirants. This court agrees that the petitioner strictly acted according to the officer's conduct rules of the Bank by obeying his supervisor's instructions on 31-03-2008 and this is evident as his supervisor NRC also signed the TL disbursement note signed by the petitioner LSR.

Hence it is hereby ordered to the respondent Bank as follows:

i. Withdraw the illegitimate penalty order dated dt.09th March 2015 imposed upon the petitioner LSR immediately

ii. Pass necessary orders for his thribble Promotion as follows:

   - Promotion from AGM to DGM (Grade-D) w.e.f., the year 2011
   - Promotion from DGM to GM (Grade-E) w.e.f., the year 2016
   - Promotion GM (Grade-E) to CGM (Grade-F) w.e.f., the year 2021

iii. Bank should file a complaint with CBI ACB, Hyderabad immediately and CBI should accept the compliant and register FIR to find out and prosecute all the fraudsters as per law in SBEMPL loan fraudulent collateral security aspect.

Conclusion

The judgment proclaimed in the previous chapter was only the predicted one just for the self-satisfaction. In reality, despite filing the Writ Petition in the year 2021, still there has been no posting of the case as on 23-01-2023. Further it is understood that especially in service matters it may take years together ranging from 5 to ten year to deliver judgment. I do not know how far it is true. Mine is just one and half years old WP and in this way, by the time the judgment is pronounced in this case, it may be year 2030 or above and by that time I must have retired from service. Thus it might be proved that the ***justice delayed is justice buried***.

We talk about so many great things like technology development, social media, digitalization of money etc etc., but we are lagging far behind in catch holding such internal and external fraudsters mentioned in this book. Unless there is commitment on the part of the management to think and act purely in terms of Bank's interest, such fraudster would be always left scot free and the scapegoats like CSO LSR will be always suppressed and harassed.

In reality in many occasions it was proved that only those who do chamchagiri will climb the career ladder fast (not all but many). The days have come where in today you can not even believe the rating assigned by the credit rating agencies also whether it is individuals or it is organizations. People have become over intelligent and know, how to increase their credit score by resorting to manipulative methods.

One NPA borrower has downloaded a different voice tone as his caller tune in his smart phone. When you call that defaulter over phone for recovery follow-up, after two or three rings a typical local lady lifts the call and irrespective of you saying hello, hello hello madam, the caller tune says in typical local language that.."Who is calling, arey who is calling, ladies ku call karke baath nahi karte kaya, police compliant dedunga". When you listen to such voice when called a defaulter, obviously the officer do not dare to call again to the same number, but in fact that lady voice was a caller tune that the defaulter has set up to avoid repeated calls from the Bankers.

On the other hand mostly Bank's credit officers' life is ending up in paradoxical statements. For example, if I say, I always tell lies, what does it means, how you understand this statement. The statement 'I always tell lies' if you believe it as a truth, then it must be a lie, just think about it for a minute. In fact it is a paradoxical statement, you do not know whether it is a true statement or a lie. Similarly, the individuals approaching for business loans especially, they project some unimaginable turnover for the future, thus request for huge loan amount which is practically impossible to achieve and Bank credit officer being chased by credit target, cannot realize that the justifications given by the clients as how they are going to achieve the turnover is only a paradoxical statement.

In this SBEMPL loan case, it appears that the present management of the Bank is not bothered to take proactive steps to do justice and to punish the internal fraudster, the reason being that this illegitimate punishment did not take place during my tenure as MD of the Bank, as ED of HRD so on so on.

No officer generally prefers to approach any court of law due to two reasons, one being the internal officer, there is always a fear that he or she may be targeted and harassed during his/her future tenure in the organization, Secondly, having a little hope that if not today, may be in future at some point justice will be done to me because my appeals will result fruitful one day.

In this specific case of SBEMPL loan case LSR has been professionally murdered. Despite so many negative angles noted below nobody bothered about them. This SBEMPL fraud loan case and subsequent illegitimate internal proceedings took place in the Bank have the following negative angles and negative aspects:

a. Fraud angle (Collateral Security is non-existing immovable property)

b. Non-adherence to RBI guidelines dt.01-07-2010 on Frauds on the part of respondent Bank for not filing FIR with CBI

c. Vigilance angle and misguiding Vigilance department by respondent Bank in various internal office notes submitted to it.

d. Conspiracy angle by giving illegitimate punishment to the petitioner by providing false information to Staff Accountability Committee so as to protect the internal and external fraudsters

e. Cheating angle (Internal fraudsters have cheated this Bank by suppressing the facts in various office notes submitted to SAC and CVO of this Bank)

f. Money Laundering angle (DGM N.R.C remitting Rs.50.00 lakhs in to this fraud loan at Rajahmundry branch to delay the inquiry proceedings)

g. Illegitimate judgment by the Bank's Appellate Authority in contradiction to the findings of Bank's Internal Inquiry Officer. This resulted in protecting the internal fraudsters

h. Cyber Crime Angle - As per Information Technology Act, Cyber Crime committed by Smt.V.K.N by submitting fraudulently purported fabricated email dt.22-6-2008 to the Bank. An email of the year 2009 was forwarded by her in the year 2008 itself by resorting to cybercrime (by changing computer PC date)

i. Discrimination, harassment and suppression of the petitioner who is a Scheduled Caste Officer in the professional career ladder for the past 12 years to protect internal fraudsters ***(this is against to the principles laid down in Indian Constitution and against to the principles of natural justice)***

One should be always optimistic and should never stop fighting for justice. Irrespective of results or the delay that has been taking place in realizing the fruits of our fight, without getting tired and without losing hope one should continue his/her efforts if they believe that what they are doing is for the right cause.

Depression, disappointment, worried thinking etc etc try to dominate you by occupying your mind when you are the sufferer and unfortunately made a scapegoat in an unrelated issue. In such context one should not be demotivated at all. It is certainly not the external circumstances that demotivate you but your internal thinking and your lack of confidence in your god given inbuilt capacity.

The so called positive thinking books, speeches etc are not just to read or listen, but to apply on yourself when such practical circumstances occur in your life. If justice is done to you during your life time, you will be called as the winner and if justice is denied or buried, you are leaving a lesson to your successors. As long as you can answer to your conscience that you have not done anything wrong, you need not fear to initiate your proactive steps in the right direction seeking justice.

Sometimes certain negative things happened in our life may give us positive results in some other aspects of our life. We should never stop searching for positivity in negativity also.

I am hopeful and I am optimistic

www.ingramcontent.com/pod-product-compliance
Lightning Source LLC
LaVergne TN
LVHW041020150826
845672LV00001B/149

* 9 7 9 8 8 8 9 3 5 9 3 2 6 *